UNDEFEATED

TIBET HOUSE US PUBLICATIONS

CONFESSIONS *of A* TIBETAN WARRIOR

PALJOR THONDUP

WITH SUSAN SUTLIFF BROWN

INTRODUCTION BY DOUGLAS PRESTON

ཨ་རི་བོད་ཁང་

TIBET HOUSE US

PUBLISHED BY

TIBET HOUSE US
22 West 15th Street
New York, NY 10011
www.tibethouse.us

Printed in the United States of America on acid-free paper.

28 27 26 25 24 23 22 21 20   1 2 3 4 5

ISBN 978-1-941312-10-0 (paper)
ISBN 978-1-941312-11-7 (e-book)

LIBRARY OF CONGRESS CATALOGING-IN-PUBLICATION DATA

NAMES: Thondup, Paljor, 1949– author. | Brown, Susan Sutliff, 1946– | Preston, Douglas J., writer of introduction.
TITLE: Undefeated : confessions of a Tibetan warrior / Paljor Thondup, with Susan Sutliff Brown ; introduction by Douglas Preston.
OTHER TITLES: Confessions of a Tibetan warrior
DESCRIPTION: New York, NY : Tibet House US, [2020] | Summary: "A personal memoir by Paljor Thondup, a native-born "Khampa"-an inhabitant of Kham, a large southeastern region of Tibet; an account of his childhood and youth shared with his friend Dupa, and the journey they and their two families take across the east-west length of Tibet, while engaging in combat as guerrilla fighters against occupying Chinese forces in the late '50s and early '60s, and their escape to the west, ultimately to Nepal. The latter part of the book deals with the growth of the two friends into businessmen in Nepal and then founders of a cultural center for Tibetans ("Project Tibet") in Santa Fe, New Mexico, where their efforts are appreciated and blessed by a visit from the Dalai Lama. The two old friends return to Tibet to revisit their birthplace and bring in funding for Tibet-language schools for young Tibetans-now second-class citizens under the Chinese-before the occupation government discovers their activities and expels them from Tibet." — Provided by publisher.
IDENTIFIERS: LCCN 2020022366 (print) | LCCN 2020022367 (ebook) | ISBN 9781941312100 (paperback) | ISBN 9781941312117 (ebook)
SUBJECTS: LCSH: Thondup, Paljor, 1949– | Exiles—China—Kham (Region)—Biography. | Tibet Autonomous Region (China)—History—1951– | Tibet Autonomous Region (China)—History—Uprising of 1959—Personal narratives, Tibetan. | Exiles—Nepal—Biography. | Khampa (Tibetan people)—Biography. | Kham (China : Region)—Biography.
CLASSIFICATION: LCC DS786 .T484 2020 (print) | LCC DS786 (ebook) | DDC 951.05/5 [B]—dc23
LC record available at https://lccn.loc.gov/2020022366
LC ebook record available at https://lccn.loc.gov/2020022367

PRESIDENT: Robert A.F. Thurman
PUBLICATIONS DIRECTOR: Thomas F. Yarnall
MANUSCRIPT EDITOR: Susan Sutliff Brown
COPY + PHOTO EDITOR: William Meyers
CARTOGRAPHER: Tsering Wangyal Shawa
COVER PHOTOS: © Paljor Thondup
COVER + BOOK DESIGNER: Vin Dang

CONTENTS

PREFACE

ROBERT A.F. THURMAN

E ARE HONORED TO PRESENT this memoir of a genuine Tibetan hero, a warrior for freedom and justice, who fought bravely from youth, and then ultimately rose to the supreme challenge and conquered the inner enemy of bitterness and hatred.

The Tibetan freedom fighter movement was founded in the 1950's primarily by the Eastern Tibetan "cowboys" or "yak-boys" from Kham and Amdo, where the brunt of the Chinese communist invasion and the devastation of Tibet was first experienced. Their first gathering was organized under the pretext of gathering resources to create a golden throne to offer to their beloved leader, the 22-year-old Dalai Lama. In spite of their valiant resistance to the Chinese takeover, the world thinks they lost, and has put the movement for a free Tibet in the "lost cause" category.

But the heart of the Tibetan battle for freedom is not the usual "kill our enemy" militarism program that all nations now use to destroy the planet. The golden throne is now seen as a museum piece in occupied Tibet, but it also towers majestically over the world, radiating from "the roof of the world" to all peoples who are suffering under internal and external violence. The Dalai Lama is a Nobel Peace Prize Laureate, and dwells somewhere in everyone's mind as a personification of hope that we can all awaken from the self-destructive chaos induced by the industrializing of greed and hatred into unsustainable consumerism and militarism.

For decades, the Tibetan freedom fighters like Paljor Thondup bravely battled against overwhelming odds, and finally lost that external battle. The Dalai Lama urged them all along to wage an internal battle of the mind, sharing his own practice of Shantideva's great teaching: Defeating the inner enemy of hatred is the real victory; there is no such victory in killing outer enemies, who just leave their corpses, get reborn, and come back at you in the endless cycle. As the great Shantideva wrote:

> Those who rise above all sufferings and conquer real enemies such as
>   hatred—
> They are the truly victorious warriors! The rest just slaughter
>   corpses.

Welcome to this fascinating history of heroic courage in battles, both outer and inner! You will discover the brave heart of Tibet—one that, no matter what, remains undefeated.

ROBERT A.F. THURMAN
PRESIDENT, TIBET HOUSE US

INTRODUCTION

DOUGLAS PRESTON

THE STORY OF PALJOR THONDUP'S LIFE, related in this book, is one of the most remarkable human stories I have ever encountered. The arc of his life, from an idyllic but rough childhood in the Himalaya mountains to Santa Fe, New Mexico, is immense in its sweep of history and geography, and especially in the human story it tells. The journey from revenge and hatred for unspeakable crimes to forgiveness through the compassion and loving kindness of the Dalai Lama is one of the greatest stories ever told.

I first met Paljor in the mid-eighties, after I quit my job as an editor at the American Museum of Natural History, left New York, and moved to Santa Fe, New Mexico, to try to make it as a freelance writer. Paljor was the founder and leader of a small group of Tibetan exiles who lived in a picturesque compound on Canyon Road, where he ran an organization called Project Tibet. It supported the small expatriate Tibetan community, organized religious ceremonies from time to time, and also ran a business selling Tibetan rugs, jewelry, and religious items. The Tibetans had settled in Santa Fe because its mountains, adobe buildings, and high-altitude environment reminded them of home.

It was through Paljor that my own life was changed. It began when His Holiness the Dalai Lama won the Nobel Peace Prize, and was planning a tour of the United States. Because of Paljor's previous relationship with His Holiness, the Dalai Lama agreed to come to New Mexico to meet with the Tibetan community, Indian leaders, and New Mexicans, as well as to teach and lecture for a week. At the time, he wasn't quite the international celebrity he is today. He traveled with only a few monks and Tibetan bodyguards, few of whom spoke English. He had no handlers, advance people, press secretary, or travel coordinators. As the date of the visit approached, Paljor asked a young man named James Rutherford, who ran the governor's art gallery in the state capitol building, to help plan the visit. Rutherford had a rare gift for persuasion and organization, he had good political contacts, and he knew how to get things done.

One of the most serious challenges was security. The Chinese were enraged over the Nobel Prize, calling it "preposterous," and they issued a furious diplomatic protest when the U.S. granted him a visa for the visit. There was a concern that the over-the-top Chinese rhetoric might inspire some freelancing fellow traveler to take a potshot at the Dalai Lama. Another problem was how to manage the local press, which was clamoring for access to the Dalai Lama. A final problem was the cost of the visit.

Pajlor called his friend Edward Bass, a wealthy investment banker, environmentalist, and supporter of Tibet, to ask for help. Bass had helped establish Project Tibet and had also founded the Biosphere 2 project, among other visionary scientific and environmental efforts. Bass loaned Project Tibet $45,000 to help cover the costs of the visit. The entire town of Santa Fe pitched in. Rutherford borrowed a stretch limousine from a wealthy art dealer, and he asked his brother Rusty, to drive it. They persuaded the proprietors of Rancho Encantado, a luxury resort outside Santa Fe, to provide the Dalai Lama and his monks with food and lodging. Rutherford called the State Police and arranged for a security detail.

Paljor and James asked me to act as the Dalai Lama's press secretary. I explained to them that I was a writer, not a press secretary, that I had no experience in that line, and that it would surely be a disaster. But Paljor wanted someone he knew and trusted, and I was honored to accept.

The Dalai Lama arrived in Santa Fe on April 1, 1991. I traveled with him from six in the morning until late at night. Paljor was constantly at his side. I could see the two were very close and that they had a deep, easy, and trusting relationship. I did not at the time know their history—the history told in this book.

One of Paljor's responsibilities was to keep the Dalai Lama on schedule. His Holiness rose every morning at 3:30 and meditated for several hours.

While he normally went to bed early, in Santa Fe he had dinners to attend most evenings until late. As a result, every day after lunch Paljor would escort His Holiness and his monks back to Rancho Encantado for a nap.

The Dalai Lama loved being in New Mexico. He was always cheerful—making jokes, asking questions, rubbing his shaved head, and laughing about his bad English. He had time for anybody, no matter how many people were trying to rush him to his next appointment, and he treated everyone the same, from billionaires to waitresses. When he spoke to you, he focused all his attention, care, and concern on you as if you were the most important person to him in the world. Feeling the warmth of his loving kindness when he spoke to you, like a heat lamp on a chilly day, is something I'll never forget.

The press converged from several states to cover the story, which was far bigger than we had anticipated. There were scores of reporters and television crews. I had no idea, frankly, as to what I was doing. But I muddled through. The Dalai Lama met politicians, movie stars, billionaires, New Age gurus, and Pueblo Indian leaders. He had a private audience with a group of wizened Hopi elders, who had come all the way from Third Mesa, Arizona. The Hopis were amazed at the Dalai Lama's appearance; they exclaimed that he looked like a Native American and asked which clan he belonged to.

On the penultimate day of his visit, the Dalai Lama and Paljor attended a lunch with Jeff Bingaman and Pete Domenici, the senators from New Mexico, and Bruce King, the state's governor. During the luncheon, someone mentioned that Santa Fe had a ski area. The Dalai Lama seized on this news and began asking many questions about skiing—how it was done, if it was difficult, who did it, how fast they went, how did they keep from falling down. Paljor was a skier himself, which amazed the Dalai Lama—that a Tibetan could be a skier.

After lunch, the press corps dispersed, as nothing much happened when Paljor took the Dalai Lama and his monks back to Rancho Encantado for their usual afternoon nap. But this time something did happen. Halfway to the hotel, the Dalai Lama's limo pulled to the side of the road. I was following behind the limo in Paljor's car and we pulled over, too. The Dalai Lama got out of the back of the limo and into the front seat. We could see him speaking animatedly with Rusty, the driver. A moment later Rusty got out of the limo and came over to us with a worried expression on his face. He leaned in the window.

"The Dalai Lama says he isn't tired and wants to go to the ski basin. What should I do?"

"If the Dalai Lama wants to go to the ski basin," Rutherford said, "we go to the ski basin. What do you think, Paljor?"

"We go!" said Paljor.

The limo made a U-turn, and we all drove back through town and headed into the mountains—the limo, our car, and a van carrying the handlers. Forty minutes later we found ourselves at the ski basin. It was the tail end of the ski season but the mountain was still open. We pulled up next to a melting bank of snow below the main lodge.

"Wait here while I get somebody," Rutherford said.

He disappeared in the direction of the lodge and returned five minutes later with Benny Abruzzo, whose family owned the ski area. Abruzzo wore jeans and a psychedelic cowboy shirt and was astonished to find, in the parking lot of his ski area, the Dalai Lama and his monks piling out of a limo.

We walked up a flight of stairs and the ski operation came into view, spread out before us. It was a splendid April day, perfect for spring skiing—the temperature in the upper fifties, the slopes crowded, the snow of the kind skiers call "mashed potatoes." The Dalai Lama and his monks looked around with keen interest at the activity, the humming lifts, the skiers coming and going, and the slopes rising into blue sky.

"Can we go up mountain?" the Dalai Lama asked.

After some discussion, it was decided that we would all go up the mountain on the chairlift. Abruzzo walked over and spoke to the operator of the quad chair. Then he shooed back the line of skiers to make way for us, and opened the ropes. A hundred skiers stared in disbelief as the four monks, in a tight group, gripping each other's arms and taking tiny steps, came forward, led by Paljor. Underneath the maroon and saffron robes the Dalai Lama and his monks all wore the same footwear: Oxford wingtip shoes. Wingtips are not good in the snow. The monks were slipping and sliding, and Paljor was like a den mother, herding them along, worrying that one would fall and bring down the rest.

We made it to the lift without spilling, and the operator stopped the machine, one row of chairs at a time, to allow everyone to sit down in groups of four. There were about twelve of us in total: three chairs full. In the confusion, I ended up sitting directly next to the Dalai Lama, in the center of the chair. Paljor scrambled into the chair on my left.

The Dalai Lama turned to me. "When I come to your town," he said, "I see big mountains all around. *Beautiful* mountains. And so all week I want to go to mountains. And I hear much about this sport, *skiing*. I never see skiing before."

"You'll see skiing right below us as we ride up," I said.

"Good! Good!"

We started up the mountain. The chairlift was old and there were no safety bars that could be lowered for protection, but this didn't seem to bother the Dalai Lama, who spoke animatedly about everything he saw on the slopes. As he pointed and leaned forward into space, Paljor, who was gripping the arm of the chair with whitened knuckles, kept admonishing him in Tibetan and even putting his arm around him and clutching his robes to prevent him from leaning out too far or slipping off the edge of the seat. His concern for the Dalai Lama was deep and powerful. Later Paljor told me that he was terrified of the Dalai Lama's enthusiastic movements in the chair, and he was begging His Holiness to please sit back and not lean out so much.

"How fast they go!" the Dalai Lama said. "And *children* skiing! Look at little boy!"

We were looking down on the bunny slope and the skiers weren't moving fast at all. Just then, an expert skier entered from a higher slope, whipping along. The Dalai Lama saw him and said, "Look—too fast! He going to hit post!" And then he cupped his hands and cried out, shouting down to the oblivious skier, "*Look out for post!*" He waved frantically. "Look out for post!" while Paljor tried to ease His Holiness back in the chair. Paljor's intense feeling of protectiveness toward the Dalai Lama was remarkable to see, and it surrounded us with a kind of warm light.

The skier, who had no idea that the fourteenth incarnation of the Bodhisattva of Compassion was crying out to save his life, made a crisp little check as he approached the pylon, altering his line of descent, and continued expertly down the hill.

With an expostulation of wonder, the Dalai Lama sat back and clasped his hands together. "You see what he did? Ah! Ah! This skiing is *wonderful* sport!"

We approached the top of the mountain. Abruzzo had organized the operation so that each quad chair stopped to unload its occupants. The monks and the Dalai Lama managed to get off the chairlift and make their way across the mushy snow in a group, shuffling cautiously behind Paljor.

"Look at view!" the Dalai Lama cried, heading toward the back boundary fence of the ski area, behind the lift, where the mountains dropped off. He halted at the fence and stared southward. The Santa Fe ski basin, situated on the southernmost peak in the Sangre de Cristo mountain range, is one of the highest ski areas in North America. The snow and fir trees and blue ridges fell away to a vast, vermilion desert five thousand feet below, which stretched to a distant horizon.

As we stood, the Dalai Lama spoke enthusiastically about the raptors circling in the thermals below, so distant that nobody else could see them without squinting. "When you are in mountains," he said, "you are above the common consciousness." After a while he lapsed into silence and then, in a subdued voice, he said, *"This look like Tibet."*

The monks admired the view a while longer, and then the Dalai Lama pointed to the opposite side of the area, which commanded a view of twelve-thousand-foot peaks. "Come, another view over here!" And they set off, in a compact group, moving swiftly across the snow.

"Wait!" someone shouted. "Don't walk in front of the lift!"

But it was too late. I could see the operator, caught off guard, scrambling to stop the lift, but he didn't get to the button in time. Just then four teenage girls came off the quad chair and were skiing down the ramp straight at the group. A chorus of shrieks went up, of the piercing kind that only teenage girls can produce, and they ploughed into the Dalai Lama and his monks, knocking some of them down like so many red and yellow bowling pins. Girls and monks all collapsed into a tangle of arms, legs, skis, poles, and wingtip shoes.

We rushed over, terrified that the Dalai Lama was injured, but he was fine and in a good humor, laughing at the incident.

"At ski area" he said, "you keep eye open always."

We untangled the monks and the girls and steered the Dalai Lama away from the ramp, to gaze safely over the snowy mountains of New Mexico.

He turned to me. "You know, in Tibet we have *big* mountains." He paused. "I think, if Tibet be free, we have *good* skiing!"

We rode the lift down and repaired to the lodge for cookies and hot chocolate. The Dalai Lama was exhilarated from his visit to the top of the mountain. He questioned Abruzzo minutely about the sport of skiing and was astonished to hear that even one-legged people could do it.

The Dalai Lama turned to Paljor. "Your children, they ski too?"

Paljor assured him that they did.

This delighted the Dalai Lama most of all. "Even Tibetan children ski!" he cried, putting his hands together and laughing delightedly. "Yes, this wonderful sport!"

As we finished, a waitress with tangled, dirty-blond hair and a beaded headband began clearing our table. She stopped to listen to the conversation. After a while, when there was a pause, she spoke to the Dalai Lama. "You didn't like your cookie?"

"Not hungry, thank you."

"Can I, um, ask a question?"

"Please."

She spoke with complete seriousness. "What is the meaning of life?"

The Dalai Lama answered without hesitation. "The meaning of life is *happiness*." He raised his finger, leaning forward, focusing on her as if she were the only person in the world. "Hard question is not, 'What is meaning of life?' That is *easy* question to answer! No, *hard* question is what *makes* happiness. Money? Big house? Accomplishment? Friends? Or compassion and good heart? This is question all human being must try answer: *what makes true happiness*?" He stopped, looking at her with a smile.

"Thank you," she said, "thank you." She finished stacking the dirty dishes and cups, and took them away.

That was my introduction to His Holiness, but it also showed me a side of Paljor I had not seen before. For one thing, he had a sense of humor that he often turned against himself, giving him a self-deprecating, humble demeanor. His dedication to Tibet and his love of the Dalai Lama was inspiring. But underneath that was an incredible sense of toughness and self-reliance. A devout Buddhist, he was also an NRA national shooting champion, something that grew out of a lifelong experience with weapons, honed as a freedom fighter in the mountains of Tibet against the Chinese occupation.

Paljor was not someone to talk about himself, and it was hard to draw him out. But in the years since His Holiness's visit, I heard bits and pieces of Paljor's remarkable story, mostly from others. I found myself asking questions and encouraging him to talk. A few years ago, my wife Christine and I went to a traditional Tibetan dinner at Paljor's house, with his wife Tsering and his son Thubten. I was determined to try to encourage Paljor to open up and tell his life story, or as much of it as I could get out of him.

It was a memorable dinner. He finally told us the story of his life, which is the story you will read in this book. It is not uncommon that a brutal military invasion and occupation of a people often brings out the worst, not just in the invaders, but in some of the oppressed people. However, a journey of redemption is the story at the heart of this extraordinary book. And it tells us of the true gift of Buddhism, which is a practical way to help us along the journey from selfishness and egoism to a loving kindness and compassion for all human beings. The heart of the book for me is Paljor's immense personal struggle with these conflicting feelings, so beautifully and movingly portrayed.

After hearing the details of his life story at that dinner, I said, "You must write a book." And that is exactly what Paljor has done. A year later, when he handed me the manuscript, I was enthralled. There is so much richness in it, so much of precious value—stories of a hard but idyllic childhood growing up in the high mountains of Tibet, his relations with his extended family and elders, unforgettable depictions of traditional Tibetan life and culture, stories of gunfights and battles with marauding neighbors, wild tales of crazy things he did with his "brother" (cousin) and best friend Dupa, and moving accounts of his struggle with and rebelliousness against Buddhist principles.

There is a subversive, Tom Sawyer–like quality to his childhood story, a mischievous sense of humor, a boyish irreverence—which all came crashing to an end with the Chinese invasion. At that point Paljor's story becomes one of survival, violence, horrors almost beyond belief, escape, and redemption. His manuscript has been further enhanced and transformed by the excellent hand of Susan Brown, who helped Paljor organize it and put it into a more standard English idiom, and who worked with Paljor to capture the details of even the most horrific and frightening moments.

But it is more than a tale of a person: it is a universal story of the human journey from darkness to light. And it is an indelible portrait of a man struggling with Buddhist values and principles amidst horrific violence and tragedy, and finally overcoming hatred and vengeance. This is a story for the ages.

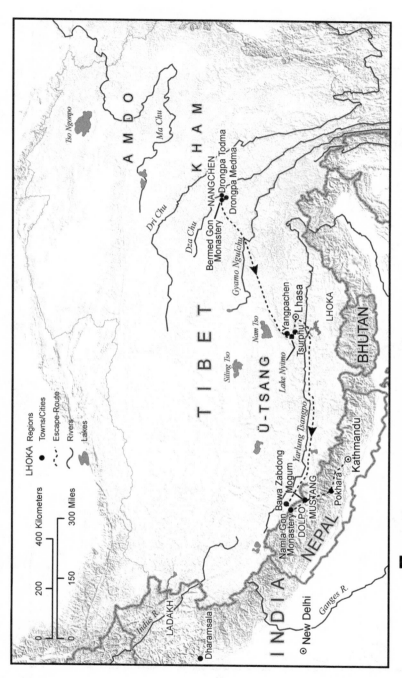

A JOURNEY OF THE GONATSANG AND KHURUTSANG FAMILIES – FROM DRONGPA MEDMA TO KATHMANDU

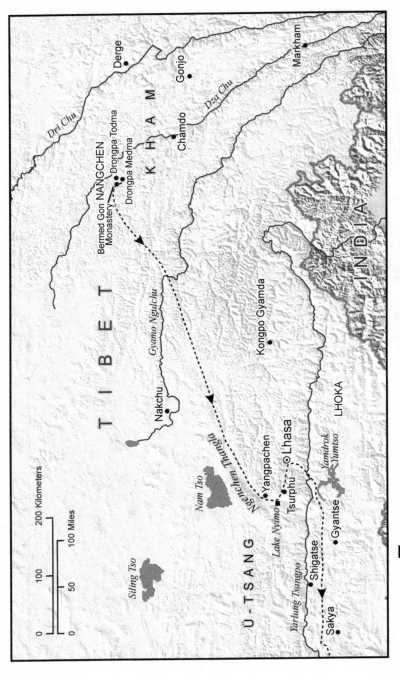

B JOURNEY OF THE GONATSANG AND KHURUTSANG FAMILIES – FROM DRONGPA MEDMA TO KATHMANDU

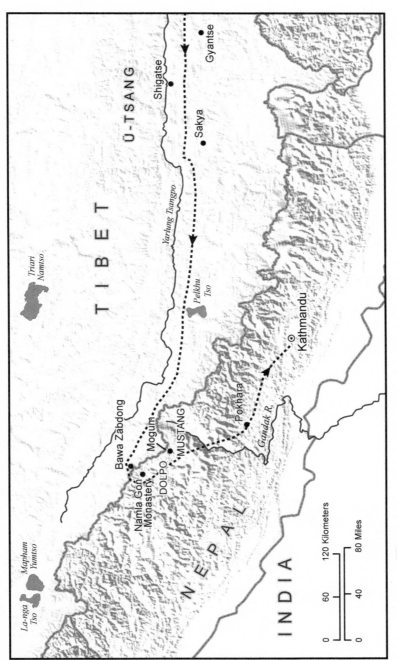

MAP ![E] JOURNEY OF THE GONATSANG AND KHURUTSANG FAMILIES — FROM DRONGPA MEDMA TO KATHMANDU

CHAPTER ONE

THE SHEEPSKIN HAT

FALL 1957: DRONGPA MEDMA, TIBET

OVERHEAD, THE VULTURES BROKE FORMATION, and the circling crows exploded with the repeated question, "What? What? What?" Running from the sheep pasture and shouting, "Chinese coming, Chinese coming," our shepherdess was insistent in the manner of official district messengers announcing militants from a rival region—*"Dabo-dai dabo-dai"* (enemies coming, enemies coming).

At first, my cousin Dupa and I, who were ten, didn't glance up from our toy soldiers. Maybe it was the wolf again? It couldn't be the Chinese. We would know. At the first sight of any armed men headed our way, the messengers would have galloped into our camp crying, *"Dabo-dai dabo-dai."* For centuries, we Khampas had been fighting each other, and it was the messenger's job to provide critical details—the enemy's home district, the number of men, and their current location—and then bring more fighters to join the border guards. Even in the mid-twentieth century, Kham in Eastern Tibet was still the Wild West—teeming with gunslingers, horse thieves, bandits, and deadly feuds. In five generations of my family, none of the men had died of natural causes. My oldest uncle liked to say, "Khampas would rather die in the excitement of battle than in their beds of old age." For Dupa and me, that was the plan.

But today, an easy autumn day in 1957, we were in a fake shootout with each other in the sheep pen. As there were no toys or any other playthings in Tibet in those days, Dupa and I had fashioned weapons from wood and soldiers from the bones of animals. The kneecaps were especially good. Pretending we were two warring enemy districts, we shouted the standard war cry, "*kee hee hee hee, lha gyalo*" (victory to the gods), and I imagined myself fighting like Pa Jatsa, one of Thirty Heroes under Tibet's legendary King Gesar. Since we were little children, we had listened to our fathers reciting the stories of this leader and his warriors, all of whom fought like magicians with superhuman powers. Today I was using a miniature replica I had made of Pa Jatsa's famous magic sword, *Yyazukaten*. Tibetans named their weapons.

Of course, since we were young children, Dupa and I owned real weapons. When I was eight, my father taught me to shoot my first gun, a black powder muzzle-loader—also called a musket. Although our families already had more swords than men, my father also gave me a custom-made Tibetan sword—one that could cut a man in half with one strike. And one day I would. But for now, I was too young, and my musket and sword were wrapped in blankets and stored away with the men's British Enfield rifles.

Suddenly, Dupa lowered his wooden gun. We both heard it. A sound like the harsh barking of a small dog alternating with the guttural clicks of a maniac's chuckle. Ravens. Above us, two of them rose and dove—graceful, shiny, black streaks—as if we had thrown two hats in the air and watched them fall. When the ravens' squawks were lazy and the clicks sounded like water dropping from a height into a bucket, all was well. However, whenever these sacred birds of the Deity Mahakala—one of the Dharma Protectors and the wrathful aspect of the Buddha of Compassion—screeched the alarm, our fathers usually took the warning seriously.

Dupa glanced at the noisy birds and shrugged. No. The shepherdess must be wrong. Since long before Dupa and I were born, no enemy had ever made it past our border guards.

Returning to our shootout, Dupa and I began debating what to do next. So far it had been a typical day. As our elders and monks recited morning prayers beginning at 5:00 o'clock a.m. and the women milked the female yaks for two hours, we lazy princes slept. When we woke—two spoiled nomad boys, the only heirs to the richest and most powerful families in the district of Drongpa Medma—it was just another easy day of play in the Land of Wild Yaks. This was our home where we were safe—the Gonatsang and Khurutsang homestead—Go-Kho Nye for short in Tibetan—going back five generations and named for our two families. Located in the county of Khetsapnye—which was named after the two original families of my grandmother and great-grandmother, Khetsa and Tsabser—our home was in one of the largest counties in Drongpa Medma district.

Dupa and I had started the day violating all the rules of our Buddhist upbringing by killing small birds. Using a sling designed for controlling sheep, we could easily strike targets within 100 yards. As our Buddhist families never killed anything they couldn't eat and always avoided small game, when my religious granduncle, Uncle Chopak, caught me killing crows for sport, he shoved a dead bird in my mouth and said, "You killed it; now you eat it." Tibetans didn't eat small animals to avoid the karma of taking more lives than necessary; a large animal—like a yak—could feed many while taking only one life. But Uncle Chopak's lesson didn't stick. The way Dupa and I saw it, cutting a bird's life short helped speed up its next reincarnation. Weren't we doing it a favor? Slaughtering birds by the hundreds every year, all day and every day during all seasons, our slings usually lasted no longer than a week. For us, it was another day, another bird.

But who was here? I glanced toward the tents. A hunter? Beggars again? It didn't matter. In Khampa tradition, we always provided food and shelter to travelers regardless of race, religion, gender, and political belief.

Then Dupa smiled. "Maybe it's pilgrims?"

I nodded. We hoped so. That would be even more fun than killing birds. As the nearest village was miles away, the land stretching for miles with no neighbors, here in a remote area of northeast Tibet, 16,000 feet above the sea, Dupa and I had only each other for playmates. For us, isolated on an eighteen-square-mile territory—the birthplace of generations of our families—religious travelers meant live entertainment.

A few months earlier, while Dupa and I sat with our chins in our palms, a group returning from a 500-mile pilgrimage to Central Tibet told us stories of the Holy City of Lhasa and our new young Dalai Lama. Like all Tibetans, Dupa and I assumed we would journey to the Holy City at least once in our lifetimes. We were set on seeing the Potala, the Winter Palace of the Dalai Lamas, which, the pilgrims said, looked like a mountain range against the sky. As my mother served the holy travelers buttered tea and *tsampa,* a Tibetan staple of roasted barley flour, they had also reported all the regional news of lamas performing miracles, gun battles between districts, tales of local bandits, news about who married whom among the rich and famous in society, encounters with ghosts, fresh information about who killed whom, the births of new reincarnations, the deaths of high lamas, and the capture of a notorious horse thief. As a special favor for our families, the lamas in the group—using damaru drums, ritual bells, and trumpets made from human thigh bones—performed the Chod practice, a ritual representing the cutting away of ego attachment.

"Maybe it's the same group." I was really smiling now. As soon as we finished our shootout, we would check.

Then we heard the dogs, and we dropped our weapons.

WHEN MASTIFFS BARK MADLY IN TIBET, everyone goes out to see what and why. With their super-power sense of hearing and smell, our mastiffs were our alarm clocks and alert system. Like most nomads, we had two kinds. The *jugche* were our spies patrolling the borders to keep away horse thieves, grizzly bears, wolves, and even rodents. Chained next to our tents were the *dhugche*, our ferocious killer mastiffs, who needed to be restrained, so they wouldn't bite travelers, pilgrims, and beggars. Now our *jugche* were spinning and yelping, and the killers yanked at their chains. I pushed myself to my feet. Okay. Time to pay attention.

As Dupa and I peered over the wall, we recognized the blurry outlines of dozens of Red Army soldiers on horseback cresting the horizon. Uh-oh. Time to hide. Even though our only visit from the Red Army two years earlier had been friendly, recently we had been hearing bad things about the Chinese. One rumor claimed that during the revolution, the food shortages were so severe that the Communists were eating the peasants who were either too old or too young to work. Although this had seemed more like a ghost story, we ducked back behind the wall of the sheep pen anyway. They weren't having us for lunch.

Instead of gunfire, however, we heard something else. The peal of hundreds of bells. What was this? I felt a prickle at the back of my neck. As the figures drew closer, we peered over the sheep pen wall again. Around the neck of each mule in a long mule train was a necklace of over 20 bells, each one the size of a golf ball. As the bells crashed and collided against one another with each step—slow, fast, and faster—the ringing scattered the crows to the bushes. Rather than the rapid and deliberate charge of a fierce invading force, the long caravan of horses, pack mules, and men coming into our camp looked like a slow and orderly parade.

As the strange procession got closer, Dupa pointed to the men riding at the front of the convoy. Beside a Red Army soldier trotted a man wearing a bright and colorful brocade *chuba* (overcoat). Then we noticed that several horsemen had saddle blankets that were beautifully colorful in hand-woven Tibetan designs. Even their horses had multi-colored headdresses. I glanced at Dupa. What was this? Riding with the Chinese soldiers was a group of local *ponpos* (chieftains), observing official protocol as they headed the entourage. From all appearances, the Red Army was just a protective escort, and the Tibetan leaders were in charge. Which explained why there had been no messenger alerts—except from our frightened shepherdess.

This was a visit from royalty, not an attack.

When my father recognized our chieftain, Pon Gyalpo, at the head of the party, he rode out to greet them. Maybe our fathers didn't trust the Chinese, but they trusted our chieftains. While our province in Kham—the Kingdom of *Nangchen*—was ruled by a king, each of its twenty-five districts had a chieftain, and our district, Drongpa Medma, had been ruled by the same family lineage for generations. In the days of my childhood, our *ponpo* was Drongpa Pon Trigyal, and during his reign, Drongpa Medma reached its peak of political power, wealth, resources, and military strength—glorious days unmatched by any other districts. When Drongpa Pon Trigyal passed away at an early age, his son, Pon Gyalpo, assumed command of our district at age fifteen. Recognized as a reincarnated lama when he was a small boy, Pon Gyalpo was educated in a monastery and trained as a Tibetan lama. Highly respected for his skills in music, ritual dance, the arts, and astrophysics, he had become the master of religious ceremonies in Lho Long–Kargon Monastery until the death of his father. Because of his ability to successfully represent our district in complex legal matters so far, our fathers had been impressed with our new young chieftain.

Now Pon Gyalpo was paying our families an official state visit with the Red Army as bodyguards.

Pushing aside the gate to the sheep pen, Dupa and I hurried toward the commotion. The new rumors about the Red Army abducting Tibetan children must be wrong. After all, the Chinese hadn't kidnapped me when I had attended one of the experimental Chinese tent schools for a day; instead, they sent me home with a picture book about Mao and two packs of cigarettes. I was six. When the platoon of six dozen Chinese militia had stopped by in that one visit to our home, they had been gracious. Even though my giant mastiff,

Mardo Sangay (Red Lion), had slipped his chain and bitten four soldiers before we got him under control, the Red Army had paid for everything they ate and drank and gave us posters of Mao, several bottles of Chinese whisky, and—for Dupa and me—pocketfuls of *shekara* candies (crystal sugar rocks).

We were hoping for candies again.

Meanwhile our shepherdess Ostok, who had cried out the traditional messenger's warning, was scowling from the entrance to her tent, her arms crossed. As the judge, jury and executioner in the world of the sheep—placing the animals that gave her trouble first in line to be butchered—our tough shepherdess was still ready to execute the Chinese soldiers, who, she believed, were coming to attack us.

Unfortunately, she was right. They were. Everyone was being tricked.

Due to the difficult terrain and treacherous passes, most places on the border of my family's territory were impenetrable, so travelers, pilgrims, and even horse thieves had to use the main road to enter our winter residence. The only way to sneak in was in full sight. The Red Army wasn't along to protect the chieftains. Appearing to come in peace—a ploy the Chinese would use throughout Tibet—they were protecting themselves. And it worked. Creating the impression that they were guarding the Tibetan officials, the Chinese were able to breach our base camp by the only passable route. In addition to fooling the Tibetan officials and border guards, the deception also deflected local rebels who might have arrived with guns blazing if they knew the truth.

Now the Chinese needed to trick our fathers.

As the entourage dismounted and the jangle of bells stilled, Dupa and I stared at the two Chinese generals, Lee Chiafung and Xu Hu Chen. One of them had all his front teeth covered in gold, unlike most people in Tibet, who had one or two gold teeth as ornaments. The same general was wearing a Khampa sheepskin box hat, the kind worn by the poor in Kham. Dupa and I looked at each other. The commander obviously didn't know. Chieftains and bigwigs wore red fox hats.

From the periphery of our camp, riling up the birds again, came the sound of Red Army troops pounding in tent stakes.

Pulling Dupa and me aside, my father looked worried. "Don't expect candies this time." Like most Tibetans, our fathers—who were brothers-in-law and sub-chieftains in our district—had been scratching their heads for the past year trying to decipher the unknown—China's real intentions. In 1957, with no communication network, all news was word-of-mouth from travelers, and the average Tibetans didn't know what was happening in the rest of their province or country. Even the Dalai Lama had to consult the Oracles to decide a course of action with the Communist Chinese. In our remote district of Kham, our fathers had only the Tibetans' ancient distrust of the Chinese telling us to be wary of the general in the sheepskin hat. And then there was my mastiff, who was snarling and pulling at his chain. And Ostok, who was still glaring at the generals.

Finally, sitting on mats, drinking buttered tea in our huge yak tent, the general with the sheepskin hat smiled pleasantly, and, crushing out his cigarette, explained the reason for the visit. The Red Army was there to help resolve a conflict between eighteen of our men and the neighboring district of Drongpa Todma. "So tomorrow is an important day. We all want the issue be resolved with peaceful dialogue, don't we?" Then he nodded to the Tibetan officials. To do the talking, the Red Army generals had "escorted" influential high lamas, chieftains and sub-chieftains (*gyenpos*) from our province. Our chieftain Pon Gyalpo explained the Red Army's proposition. If our eighteen men would turn themselves in "without further incident," they would be taken to the main Chinese garrison in the nearby Dzatu-Shen district, tried in the Chinese military court, and—after paying court costs and fines—"be released within a few days." Allowing Tibetan officials to mediate created the impression that a delicate negotiation would be handled justly and fairly by non-biased fellow Khampas.

Now my father looked really worried.

The conflict in question had actually ended in a deadly shootout. It all started when horse thieves from a third district stole several horses from the Chinese troops stationed in Drongpa Todma. In Tibet, horse thieves were common, and, next to boundary disputes, the primary reason for bloodshed in Kham. To make it appear as if we had stolen the Red Army's horses, the thieves brought the horses through our territory. Because our district—Drongpa Medma—and the Drongpa Todma district had engaged in bloody battles for decades, when our scouts on border duty spotted a camp of armed horsemen on our land, they mistakenly presumed that Drongpa Todma men were on their way to attack us again. They weren't. The armed men from that district and the Chinese soldiers were following the horse tracks through our district to pursue the real thieves. Neither the Chinese nor the Tibetans had any conflict with our families.

But it was too late. As was the local tradition—*ga-ngazen chezen* (whoever saddles his horse first goes first to the battlefield)—the initial responders, eighteen of our close relatives, friends, and village men, decided to ambush the encampment on their own, without waiting for backup. In the early morning, while the armed intruders were sound asleep, our men attacked, and, before the camp surrendered, they had killed one Tibetan and two Chinese. When our men discovered that the search party was mostly Chinese soldiers who weren't there to attack us at all, our men were shocked.

Unfortunately, what was done couldn't be undone.

Slowly lowering his silver-trimmed wooden drinking bowl, my father glanced at Dupa's father. This wasn't good. Not at all. Our officials didn't get it. Arriving with smiles and handshakes disguised as a peace mission, the Chinese authorities had come for vengeance. The Chinese had never meant Tibetans well. In the past, there had never been room for peaceful dialogue or logic. However, our fathers' challenging the chieftains and lamas would have been like an American citizen telling the State Department what to do.

Faced with the Red Army's apparently innocuous behavior, our families, who were practicing Buddhists of the Karma Kagyu lineage, were obligated to act on the Buddhist tradition that we treat no one as an enemy who showed up at our doorstep. Buddhists believe that everyone is the same in the eyes of Buddha and under the law of karma, and all things living deserve our respect. Even the Chinese.

Had our fathers known about the pending arrest and subsequent life sentences for eighteen of our people, there would have been bloodshed right there and then—even if it cost us our lives.

The Chinese knew this.

To keep us further off guard, the generals also brought with them a couple of chefs who, with a noisy clanging of pots, prepared for us a special noodle soup called "thenthuck," which was usually reserved for the top brass. Soon steam from the soup filled our tent. Although the flat noodles and broth weren't candies, they were almost as good. Dupa and I had seconds. To continue the deception, the Red Army leaders didn't immediately mention the shootout again, but spun hopeful visions of a shared future between our homeland and our Communist neighbor. After the chefs had taken away the bowls and everyone was full, sitting relaxed in a half circle on rugs, the general with the golden teeth took a few puffs on his cigarette and began painting glorious pictures of the impending Cultural Revolution:

I'd like to take this opportunity to say a few words about the wonderful plans of our great Chairman Mao. Mao, the greatest leader in the world. He has the biggest and best dream for China. You may already know some or all of it, but I'll repeat it again to make sure we are on the same page. As you know, both China and Tibet struggled badly in the past due to the old dysfunctional systems, bad governance, and a lack of modern facilities. Today, we are about to embark on the glorious road to happiness. Thanks to Chairman Mao! We have come here to help Tibet to modernize the standard of living equal to none by building roads, bridges, airports, hospitals and schools. How does this sound to you, my friends?

I was nodding. Okay. That sounded good. But only to me.

Our Tibetan officials had stopped sipping their tea and were looking at each other. Yes, the hypothesis of a common government for a common cause and common properties with common ownership by common people appealed to common Chinese peasants who longed for freedom from exploitation and suffered tremendously under their own emperors and foreign domination. But we weren't a people with a history of living under brutal regimes run by iron-fisted dictators. Why would we want to "modernize"? Khampas had thrived for centuries with our system of districts, a loose collection of fiefdoms. Our community of nomads, like everyone in our district, would be content to remain this way for another few centuries.

Swirling above our camp, the ravens sounded almost human, similar to parrots imitating human voices.

Finally our chieftain asked, "When are you going to implement all these plans?"

The general with the sheepskin hat knocked the ash from his cigarette. "As soon as you're ready and we're ready."

In answer to the question, "Who's paying and who will do all these tasks?" the general turned a golden-toothed smile on everyone in the circle. "Don't worry about this. Our government, the People's Republic of China, will pay for everything, I mean everything." He motioned over his shoulder toward the soldiers camped outside our tent. "And we'll bring in our own workers to do it all. You just stay put."

I glanced at my father. Tapping some tobacco onto his thumbnail from his *nara,* a tobacco container made from deer horn and silver, my father paused before taking a sniff. His body language was, as always, unreadable, but, looking back, I now realize what he was thinking. Thousands of Chinese workers. That would be an invisible invasion.

Pon Gyalpo wasn't smiling either as he poured himself more tea and addressed the general. "So how long do we stay put?"

The general's teeth sparkled. "As long as necessary."

Outside, the squeal of brass brushes against metal bit into the air as the Chinese soldiers loaded their bolt-action rifles. In plain sight, they were snapping magazines into their submachine guns.

One of the high lamas joined the conversation. "So everything remains to be seen?"

When the general didn't answer, my father placed his tobacco holder at his side and looked at Dupa's father again. A Chinese wolf couldn't fool all the Tibetan sheep. Our fathers knew the nature of wolves too well. However, no one could have imagined the barbarous invasion of Tibet that "remained to be seen," even the officials there that day who weren't actually innocent sheep. A few of them had been guests of the Beijing authorities and hadn't revealed what they really saw in China or how many boxes of silver coins they received for keeping quiet.

At this point, all we knew and could prove was that the Chinese high command had brought their cooks to make us fancy soup.

When the gold-toothed general showed us a brand-new, small semiautomatic pistol wrapped in a red handkerchief, which he kept in his pocket instead of a holster, Dupa and I leaned in for a close look. Everyone was impressed. I wanted a pistol like that for myself. Or maybe one of their other guns. The M44—the Russian version of the Mosin M91/30, but much shorter—was the right size for me. Although showing off guns followed by a competition was the custom for both the Chinese and Tibetans, on this occasion, the Red Army generals had a different goal. To waste Tibetan bullets.

As the other general pulled out his handgun—which was the size of the Walter PPK—the Chinese commanders invited the Tibetan officials to join them in pistol shooting. As we stepped just outside our tent, I frowned. What was this? The generals didn't set targets but began firing, one by one, countless shots into the sky. Even though bullets were invaluable to Tibetans—we once heard of a man who traded a sheep for one bullet—the chieftains felt they had no option but to do the same. I looked at my father. His jaw was clenched. On the doorstep of our tent, the shots fired into the targetless sky sounded like firecrackers going off one at a time.

I saw Dupa's father tuck a pistol in his *chuba*.

But the Chinese were steps ahead of us. They also knew our family's reputation. Our district and our fathers were undefeated in Eastern Tibet. My father, Gona Gedum Sherab, respected throughout the district as a strategist and leader, was especially gifted in guerrilla warfare. And Dupa's father, Khuru Ngajam, was a local legend. In addition to owning many guns, Dupa's father carried a sword which came from the Mahakala Temple of Tsurphu Monastery, the seat of the Karmapa Lamas, and which was believed to have belonged to one of the Thirty Legendary Warriors of the great King Gesar.

And everyone in Kham knew about Khuru Ngajam's horse, Ta Tongrie, which he purchased as a stolen horse from a distant relative who was a notorious horse thief. Although the horse had been purchased for the highest price ever paid for a horse in Kham—2000 sheep—and then stolen and sold to Khuru Ngajam for pennies, he never even changed the horse's name. Because Dupa's father was a powerful sub-chieftain in Drongpa Medma, the most powerful district in the area, no one would challenge him, not even the former owner. I loved to watch Khuru win the dangerous downhill horse race, shoot targets from his full-running horse, and pick up objects on the ground by reaching down from one side of Ta Tongrie. But that was during the annual village festivals. Heading into a battle, with Ta Tongrie's hoofs kicking up clots of earth, Dupa's father was a dangerous warrior who feared nothing. And that would certainly include the Chinese. Both our fathers were famous for always riding first into battle.

To avoid any possibility of engaging with our fathers, the commanders and their bodyguards left their own tents empty and insisted on eating, talking, and sleeping in our home tent with us and the Tibetan officials. Dupa and I found this very amusing. The chieftains, who were used to living like royalty, found themselves on mats crowded together like dogs, everyone smelling one another and almost touching. Mingled with coughs and the thump of an elbow as someone tried to turn over, the breathing in the tent sounded like dozens of bellows out of synch. The Chinese ploy insured that if anyone made a move, all the others would know it at once. Sleeping so closely together made it impossible for us to kill the generals. Which they knew we'd do once we realized what they were up to.

For us, a life devoted to Buddhism and the Dalai Lama posed no contradiction with the Khampa revenge code. We built a Fire Puja to bless a battle, memorized an entire prayer book while also memorizing long passages from the bloody tales of King Gesar, and observed the Buddhist principle of compassion for all sentient beings—except when we had to slaughter our enemies. While the elders taught me never to forget the lessons prescribed by His Holiness, when teaching me to use my new sword, my father told me, "Khampas teach their enemies lessons they'll never forget." This was my upbringing. If you're about to be shot, do you fight back, run away, or conduct long metaphysical debates with yourself? A dead man can't practice Buddhism. That's how a Khampa thinks. If we killed one enemy to save two, that was our karma. That's how a Buddhist thinks.

The problem was no one knew how to think. No one knew what to believe.

Even though our officials may have been wary of Chinese promises, they had no other choice other than to go along with the battle-hardened and better-equipped Red Army and their unlimited ammunition. The Tibetan officials were out of bullets.

In the morning, the generals again promised that no harm would come to our people and that, after a few days at the army base, our men could return home. Among the eighteen were Kure Awake, who was married to my father's oldest sister; my two favorite grown-up cousins, Khetsa Kun-nam and Khetsa Gyalgyal; and my uncle Tsepser Sangrab. The rest were close friends, some of whom spent weeks or months with my family every year. There was no mention of arrest.

To further convince us that our men weren't in danger, as the Chinese led our men away, they didn't handcuff them.

With one palm resting on my mastiff's warm fur, shading my eyes against the bright autumn sun, Dupa and I watched from the entrance of my family's tent.

Trotting beside the Red Army horsemen on the outskirts of our camp, our men disappeared within minutes, and we never saw them again.

WHEN, WEEKS LATER, the messengers arrived with the news, my father banged his fists against his head. "How could these *pharo zaju* (dead father eaters) ever think of doing such unimaginable things to other humans?" *Pharo zaju* is a typical Khampa curse, but I'd never heard my father use it before. Around us, people were weeping and kicking at the dirt. Wrapping her arms around herself, my mother cried out, *"Karmapa Chenmo"* (May Karmapa Bless Us All). Bent over, almost vomiting, my monk uncle whispered *"Om Mani Padme Hum"* (Hail the Jewel in the Lotus), the mantra for generating compassion.

Soon, the pungent order of smoldering juniper settled around us like a mist as the families of our eighteen men began lighting Fire Pujas. Superstition played a significant role in the views of the older generation of Tibetans, and our family was already wary of the number eighteen. Legendary in our history was the famous battle, the Killing Field of the Eighteens, in which my Uncle Chopak was the lone survivor as eighteen men were killed on either side of a border dispute. And recently in our village a child was killed by lightning on the eighteenth day of the month in the Tibetan calendar. Now eighteen of our men had been taken by the Chinese. Throughout our camp, the families of the arrested men performed religious rites and prayers to prevent the souls of our loved ones from turning into evil spirits due to anger and hatred.

It was clear enough who the evil spirits were. Instead of being given a fine and set free as promised, our men had been taken to the capital city of the Chinese-created Qinghai Province, tortured, and sentenced to life in the labor camps.

With the terrible report from the scouts that we would never see our men again, a new chapter in the lives of our two families was about to begin. In the Chinese double-standard system, all family members of a Tibetan who kills a Chinese—even in self-defense—can be arrested and executed as accomplices.

The Chinese would be back.

At ten years old, my idyllic life in the Land of the Wild Yaks on the Roof of the World was over.

CHAPTER TWO

THE LAND OF WILD YAKS

FALL 1957 TO SUMMER 1959:

CROSSING EASTERN TIBET

A WAY FROM THE TENTS where they couldn't be overheard, our uncles and fathers plotted our escape. With the temperature in the Himalayas dropping, Dupa and I, in our fox fur hats, listened, watching our breath float in the air before us. What was the soonest possible date to depart? Who should know our plans, who kept in secrecy? Which traveling companions would join us later? What was the best route to travel the 500 miles to safety in Central Tibet? The plan had to be foolproof. The sudden disappearance of two powerful families from our district—our fathers were *gyenpos*, second only to the district chieftain in Drongpa Medma—would make the Chinese very suspicious, especially when we were related to some of the prisoners by blood and friendship.

We would be next.

In fact, as we learned when scouts arrived with more news, all of Eastern Tibet would be next. After the 1956 uprisings and the ongoing attacks from bands of Khampa guerrillas, the Chinese appeared to have a special vendetta against the people from Kham. Just as the Chinese had used the deception of placing Khampa chieftains at the head of the parade when they came to arrest our men, the wolves were moving slowly and surely throughout the Eastern districts, playing friendly before committing unimaginable atrocities—

beheadings, public humiliations called *thanzings*, forced public sexual acts, bombings of monasteries, and the mass slaughter of women and children. When we'd hear new stories of the rape and dismemberment of nuns, Dupa and I could only look at the ground instead of each other. I knew this had to be the work of Lucifer. How could human beings do such terrible things to other human beings? The Khampas killed their enemies, but they never tortured people. Waterboarding would be a pat on the shoulder compared to the various gruesome acts of cruelty used by the Red Army. My father's voice had been grim: "The uncertainty about our future is no worse than the knowledge of the coming Chinese invasion."

At night, as I lay awake listening to the wind whistling through the tall grasses, I would flinch at the rustle of my mastiff's chain or the distant cry of an owl. No one, not even Dupa—who slept in his own family's tent—knew that I was afraid to close my eyes. When I did, I saw real-life zombies with gold teeth and sheepskin hats.

But we weren't just worried about the Red Army. When, as a young child, I was taught to cut a man in half with a sword and to shoot from a galloping horse, it wasn't to fight foreign invaders. While fleeing the Evil Empire, we also had to get past our Tibetan enemies. An unresolved feud with an enemy district in Kham could prove as deadly as a Chinese ambush. The first three days of our flight would require sneaking through Drongpa Todma, the district whose man our fighters had just killed in the ill-fated shootout. My nightmares now included snarling Khampa warriors, their swords drawn. With a caravan of eighteen people, a few goats, twenty horses, a mean mule, a dozen dogs, 300 yaks, and about 2000 sheep, we'd also be trespassing through a district with whom we'd been bitter enemies for decades, especially after a humiliating and legendary battle when fifteen of our men held off 500 Drongpa Todma fighters.

This famous story—one of my favorites—was well known around campfires throughout Nangchen Province. Originally, our forces would have been evenly matched. When district messengers reported the rumor that Drongpa Todma was recruiting over 500 fighters to engage us in the largest battle ever between our two districts, our district called in about 600 militiamen. Then the two sides posted their men at the border. When, after several months, the enemy still hadn't advanced, our fighters decided the threat was intended as psychological warfare and everyone left for home except for fifteen men, including Dupa's father and mine, who stayed behind to feast on a freshly killed blue sheep.

When the sound of footsteps on dry grass woke our sentry—the enemies were surrounding our camp ready to kill everyone in their sleep—our man fired his rifle and it became a battle of fifteen men against 500. In the pitch dark and through the foggy early morning, fighting lasted several hours. When our reinforcements arrived mid-day and our men killed two of their sub-chieftains, the men from Drongpa Todma finally retreated. They'd lost two of their top men and suffered the humiliation of being held at bay by fifteen men for half a day. In districts far from ours, comparisons to King Gesar and his Thirty Heroes was always part of the story and turned our fathers and our men into legends. Fifteen fighters, no matter how skilled, were no match against 500 anywhere on earth and under the sky. Although I knew the story was true—our fathers always told us the truth—I also knew that that victory had required some luck and a miracle.

We could certainly use some luck and a miracle now. Once we made it through Drongpa Todma, we'd still have many more foes than friends. Because our district had been undefeated for decades in bloody battles and long-standing rivalries among most regions in Kham, any of these territories would be only too happy to catch us trespassing.

Every day for weeks, as Dupa and I rubbed our hands together in the chilly air, our mastiffs milling about our legs, our fathers and uncles, coolheaded and at ease, strategized, punctuating their comments with *mudras* (symbolic hand gestures), pointing, slashing, and waving. As usual, the sense of urgency everyone was feeling was not measured in real time. Typically nomads live beyond time and space. A nomad would never say: "Oh, no, I'm five minutes late for a meeting." He might say, "I'm three months early for a meeting."

Finally, by the last weeks of winter, the plan was meticulous. First, we would circulate rumors that we were moving to our summer location earlier than usual. Once there, we would create a decoy camp and flee into the night toward Central Tibet. Because nomads only left their tents during daylight in the winter, we would travel after dark. And, because our district was well known even far away, we would keep our real family names secret.

While the men were finally happy with their scheme, I wasn't. Cozy at night in our large family tent, I was pretending this wasn't happening. And I wasn't about to go to sleep. My nightmares were no longer only filled with Khampa enemies and ghoulish Chinese soldiers with fake smiles. Now, if I closed my eyes, I saw the black, dark unknown. We, like most Tibetan nomads, never moved our tents and animals beyond the borders of our own property.

Dupa and I had never been further from home than the local village. Now we were fleeing 500 miles to Central Tibet.

Although, under normal conditions, moving all our animals and possessions between our summer and winter locations each year was no easy task—in most cases taking a day—the world was now a very different place from the lavish and extravagant world in which I was contentedly happy to be an only child in the most prominent family in the district, one in which my father was always buying newer guns and better horses and my grandmother—who always added more salt to everything, even food prepared by others—had boxes of treasures.

Fleeing for our lives, we would be traveling light. After packing the basics—like our copper, brass, and aluminum pots of all sizes, depths, and designs for cooking and our metal fireplace, which could be taken apart and reassembled while traveling—it was time to choose which possessions of sentimental value—most of them collected over centuries—wouldn't go with us. That old saddle that had been in the family for five generations? This folding table that was given to the great-grandfather of my great-grandfather by a high lama? A sword that was a gift from a former chieftain to my granduncle? Tibetans didn't have the custom of auctions, and giving away ancestral collections would be considered a family disgrace. While offering them to a lama might be a good idea, this might reveal our secret plan to flee.

There was no choice. Our fathers ordered everyone to make piles of our ancestral treasures, and we burned them to ashes.

As Dupa and I stood at the edge of the fire pit, Dupa's mother, who, in her prime of life, had had a terrible stroke that had paralyzed the left half of her body, limped to the pit and, with her good hand, tossed an ancestral wooden stool into the flames. Her expression was calm. Although she suffered tremendous physical pain, mentally and morally she upheld her dignity and worked as hard as anyone able-bodied. Meanwhile, my mother, who was more sentimental, busied herself in our tent as a colorful blanket from her great-grandmother disappeared in the fire.

Of course this was not a conflict for me, an innocent and ignorant kid of ten. I thought, "So what and who cares?" It scared the hell out of me to have so many dead people's belongings around all the time. I often wondered if we had anything that hadn't belonged to a dead person? I didn't bother to ask because I was afraid of being told, "Your gun belonged to a murdered man," or, "The previous owner killed a neighbor." I didn't want to know. I wasn't afraid of the objects, but I sure was frightened of the spirits behind them. If I had to shoot someone, I would do it myself. I didn't want a dead man's spirit pulling the trigger.

Most emotional for me was reducing our huge family tent—which normally took three yaks to transport—into one small enough for a family on the run. In Kham, the size of a tent reflected the size and wealth of the family, and our tent had been one of the largest in the province—large enough to hold tribal community meetings with more than 100 people. As I stood watching, a baby goat squirming in my arms, it felt as if my father and uncles were taking down a huge palace brick by brick to build a small hut.

For me, as for all nomads, the yak-hair tent was a true miracle. In dry weather, the fabric opened or loosened up, giving us a see-through, wind-friendly barrier. While we sipped tea in the mornings, the world outside was only a paper-thin wall away, and the air was as fresh in the tent as outside. We were that close to Mother Nature, and I always felt inside and outside at the same time. In a downpour, the yak hair, as it did on the living animal, tightened, and its tiny holes closed, making it waterproof. In winter, as we sheltered as many as 30 baby yaks for safekeeping, our tent was cozy as can be, humans and animals keeping each other warm. Even today, I still fantasize about being in my family tent—although only in a free Tibet.

Choosing the newest and best parts of our old tent to make a much smaller one, it took three days for my mother and grandmother to spin the threads and my father and his brothers to sew the pieces together. On the final day, as I stood watching our tent packed onto one yak, I was trembling so violently that my baby goat began to kick, one tiny hoof banging against my chin.

Then I felt my father's hand on my arm. Nodding toward the grazing horses, his voice was warm. "Let's take a walk."

AS WE STOOD ON A ROCK LEDGE looking at the mountains, my father waited for me to speak first, but I couldn't think of what to say. I couldn't tell him I was afraid of the dark. And the Chinese. And the future. I was ten years old. I had to come up with something. I took a breath. "Aba, when we get to Central Tibet, will I still have to be a monk?" Based on the Buddhist tradition that one child in every family join a religious order, this had always been my mother's expectation for me.

In her version of the future, I would join the Barmed Gon Monastery, which my parents supported with annual donations. This monastery had special meaning for my family. My oldest uncle was a monk who lived part-time with the monastery's four reincarnated lamas including our root lama, Serze Tulku and the youngest, Bhayu Tulku, our childhood friend who played with Dupa and me when his entourage visited our camp during the summer. Bhayu Tulku was no ordinary lama. As a child, he was clairvoyant. Although no one had seen us do it, when we used a rat for target practice and I killed it with an arrow to the neck, Bhayu Tulku knew. When he said, "Who shot the rat in the neck and killed it?" and then refused to play with us, Dupa and I got goose bumps. He seemed to be reading our minds and seeing everything, inside and out.

But being even an ordinary lama wasn't my dream. I kicked at the dirt. "I don't want to be a holy man."

Looking toward a snow-capped peak, he seemed to consider my question, then smiled. "No, Bu (son). You can't be a monk. Because you're the only child in the family, you will have to inherit my position as *gyenpo* and carry on family tradition."

Really? My fingertips began to tingle. Was this the good news I thought it was? Did my father believe we would come home again? That going to Central Tibet was only temporary? He hadn't said so before. I could feel my shoulders relaxing. Okay. So we just had to kick the Chinese out of Tibet.

Meanwhile, I wasn't so sure I wanted to be a *gyenpo*. I offered my father's youngest brother in my place. "Uncle Delshik is only six years older than me, and he could fill in."

My father laughed. "That won't work. It's tradition. Only the first and oldest son has that responsibility, and you're the only son."

I met his eyes and nodded. Okay. My mother would be sad I wasn't a monk, but I could see it now—the colorful headdress on my pony. Together Dupa and I would continue our families' centuries-old heritage as the powerful and rich leaders of our tribe. Things were looking better.

Above us, one small patch of clouds in the vast blue sky suddenly produced a brief rain shower followed by bright double rainbows. A sign.

And then the conversation took a prophetic turn that would guide my life once my father was gone. As if he were trying to identify a birdcall, my father paused. "Yes, but so much for tradition. You can also do away with being either a monk or a *gyenpo*. Things change in time."

"Really?" I frowned. "What do you mean?"

"Nomadic life isn't easy, so many problems, such hard work to live with animals day and night. Some nomads become like the animals themselves—not knowing anything better or anything about the world outside. They know nothing except how to behave like their animals."

What? Why was he saying this? Nomads had a blessed life in the arms of nature—content, affluent, powerful, carefree.

"Being a *gyenpo*, or a *ponpo* for that matter, isn't such a big deal either." He squatted and ran his hand across the dry ground. "You may be better off being a big trader or merchant because businessmen can travel freely all over Western and Central Tibet and beyond into Nepal and India. You could widen your knowledge and enjoy a life of prosperity and fame." Then he told me about Sadre Tsang and Panda Tsang, former chieftains from two famous Khampa families, who now ran successful businesses in Eastern Tibet. He paused to look at me again. "We don't know the future."

I felt my skin heat up. Why was he saying this? What did he mean about nomads and merchants? Right now everything was upside down. Why would I want to travel if I was going to be a sub-chieftain in Kham? And why would I want to leave Kham at all? Many of the highest Tibetan lamas were born in Kham at one time or another during their successive reincarnations, and some of the greatest Tibetan scholars were Khampas. Famous warriors, bandits, notorious horse thieves, and cutthroats happened to be from Kham.

As we headed back to camp, his voice was soft. "Bu, you must dance according to the sound of the drum."

I couldn't swallow. A drum? How would I know what it was saying?

In Tibet, in 1957, no one was sure what the drumbeat was saying.

AS I RUBBED MY SHOULDERS—stiff from struggling to arrange my skinny body into a comfortable position on the rocky ground throughout the night—it took me a few minutes to remember this was the final day we would stand on our own soil. Stepping from my small sleeping tent, I stared at the brown stony earth and hugged myself as the sub-zero winds smacked my skin. Instead of our usual summer site with its grasslands and wildflowers, we were in a barren and rocky corner of our property, which our fathers had chosen as the site of our decoy camp.

Although it was still winter and this location was remote and empty—except for wild animals—and no one was likely to pass by, our fathers were cautious. To produce the illusion—once we'd fled—that the bogus camp was active, our fathers used leftover materials from our old tent to set up a new one on high ground where it was visible at a distance. To simulate a nomadic lifestyle in full function, we also left a few weaker animals roaming about, and my half-brother and his mother would stay on to light a daily fire.

Shaking off last night's nightmare of fire-breathing Chinese soldiers, I headed toward our family tent where a warm fire was burning. For breakfast, my mother made *churthok*, a sour stew made of yogurt and minced lamb-meat, appropriate since this day was a sour one for all of us. We weren't just leaving behind our home. We were leaving behind our local villages and Barmed Gon Monastery where my monk uncle studied. As we loaded the pack animals, everyone was numb. Even though I was only ten, I sensed something life-changing was happening in the history of my country. But while the adults were pondering such questions as, "What will become of our ancient civilization?" and "Will Tibet simply fade away from the map of the world?" I had only one question. "Will we ever see our home again?"

Since I was a little child, I knew that Tibet was special. For thousands of years and countless generations, Tibet was the home of the Dalai Lamas, the enchanted land where the great yogi Milarepa set the example of man's quest for enlightenment within one lifetime, and the country where Guru Rinpoche left behind his profound teachings of Vajrayana as a means for a shortcut to the Buddha-field. Here the great King Gesar conquered eighteen evil empires, mythical snow lions leapt from mountain to mountain, and magical dragons sprawled behind the clouds and manifested thunder, lightning, and hail. Dupa and I grew up on these legends and myths.

The most striking feature of this land was the grass, called *pang*, unlike any other in the world—the roots interwoven so tightly that the surface of the ground was like a mown lawn. One could lick yogurt from this grassy surface and never encounter a speck of dust. In summers, Dupa and I glided on our smooth-soled shoes down the hills—like ice-skating. Once the weather dipped below zero and the snow fell, we would speed down the same hills on sleds made out of fresh yak dung, which we had molded into the shape of saddles. Overnight our dung seats would freeze solid as rocks. Then, by dipping the sleds in water several times, we made the bottom surfaces icy and slippery. Would Dupa and I ever fly down these icy hillsides again?

Suddenly, my mother, who was always brave, pressed her fists on her knees. "What will happen to my son? Will I have grandchildren to see in my lifetime?"

We all looked up from our stew.

Squatting next to her, my father touched her shoulder. "*Gaga* (Dear), we're not alone. Many, many millions of Tibetans are feeling the same and thinking the same as we do."

Watching her distress, I felt sick to my stomach. She was the gem of our family, who, with love and caring, spent each day making our home a place of welcome and warmth. As she was with all travelers who came to our door, my mother was a woman of equal kindness and generosity for beggars or kings. And now I was causing her pain by simply being her son. I told myself it was our collective karma manifesting our true bond. Then I frowned. What was this about grandchildren? What happened to her dream that I would become a monk? Everything was confusing.

When she didn't stop crying, my father stood and brushed the dirt off his pants. "We need to be strong and brave to survive and to struggle against the sea of troubles caused by the evil forces of Red China. We must fight for the freedom of our country and for our people. We are all in it together and must face it together. United, we win."

Of course, like all Tibetans at the time, he assumed this was true. So, I did too. When we fled our homeland in the winter of 1957, everyone expected we would eventually return. We would bond together, beat back the Chinese devils, retake our homeland, and retake our lives.

Although he was committed, my father also wasn't naive. By giving me permission to have a different life than that of an insular nomad, my father was acknowledging the uncertainty of the future. Before each battle, his warning to his men was, "Expect the unexpected, and be prepared." He wanted his only son to be prepared.

I wasn't. Resting my cheek against my pony's muzzle, I swallowed, then blinked.

As the sun disappeared behind the mountains, we left our homeland for the first time and stepped on our own soil for the last. In full motion and on the run, we disappeared into the darkness, not looking back.

TRAVELING DURING THE NIGHT WAS TOO QUIET. The noises of the animals' footsteps sounded so thunderously that my heart pumped like bellows, and the distant barking of dogs made me feel like an escaping prisoner. In the shadows, I saw armed men behind every tree and rock. Even the tall nettles and sunflowers had human faces, and the stalks moved like humans in the wind.

Although we had kept our dogs close so they wouldn't bark, I was sure the men of Drongpa Todma could spot us. Ghostly forms in the night, several thousand paces in length with 2,000 sheep and 300 yaks, we looked like a slow-moving, ghostly train from a distance. On the narrow path, only two or three yaks could walk side by side, so each family member was positioned behind a number of animals to make sure they traveled in an orderly queue. At an even greater distance, our entourage might have appeared like an army of dark ants following their queen.

And then there were the owls, which, my Uncle Chopak told me, were the pets of ghosts. He used to scare Dupa and me with owl tales, saying, "If you don't behave properly, the owls might snatch you for dinner." All those ghost stories I'd heard from my granduncle? I believed them. I was as superstitious as the elder Tibetans.

As we trotted beside each other, I wished I were as brave as Dupa, who wasn't even afraid of owls trying to eat him. Unaware that, since the arrest of our men, I was having night terrors about Chinese zombies, he just knew me as a young nomad boy, running free in the Land of Wild Yaks, who had feared nothing. Not even an angry vulture. Everyone knew the story.

At six years old, when I came upon a dead horse being eaten by a group of vultures, I had attacked one bare-handed. After all the hideous birds scattered except one—its head deep inside the horse's stomach—I had gripped the straggler by the tail and yanked. The bird bucked and thrashed, hissing when it couldn't reach me with its beak. Because in the Tibetan custom of Sky Burial—in which dead humans are dismembered and thrown to circling vultures—my grandmother called vultures "hungry ghosts." If I had lost my grip, this hungry ghost would have eaten me alive.

When no one came by after two hours, I was getting tired, so I dragged the giant bird to the riverbank and flung it into the water. As it swirled away in the current, its wings flapped, tossing sprays of water. Although the vulture could have carried me to 1000 feet above the ground and dropped me to my death, by drowning it, I felt I was the smarter one. We certainly scared the hell out of each other.

Although my father said I was silly to challenge something that was stronger than I and could have torn me into tiny pieces, in the village, all the children—even the teenagers—thought I was a hero. No one my age in the history of our area had fought a vulture one-on-one.

Well, I was no hero now. At every strange sound, I closed my eyes and clutched the mane of my pony. Luckily, my little horse knew how to pick his way through the dark. A special breed called Dorshu Sheruk, known for its toughness in the mountains, he could climb rocks like a goat and run as fast as an antelope. My father bought him for me as a baby. Named *Ngotza* (Bluebird), my pony was not just a means for transporting me places, like some lifeless car. Next to Dupa, he was my best friend. But Bluebird didn't make me feel safe tonight.

AT SUNRISE, AFTER A FULL NIGHT OF TRAVEL, we camped in a location far from normal travel routes, and, to avoid the appearance that we were running, set up our tents as usual, putting all our belongings inside, letting the animals loose to graze. Running in awkward circles over the grassy hills around us, the yaks were sharing all sorts of serious yak complaints—communicating as they did, like Tibetan monks with deep rhythmical chants, *"Om Ah Hum whooha-haa."* Clumsy animals anyway, routed from their usual routine—now that they were walking instead of sleeping during the night—they were behaving like they did in yak races during the village festivals, when they often ran in the opposite direction of the finish line and threw off their riders.

At the same time, to nomads, yaks weren't just laughable creatures. They were essential to our survival. On our journey into the unknown, yak hair would supply our tents, clothes, ropes, and thread. From the female yak, known as a "dre," would come our milk, butter, cheese, and buttermilk. Its leather would become our boots, belts, and saddles. Once we had survived the 500-mile journey to Central Tibet, we would celebrate with a feast of yak meat, a delicacy for Tibetans. My mother called yaks "wondrous living jewels." If today had been a normal day, Dupa and I, like all Tibetans, would be giving thanks to our country's yaks for taking care of more than half of Tibet's six million people. However, as we crawled from our tents for another night of travel and struggled to maneuver the stubborn and confused animals back into formation, we didn't feel much like thanking them.

But I understood. Like the yaks, we were all disoriented—traveling in the dark, and trying to sleep during sunlight hours, our guns next to us, ready for an enemy attack—either Chinese or Tibetans. While we were physically moving forward, mentally we were still attached to our home. For every step forward to make our great escape, we were pulled back two steps by the gravity of our emotions and our attachment to the land, the love of our country, our devotion to our Buddhist way of life, and our faith in the young Dalai Lama.

Once we had made it over the border of Drongpa Todma, as we headed on through the next enemy districts, no one was talking about tomorrow. In fact, no one, not even Dupa and I, was talking at all as we spent the next months groping along remote, untraveled routes in the pitch-black darkness. Traveling only five or six hours a night because our animals were weak and needed rest and grass, we were still hundreds of miles and a few months away from the safety of Central Tibet.

Then, one day, we had some luck, almost a miracle. A scout came riding into camp with the good news. The famous lama, Tai Situ Rinpoche, and his entourage were on the route just ahead. Our family belonged to the same Karma Kagyu lineage.

Traveling with Tai Situ for the next few months, our families finally felt safe enough to travel during the day. Because Tai Situ was well known throughout Tibet as one of the four highest lamas of the Karma Kagyu lineage, we felt especially protected. He travelled with a group of three dozen lamas, monks and lay people—all well dressed in the traditional Tibetan Buddhist robes—who were disciplined, well organized, dedicated to their teacher, and very well armed. Most importantly, they were very visible. Even Tai Situ's horse was highly decorated with an elaborate headdress and ornamental objects from head to tail. And, as it turned out, we needed the lama's protection.

Just when it seemed we had escaped and the darkness pervading our lives and seeping into our skin was beginning to lift, I woke one morning to the squeak of metal on metal. We were camped in a remote section of Nagshog Tagdrokma district—another territory with which we had had a bloody rivalry for decades.

WHEN I SHOOK DUPA AWAKE, we found our fathers cleaning their rifles, and my monk uncle had built a Fire Puja. My grandmother had tied up the loose dogs, and, all around us, the killer mastiffs were yanking at their chains.

From Dupa's father we learned the story. Even though we'd tried to keep our family names secret, when people from Nagshog Tagdrokma had come to our doorstep asking for food, some of the locals recognized our fathers. As soon as a group of agitators learned that the Gonatsang and Khurutsang families were among Tai Situ's group, they prepared to attack our camp and take our animals. That's what happens when a pack of hungry wolves sees 2,000 sheep and 300 yaks roaming around. Due to a terrible snowstorm that had killed most of their animals that winter, the people in this district were starving. Because of our old rivalry with their district, the robbers assumed the people of the district and the chieftain would back their plan.

While Dupa remained to watch the men cleaning their swords over the fire, I was so pale that my mother banished me to the tent with the women. There, I refused tea and wouldn't eat, my mind too busy having a horrible nightmare while I was awake. What was going to happen? Weren't we outnumbered? When attacked, Khampas fought to the death. Had we escaped the Chinese only to lose our fathers to Tibetans? We needed a miracle.

Then Tai Situ's tutor performed one.

As my father reported, when the chieftain of Nagshog Tagdrokma appeared at the tent of Tai Situ's tutor with a greeting scarf and the offer of safe passage for the religious members of the party—that is, if they abandoned us—the courageous tutor made the boldest statement that could ever come from a highly respected Buddhist lama. He was willing to risk the life of Tai Situ—one of the highest lamas in Tibet—and place all the monks and lamas in the crossfire, rather than desert us. Explaining that our two families were "the most devoted disciples of Tai Situ," the tutor warned, "Any attempts to prevent these families from traveling with our group will result in a bloody ending." Because most of the monks had rifles to protect their precious teacher, the chieftain knew the tutor wasn't bluffing. In the end, the chieftain guaranteed safe passage to everyone, including our group. In a rare moment for Khampas, two coolheaded diplomats resolved things more easily than hotheaded mobs shouting and pointing guns at each other.

Of course, although we had just escaped our Khampa enemies, someone had seen some Chinese soldiers in the area. The Red Army wouldn't be impressed at all with the intervention of a Tibetan high lama. Back in Kham, the

Chinese were murdering holy men and bombing monasteries. So, a week later, when a religious dilemma threatened to slow down our escape, the lamas had to perform another miracle.

While we were collecting baking soda—which substituted as soap for cleaning everything, including our hair—from the thick deposits all around Lake Neru-butso, a yak was killed by lightning. I knew immediately that this couldn't be good. Although I wasn't religious, I was superstitious.

Sure enough, the next day, another of Tai Situ's tutors became suddenly ill and two days later died in the lotus position of meditation—called *thugdam*—as do many highly realized practitioners in Tibet. For the consciousness to leave the body after such a death typically took a long time—usually three, seven, or even more days, usually in odd numbers for some reason. While dying in this position is considered a sign of spiritual achievement, similar to enlightenment, it did create a problem for the living lamas. We couldn't wait that long.

Finally, a solution. While Dupa and I watched, the lamas recited a special prayer to request that the consciousness of the tutor depart his body "immediately." Although I wasn't exactly a practicing Buddhist, I believed in the power of our lamas. As we watched, the junior tutor's head fell forward and some blood trickled from his nose—signs that his essence had left the body. Dupa and I moved closer to see the blood. *Wow*. It worked.

Then it was time to pack up and run. Again.

Until, that is, another miracle occurred. As we were crossing into Central Tibet, the Chinese Army apparently lost any interest in apprehending Khampa rebels. We found ourselves sharing the same road to the Holy City of Lhasa with men in Mao's blue uniforms.

CHAPTER THREE

THE WOLVES AND THE SHEEP

SUMMER 1958 TO MARCH 1959: CENTRAL TIBET

W HEN A BOY from one of the Central Tibetan villages told Dupa and me that he'd seen "many strange monsters" the night before, "running fast and farting with smoke and a terrible smell," he kept bouncing on his toes and looking over his shoulder, ready to flee. "The parents are as big as our tents, and the kids are the size of five wild yaks put together. They had big bright shining eyes and bodies shaped like boxes."

"How come they didn't eat you?" I joked.

He didn't laugh. "Perhaps they didn't see me."

The next day, when Dupa and I saw several military trucks and jeeps convoying one big truck, we didn't laugh either. Two jeeps went in front of the big truck and the military trucks were behind, followed by a few more jeeps. The village boy's depiction of what he saw fit this tableau, where the trucks seemed to be the parents and the jeeps the children. The backfiring of diesel-fueled trucks did resemble the sound of farting.

Then, two days later, Dupa and I noticed someone coming from a far distance, riding on something smaller and thinner than a horse but very fast. Jumping on our own horses, we galloped toward it. As we came close, a man got off the strange thing, pulled out a Mauser pistol, and aimed at us. Dismounting, we waved in a friendly gesture and called out, *"Arok"*—"hello" in

Kham dialect. He remained shaking his weapon, but not shooting. Finally, when we smiled, he let us come closer to see his funny little horse on two wheels. We patted its small saddle. The man was surprised we'd never seen a bicycle before. I was surprised anyone would choose a metal horse over a real one. I whispered to Dupa that a thing like that wasn't going to replace Bluebird.

Although we finally felt safe enough to travel in full sight, we were also leaving behind the primitive landscape of Eastern Tibet and coming out of the closet of ancient civilization into the technologically advanced modern world. As well as hundreds of men in blue uniforms, all kinds of strange mechanical beasts were pouring into Central Tibet to "modernize" our country. Thinking about the golden-toothed general's disturbing vision for the future, I remembered my father's worried look then. He was certainly alarmed now. The wolves couldn't fool the men from Kham. We had seen too much. This was a subtle occupation.

Our fathers decided to remove us from the line of fire.

After taking out some spiritual insurance, our fathers led our families and animals through the Nyenchen Tanglha Pass, to a remote area near Lake Nyimo, 70 miles west of Lhasa, far from the action. Before Tai Situ Rinpoche's entourage left our group for Tsurphu Monastery, we sought blessings from Ngenchen Thangla—one of the most important mountains in Tibet, whose spirit is worshipped as a local deity to protect our nation—and its "consort," Lake Namtso, known for its female energy. Blessed with the deities' protection, nine members of my Gonatsang family, seven of Dupa's Khurutsang family, and two animal caretakers—eighteen of us in all—and all our animals settled about 19,000 feet above sea level in the remote, lush, upper Yangpachen area, where we were the only group.

And then—the real miracle. It appeared that, instead of fugitives, we would be living as nomads again.

While the men set up the tents, Dupa and I explored the valley with its grassy hills covered in wildflowers. The lowing of our grazing sheep mingled with the sounds of distant thunder, the cries of wolves, the splashing of a waterfall, and the songs of birds. Ravens, vultures, and eagles swooped above us calling to each other, and, in the mountains wandered snow leopards, blue sheep, bighorn sheep, brown bears, and foxes. It was also the perfect climate for snakes. Living and moving ropes were everywhere. Seeing them for the first time, I wondered how they moved so quickly without any legs and no one pulling them. Dupa and I spent many afternoons poking about in the brush looking for them. Not only were they able to stand half of their bodies up like arrows, the thorny bushes didn't seem to hurt their silky skins.

After a few weeks, not knowing if or when we would ever return to our home in Eastern Tibet, Dupa and I slowly accepted that this area with its excellent grazing was our new home. Our families were happy in this lush valley, smiling again, and taking the time to watch a lamb learning to walk. Dupa and I, now eleven, began to believe we might stay here with the living ropes forever. Far from the hoofbeats of the Chinese army, we even felt safe enough to settle into our old routine from home. During the day, our mothers and grandmothers were chattering again as they drank tea with homemade cookies while gossiping and playing pebble games. The object was to pick up some pebbles from the ground while catching one that was thrown in the air.

Our fathers divided their time between playing Mahjong, tending the herds, cleaning their weapons, and engaging in target practice. Sometimes they read poetry and sang songs in groups or solo from the Legend of King Gesar. When we weren't shooting birds, Dupa and I played dice and Tibetan checkers. As we had back in Kham, we also watched the others work hard while we spoiled boys stayed put. And, instead of a boy afraid of ghosts and riding my pony with my eyes closed, I was beginning to feel like one of King Gesar's invincible heroes again. Or at least a cowboy.

The decision to grab the leg of a stampeding bighorn sheep had, however, been spontaneous. First we heard the loud crack. Then the ground rumbled after Dupa's father shot and killed one of the sheep from downrange. The gunshot, loud as a thunderclap, sent all the bighorns—30 of them—headed full speed toward the riverbank above Dupa and me as we camped below with all our baby goats and lambs. Unable to see us or to stop, the bighorns leapt one by one from the edge of the bank over our heads to the river's shore. Gritting my teeth, I reached up and caught one of the sheep by the leg. Similar to my grabbing a vulture's foot when I was six, it made no sense. I was dragged at least 50 yards along the river, my arms almost yanked from their sockets. Of course, it was stupid, especially since the ram shook me loose. But it was also irresistible. As with grabbing the vulture, to hold something in my own hands that could leap so high and live so free was breathtaking.

No one but me was impressed, however. The general consensus: I was fortunate not to be stomped to death. Still shaking his head, my father, who was a wonderful cook but always humble about his skill, prepared a delicious meal of the bighorn sheep Dupa's father had brought down the usual way—with a bullet. I'd hoped taking down a wild beast would demonstrate my strength as a man. Instead, my family laughed at me for being foolish enough to challenge a beast stronger than a pony. At least we were all laughing again.

When our fathers and most of our men left camp in the early summer, we didn't ask questions. We assumed that, as usual, our fathers were hunting or scouting.

Each night, after allowing the fire's embers in the big tent to keep us warm during the evening, we would then leave for our sleeping quarters in the smaller tents and unchain the killer dogs. While the *dhugche* prowled the camp sniffing the air for wolves or bears, Dupa and I slept with pistols under our pillows and daggers at our bedsides—just in case.

Sometimes, just before going to sleep, Dupa and I would whisper about our fathers. What were they doing? Were they all right? Of course they were. They always were.

By the end of the summer, however, when we still had no word, I was watching the horizon during the day and having trouble sleeping at night. It had been over three months. Where were they?

THE "BANG BANG BANG TATATA TATATATATA" sounded like a speeding avalanche of different-sized rocks, and Dupa and I noticed there seemed to be a special order for the gunfire. Rifle shots were followed by submachine guns and then regular machine guns. While Dupa, two uncles, and I—the only men left in the camp when our fathers disappeared—hid in a cave for three days, a battle raged in our backyard. Close enough to hear the gunfire from both sides, we could actually see Red Army soldiers running, hiding, and shooting their weapons. As the Chinese were too busy saving their own lives to have a tea party with us, our staying in the cave was just a precaution. In fact, the females in our camp didn't even bother to hide. If the Red Army had come over the hill to attack us, however, Ostok, our lady sheepherder—the one who had sounded the alert when the Chinese came to arrest our eighteen men—would have poisoned their tea. She always had lots of creative ideas about how to get even with the Chinese.

But no one had an answer to the real question. While a major firefight was exploding in the neighborhood, where were our fathers?

They never said where they were, but when they rode back into camp a week later, our fathers had very vivid details about the fierce battle that we had witnessed from the cave.

Staring into my bowl of soup, I frowned. How did they know about that?

Although typically composed, my father became animated, accenting his narrative with hand gestures as he boasted about the Khampa freedom fighters and their victory in the gunfight we had just seen, the Battle of Lake Nyimo. From my father I first heard the name *Chushi Gangdruk*, as he described Gompo Tashi and the secret resistance movement he had founded. Taking a sniff of tobacco from his deer-horn holder, my father told us how several thousand Red Army troops surrounded Tashi and a small platoon of his men at their secret Lake Nyimo outpost. Intending to mount a surprise attack, the Chinese had cannons, automatic weapons and grenades. My father was smiling as he continued. When Gompo Tashi ordered the buglers to announce a charge, the freedom fighters sounded the war cry, *"Kee hee hee, kee hee hee heee, duo ahe thee!"* (Got you!) and charged into the PLA (People's Liberation Army) ambush.

For this battle, as Dupa's father continued the story, the PLA had done the math. They always calculated they needed ten to fifteen Chinese soldiers against one Khampa. He smiled. "However, this time their projections were wrong." Creating a dramatic pause, he was now laughing. "Drastically outnumbered, trapped, outgunned, and unprepared, the freedom fighters had nothing to lose." It was true. The men from Eastern Tibet had witnessed atrocities against their own families and been cast out of their homeland by the PLA.

As our fathers told the story, the Chushi Gangdruk, on their galloping horses, hacking at the Chinese in hand-to-hand combat, sent the Red Army panicking and scrambling.

At this point, one of our other men added, "They fought like King Gesar and his Thirty Heroes."

I nudged Dupa. The story about this real battle was much better than folk songs about mythical warriors. These were live human beings fighting the actual forces of evil. But how did our fathers know all these specifics? Our families, like most Tibetans, had heard rumors about the existence of Tashi's secret organization, but no one knew the details.

My father then described how Gompo Tashi Andrugtsang, a businessman from Kham, had founded the Chushi Gangdruk secret resistance movement.

Under the umbrella of trade and using the cover story of collecting offerings to present the young Dalai Lama with the gift of a golden throne, Gompo Tashi and other businessmen from Kham had moved throughout Eastern and Central Tibet in 1957, building a secret guerrilla force to fight the Chinese. When my father described seeing two of the resistance organizers during his mysterious summer away, I blinked. What? Sadretsang and Pandatsang? The models my father used when he urged me to become a businessman instead of a nomadic chieftain? Apparently since the Chinese invasion, "Khampa businessman" had become a different job. Now they were freedom fighters?

Dupa whistled.

But where had my father just seen them? It was soon becoming clear.

From Dupa's father, Khuru Ngajam, we heard about the official founding of the top secret Chushi Gangdruk (Four Rivers and Six Mountain Ranges) on June 14, 1958, exactly at the time our fathers had gone missing. Khuru Ngajam nodded at Dupa and me. "It was time to unite." Forgetting past feuds, he explained, Khampas had to be "logical and pragmatic." To defend Buddhism against the Communist Chinese, freedom fighters from warring districts all over Eastern Tibet joined together at the home of Gompo Tashi near Lhasa. Committed to die for our people, our country, and our religion, all the Khampas bonded together as brothers, fighting for a common cause against our common enemy. Turning Khuru Ngajam's words into images in my mind, I pictured the huge display of force led by the cavalry under their new flag—crossed swords on a yellow background. Then, Dupa's father leaned forward as he told us that the fighters took an oath never to reveal the names of other Chushi Gangdruk members or the locations of their camps—"even under torture."

I let out a breath. *Wow.* This really was much better than the tales of King Gesar. And our fathers certainly never revealed their location all those months they'd been missing.

Adding to the mystery, my father also knew specifics about a top secret Chushi Gangdruk mission in which Gompo Tashi and his men seized weapons and ammunition from the Tibetan government armory at Shang-Gaden Chokhor. According to my father, to avoid further infuriating the Chinese, Tashi made a prior secret arrangement with the Tibetan government to make the seizure look like robbery conducted by the Chushi Gangdruk at gunpoint.

Finally, settling onto his mat and taking a breath, my father surprised us with his extensive inside knowledge about politics in Lhasa. Describing how Chinese commanders and thousands of troops were now a presence in the

Tibetan capital—first arriving with diplomatic overtures, but slowly appropriating houses and food supplies—my father explained that the Chinese were working to slowly and subtly erode the power of the Tibetan Cabinet. Then he paused. "Even the most naïve Tibetans now understand that the key strategic objective of the Chinese People's Liberation Army is to complete the illegal occupation of Tibet—" He paused again. "—by capturing the Dalai Lama."

I felt a jolt shoot through my chest as if I had been punched. *Capture* His Holiness?

My father looked at each of us in turn. "The Chinese plan is to seize power by seizing our leader." If His Holiness were physically in Chinese hands, my father told us, they could not only subdue the Tibetan government in Lhasa, but also take control over the entire country. Nodding at Dupa's father, he added, "Not all Tibetans in Lhasa are naïve about this." I thought of the officials from our home district who had been to Bejing. Collaborators. Traitors.

But how did my father know any of this? Even in Central Tibet, the average Tibetan had little or no knowledge about politics in the countryside or the next district, much less in the Holy City. Although he was one of the few informed men in Tibet, Gompo Tashi was constantly on the move and had little or no idea what was going on in Lhasa. Couriers from the capital of Tibet would ride for weeks trying to catch him with news about the growing resistance effort.

As I review the story of my family during those years, I understand that, although it would have been dangerous and against Tashi's orders for our fathers to tell us, our men must have been at Tashi's home the summer of 1958 for the founding of the Chushi Gangdruk. They knew too much. The timing was right, and, upon their return, our men had shiny new M44 Russian 7.62 × 54-caliber rifles, the same Russian-made guns which Tashi had personally bought and distributed to his fighters for the opening ceremony. We knew our fathers hadn't had animals to trade or enough money to buy such weapons. I pictured Dupa's father, Khuru Ngajam, marching on his famous horse, Ta Tongrie, in formation with Tashi's cavalry under the Chushi Gangdruk's yellow flag. It would logically be at this ceremony that my father had seen the Khampa businessmen who turned resistance organizers. And then there was the location of our campsite. Had our fathers purposely chosen a home base near the secret Chushi Gangdruk outpost at Lake Nyimo? Had they been next door the whole summer?

Our fathers never said, and Dupa and I will never know for sure, but the facts speak loudly. Although it would be two years before our families would leave Tibet to join the revitalized Chushi Gangdruk movement operating out of Nepal, it appears that, as we huddled in the cave, our missing fathers had been next door in the stampede of freedom fighters cutting the throats of Chinese soldiers and slashing their way out of the Red Army ambush.

Then there's a final question about which I'll always wonder. If our fathers had been at Tashi's home in Lhoka, had they encountered a Khampa named Gyen Bawa Yeshi—the real wolf in my family's tragedy—who was training in that area the same summer? Did our fathers' conflict with Yeshi have its origins in that summer?

After our fathers' return, one thing was clear. We could no longer stay in our bucolic new home at Lake Nyimo. The genocide and torture taking place in Eastern Tibet was now a tidal wave surging toward Central Tibet and the Holy City.

Most upset were Dupa and myself—the children. We felt safe in our new home in the land of living ropes and had innocently believed this would be our life forever.

But, in early fall of 1959, the adults knew it was time to seek higher ground. In this case, higher ground was Tsurphu Monastery with Tai Situ Rinpoche. Surely we would be safe in a holy institution? For Khampas, "safe" meant strong horses and Russian-issue rifles. But for Buddhists, safe meant holy men, blessings, and divinations. And we needed to know what to do next.

THE SMELL OF INCENSE from the Fire Puja spread like the fragrance of midsummer's wildflowers, and the thick smoke sprawled out of the chimney in the shape of a flying blue dragon. Our fathers had offered 100 animals—horses, yaks, sheep, and goats—to have the Sixteenth Gyalwang Karmapa perform the rare Black Hat ceremony. Arranging the ceremony had required connections. Based on the intervention of Tai Situ Rinpoche—our highly respected teacher with whom we had traveled and whose tutor had saved us from a bloody battle—and the fact that our family belonged to the same Karma Kagyu lineage, the Gyalwang Karmapa finally agreed.

In his monastery, the pets of the Karmapa—many different kinds of birds and little rodents—were either flying or running all over the rooms. It was like a small zoo. There were so many animals everywhere that Dupa and I couldn't count them. Outside the walls of the monastery, which was situated in a deep valley with a high rocky mountain in the back, forested hills in front, and a small river running through the valley, there were snow leopards, brown bears, and panthers. Sometimes we would hear dogs barking during the day. By the next morning, they were silenced. The panthers ate them.

Dupa and I were just glad we were safe. Of course, we also knew that, like everything in our lives, "safe" was temporary.

Waiting for the Black Hat ceremony to start, Dupa and I saw the awe on the faces of hundreds of families from across Tibet who had congregated to receive the greatest and most precious blessings from His Holiness the Sixteenth Gyalwang Karmapa. As the monks sat in meditative positions while praying to make this day beneficial to all sentient beings, the audience chanted, *"Karmapa Chenmo, Karmapa Chenmo, Karmapa Chenmo"* (May Karmapa Bless Us All).

Then everyone saw it at the same time. Dazzling double rainbows appeared like magical gates to welcome us all. *Wow.* How did the Karmapa do that?

Everything was going well except for one confusion. I kept looking toward the doors. Where was the Karmapa? Everyone was waiting for His Holiness Gyalwang Karmapa to perform the Black Hat ceremony. On the throne, where the real Karmapa was supposed to be, sat a statue. I admired the craftsmanship of the artist who made the Karmapa look-alike. As time was never an issue in Tibet, everyone waited patiently. When a monk appeared, holding high above his head a round box covered with yellow silk, the chanting and religious music stopped, and silence filled the cosmos.

Suddenly, what we believed was a statue of the Karmapa moved and two monks rushed over with the box. As part of the ceremony, the live Gyalwang had been frozen in time and space in a contemplative state of mind. Now lively and brilliant, like a bright star in broad daylight, he emerged as the living Buddha of Compassion. Taking the Black Hat from the silk box and placing it on his head, the Karmapa steadied it with his right hand and held a crystal mala in his left hand, while he recited the Karmapa mantra, "Om Karmapashe Hung." The ceremony lasted 108 seconds.

Everything changed in that moment. The entire audience was hushed by the miracle of the Magic Crown. Feeling blessed in their hearts, the audience wept tears which turned to holy water of happiness and bliss. For me, with a liking for spectacle but little interest in the spiritual, this was a moment beyond words and emotions. For the first time, I had a glimpse of the mystery.

The Karmapa's blessing couldn't change history, however.

When the four lamas from the Barmed Gon Monastery in Drongpa Medma—the one to which my monk uncle belonged—arrived at Tsurphu Monastery, they brought the bad news. During the year since we had left, most parts of Kham, including our district, had been overrun by the Chinese. Over a thousand people from Drongpa Medma, including our chieftain, Pon Gyalpo, had left for Nepal and India, all in small groups and all taking different routes. Not all of Pon Gyalpo's family escaped, however, and Dupa and I heard firsthand about the torture of someone we all knew.

Pon Gyalpo's uncle, Thupten Nyangpo Rinpoche, a highly realized lama, had been put on trial by the Communist Chinese, during which a mob tortured the defendants to near death and killed others, depending on the nature of the supposed crime (which they never committed in the first place). Many years in prison and horrific torture were Thupten Nyangpo Rinpoche's sentence, not only for being the brother of a chieftain (Pon Gyalpo's father), but also for fitting the basic criteria to receive the torture and death penalty for innocent Tibetans under Communist rule: of Tibetan origin, an intellectual, a lama, a Buddhist practitioner, a leader, an aristocrat, a democrat, a rich landowner, and a man who believed in freedom. Any of these would qualify someone for criminal charges against national security. No one actually needed to commit a real crime—in the same way that *all* Jews qualified for execution by the Germans.

The Lama's spiritually inspired method of resisting Chinese law was the exciting part of the story. According to the monks telling us the story, during the public trials in the daytime, Thupten Nyangpo Rinpoche endured tremendous beatings and injuries, but at night all his injuries were healed completely and the chains that were put on his hands and legs were found mysteriously melted away like butter. The Chinese officials, who were not supposed to believe in such phenomena, tried to hide this.

Ironically, as the monks reported, unless a person was in prison, no one knew who went where, or who got killed, or who escaped. Families were separated, and people were missing. As we heard about our own relatives and friends who were killed, wounded, and captured, I watched my father's face. He looked like he did two summers earlier when he loaded a gun to track the wolf that was killing our lambs.

My father's expression was even grimmer when he returned from a fact-gathering mission to Lhasa. Although travelers were still spreading news of Gompo Tashi's victories, in January 1959, the reality my father now described was not so glorious. The Chinese, he told everyone at Tsurphu Monastery, were now in complete control of the capital. "It's clear that the Chinese are ready to take their most valuable target." In addition to praying in the morning, my Uncle Chopak continued his prayers throughout the day. In February 1959, all of Tibet was praying for the safety of His Holiness.

My own prayers had a more selfish spin, however. Did the Chinese takeover of Lhasa mean we weren't going to see the Dalai Lama and his golden throne? We all knew the details: it weighed over 3,000 tolas of pure gold and was studded with priceless precious stones. For weeks, my Uncle Chopak and my grandmother had been preparing for our pilgrimage. But, like so many other things that hadn't come true, our seeing the Winter Palace looking like mountains against the sky seemed to be a dream. We couldn't go to the Holy City while its streets were overrun with Chinese devils, could we?

When Dupa and I woke the next morning, my Uncle Chopak was hooking up a yak-drawn cart.

Dupa and I moved closer. What was he doing?

"This is for your grandmother." He tightened the harness with a yank. "The rest of us will be going on foot."

THROBBING WITH THE "DANG, DANG, DANG" of religious drums and the wail of conch shells, cymbals, and horns, the Holy City of Lhasa churned below us, and throughout the city, smoke curled from Fire Pujas calling on the deities to protect our leader.

Explaining that the Chinese were waiting for the end of a month of religious ceremonies before they would attempt to abduct His Holiness and initiate the collapse of our thousand-year-old civilization, Uncle Chopak had led Dupa's parents, my grandmother in her yak-drawn cart, and Dupa and me on the two-day journey from the monastery to Lhasa. Now, from a rooftop, Dupa and I were witnessing the historic spectacle of the 24-year-old Dalai Lama carried on the shoulders of his attendants in a specially built golden palanquin. While the procession moved from the Norbulingka, the Jewel Park, to the Jokhang Temple, where His Holiness would complete the final examinations in his Buddhist studies, the thousands who had arrived in Lhasa that month to celebrate the Great Prayer Festival of Monlam Chenmo, as well as the Fourteenth Dalai Lama's final religious examinations, chanted, *"Om Mani Padme Hum"* (Hail the Jewel in the Lotus).

To guard the temporal and spiritual leader of Tibet, the full Tibetan army lined both sides of the roads, the commanders wearing British uniforms and the militia in *chubas,* or long overcoats. Ready to shoot, the soldiers swiveled their guns in wide semi-circles. Many of them had American-made muskets, like the first gun my father gave me. Pressing in behind the Tibetan soldiers, ready to protect their leader, stretching out as far as Dupa and I could see, were tens of thousands of ordinary Tibetans from all walks of life—many with babies on their shoulders. Uncle Chopak had heard that the number of refugees from Eastern Tibet, most of them Khampas, was over 100,000. Also among the crowds were many restless young Khampas—Chushi Gangdruk who had infiltrated into the Holy City from Tashi's stronghold in Lhoka, recognizable by their khaki *chubas,* which were tucked higher than those of Central Tibetans, and by their shirts with much longer sleeves for hiding weapons. Shouldering through the crowds, the young freedom fighters blended in, their guns well-hidden. Excited, Dupa and I got busy locating them in the seething crowd.

Meanwhile, quietly threading their way through the Tibetans, hidden in plain sight but moving slowly and carefully, were the Red Army soldiers in Mao's blue uniforms. They were in no rush to finalize the occupation. The goal of Communist China, Uncle Chopak told us, was "a peaceful surrender" by the Tibetan government and its army. Bloodshed would have sabotaged the Red Army's pretense that this was a "Peaceful Liberation of Tibet." And the influx of refugees and the unprecedented hundreds of thousands of Tibetans like us in town for the festivals was complicating that goal. The Chinese were willing to wait. However, in preparation, they were filling the Holy City with soldiers. And more were coming.

On our two-day pilgrimage on foot to see the Holy City for the first time, we shared the route with hundreds of Chinese military trucks and jeeps emitting stinking smoke and backfiring. As there were no paved roads in Tibet, the convoys kicked up trails of dust which, with the help of the wind, became billowing clouds. We had to cover our mouths as they rumbled past us. The Red Army trucks, I pointed out to Dupa, usually traveled in groups of ten—ten soldiers in one unit of the army, ten in each truck, and often ten trucks traveling at a time. Although the soldiers had also been heading for Lhasa, it was to abduct His Holiness, not honor him. While Dupa and I were busy counting

Chinese trucks and waving to the soldiers who never waved back, Dupa's father was silent. He never even turned to look as the next Red Army convoy rattled up behind us.

For today, however, the Red Army, the Tibetan army, and the Chushi Gangdruk walked the same streets of Lhasa in a tense cease-fire.

The only actual violence we saw on the streets involved Tibetan holy men. Around Lhasa alone the monasteries had as many as 8,000 to 10,000 monks, all of whom had come for the festivals and were jostling about the Holy City. Although Dupa and I wandered through all the temples, including the Winter Palace, when we tried to walk the streets, they were so crowded that it took us an hour to go a hundred paces. To prevent injuries from all the shoving and brawling, especially when the monks were coming out of the temples after their daily prayers, the temples provided *Dhub-dhub*—monk police—to manage pedestrians. In a rowdy crowd, people could be stomped. Under their robes the monk police, looking giant and fearsome, wore shoulder pads like football players in America. Well-trained in hand-to-hand combat, they carried big metal keys with leather handles for reaching above the crowd and hitting brawlers on the head. Weapons in disguise, these keys were as powerful and deadly as sledgehammers. The tallest people received the most beatings. Although I always wanted to be taller, I felt lucky to be short in the Holy City of the Gods.

On the roof, we were safe from being trampled or beaten, and, even better, we had the best view in the city to see our leader at this critical moment in Tibet's history.

When seeing the Dalai Lama as a real person and not a gold statue, I couldn't breathe. Golden statues didn't come to life like this young holy monk who was talking with the lamas walking next to him and gesturing with his hands. In the warm midday of that February, my heart was thumping. Perhaps His Holiness was too young to be the national leader, but the tragic circumstances of the Chinese invasion forced him to take on the leadership role he inherited as the Fourteenth Dalai Lama of Tibet. In our family and for most Tibetans, the Dalai Lama's young age and political inexperience didn't matter all that much. For us, he was the true living Buddha of Compassion, and he still is. My father's name for him was *Gyalwa Yeshen Norbu* (the Victorious Wish-Fulfilling Jewel).

Then a murmur turned into a roar as the crowd swirled below Dupa and me. Under the huge portal of the Jokhang Temple, opening out the front to the public, the Dalai Lama made his way to the famous golden throne. Immediately, as if trying to pick a fight with His Holiness, several monks began shouting at him simultaneously. What was this? It was impossible to hear. Circling the throne, holding prayer beads in their left hands, the monks—who were the most educated debaters of complex Buddhist philosophical thought, logic, and metaphysics—clapped their hands in the face of the Dalai Lama. Only when one of the observers on the roof explained that the monks were conducting their debate in accordance with tradition did my shoulders relax. But not for long.

Even though the young Dalai Lama successfully passed his last monastic test, the mood in the Holy City was mixed. The festival was about to end, which meant that so was the fragile détente in the Holy City. What would happen now?

Back at camp that night, as Dupa and I whispered about His Holiness, his Winter Palace, and the golden throne, the adults weren't talking. Uncle Chopak was praying under his breath, and Dupa's father was packing. No one wanted to talk about what was going to happen. Everyone had too many questions about what to do next. Especially our fathers.

TO CALL THE FAMOUS YOGI, Chewang Tsempa, to the small window of his cave—which was completely sealed inside solid stone walls with only one opening—my father banged on a flat stone. From inside the cave came loud shouting: "Why don't you leave an old man like me alone?" However, he was already at the window. Dupa and I started to laugh. Apparently this was his way of greeting guests. As he had no supplies stored in his cave, Chewang Tsempa depended on visitors like us to bring him food. At a nod from my father, I placed our *tsampa* offering on the stone sill.

As we waited for the yogi to eat, I bumped my shoulder against Dupa's. This was going to be like magic. Here was an actual yogi, like the great yogi Milarepa. This was Chewang Tsempa—Chewang the Mediator—famous throughout Tibet for his accuracy in divinations. And we needed advice.

When we had returned to Tsurphu Monastery from the Holy City in early March, 1959, our fathers had been struggling with the same questions facing all Tibetans. Should we stay or flee? Was it better for us to leave Central Tibet and fight the Chinese from across the border or stay and fight on Tibetan soil?

For ordinary Tibetans like us, a divination from a highly realized lama would be a serious determining factor in our choice.

Because the Gyalwang Karmapa was giving only blessings, we had to seek out Chewang for the answer. Similar to a Pope's blessing, a Karmapa's blessing had no political implications and was dispensed freely, openly and publicly, but without advice. For divinations—which included predictions and guidance—the Karmapa sent us and other Khampas to Chewang, who was not a public figure like the Karmapa, but a highly accomplished practitioner, and whose cave was walking distance from the monastery. Thinking him just a poor old monk staying in a cave, the Chinese left Chewang alone, even after they fully occupied Tibet.

In Kham, there were many holy men living in caves, and, when we were young, Dupa and I mistook these great yogis of Tibet for crazy homeless cavemen. Or horse thieves, perhaps? Luckily, we never created the bad karma of attacking one of the caveman yogis with our slings. In our next lives, or even possibly in this lifetime, we would have been stoned to death. With religious figures we had made from bone, Dupa and I performed made-up rituals, mumbling nonsense phrases, sometimes even pretending to be yogis. This was no pretend yogi.

When we asked Chewang our question, his reply came in the form of a surprising riddle: "What would be the difference between the wild yaks roaming in the mountains and the sheep lined up in the streets for the butchers? Is there any difference?"

Our fathers interpreted the yogi's divination to mean we should be wild yaks roaming the Himalayas, staying on in Tibet to fight for our homeland.

As it turned out neither choice—yak or sheep—would have saved us.

Scouts arrived at the monastery with the news. In less than a month after the Dalai Lama had passed his final test as the reincarnated Dalai Lama of Tibet, ruthless Chinese troops had destroyed the Holy City. However, before the Red Army could kidnap His Holiness, the Dalai Lama was rescued by the Chushi Gangdruk. Fleeing Lhasa in disguise on the night of March 17, 1959, His Holiness safely crossed the border into exile in India. I was impressed. Uncle Chopak's praying day and night had worked.

In the fateful Lhasa Uprising that followed, in their last desperate attempt to challenge the overwhelming forces of the Red Army, the monks and common people in Lhasa tried to secure weapons from the Tibetan government stockpile which were hidden in the Winter Palace. They found the doors locked. Those who finally broke in found that the guns were useless with no functioning bolts and that all the bullets were locked in different rooms. Some Tibetan officials had aligned with the Chinese. It was a typical story of traitors.

Red Army units were also aggressively scouring the countryside to destroy the Chushi Gangdruk, which, to the Chinese, meant all Khampas.

My father and uncle gathered us together. "It's clear," my father told us, "Central Tibet is also no longer safe, not even in a monastery." According to the scouts, thousands of Tibetans were fleeing toward Western Tibet and the Nepalese border.

My father looked at each of us. "We can't let this happen. It's time for Tibetans to fight back. We're going to stay."

I felt my heart thump.

With Chewang's ambiguous message fresh in their thoughts, our fathers led our group on a two-days' ride from the monastery—about sixteen hours on horseback—to a site on top of a group of hills which had the strategic advantage in a gun battle. Mounting an uphill attack, the Chinese would find it hard to maneuver, and they would be more openly exposed as easy targets. Close to an escape route to the border, our new base camp was also far from any other nomads who might report our location to the Chinese.

No longer lazy princes, Dupa and I, now twelve, worked alongside the men securing what animals we had left. To buy Lee Enfield rifles, a few thousand rounds of bullets, and other supplies from Khampas heading for the border, we sold many of our animals, leaving us only about 700 sheep and 150 yaks or less than half of what we'd brought from Kham. We needed the guns, and most importantly the bullets, Dupa's father explained. This was war. We were no longer nomads or refugees. We had to be fighters.

For almost two years, fleeing five hundred miles, we had managed to evade a Red Army attack on our camp. Now they were coming, covering Central Tibet like a red wave.

After carefully preparing our camp, we were ready, even for the unexpected. With good accuracy for a down-range position in the battlefield, our Enfield rifles would have the upper hand. But this time, the unexpected was something for which we couldn't prepare.

We couldn't fight airplanes with bullets.

ON THE AFTERNOON OF MARCH 23, 1959, while Dupa and I were playing *Sho*—a Tibetan game of dice—in the sheep-yard, we heard a distinct noise that sounded like Chinese military trucks, but much louder and coming faster. I dropped my dice. What was happening? We were camped on a high hill, and the sound seemed to be coming from below us. As we looked about in every direction, suddenly, with an earsplitting growl, an airplane appeared from below us, then rose next to us, and finally roared above our tents.

At first, when we heard the loud sputter, Dupa and I thought the Chinese airplanes were doing the same thing as their trucks did, backfiring in a volley. However, when the plane was just above us, streaks of fire and smoke pierced the ground, and spent casings—six or seven times the size of normal rifle bullet casings—thudded all about us. The bullets had been fired from some kind of cannon. Because Khampa yak-hair tents were larger and had a different shape from those of local Tibetan nomads, the Chinese had recognized us from the air.

As Dupa and I ran for cover in the bushes, the dogs ran away, and, spooked by the plane and the rattle of machine-gun fire, the yaks were running in dizzy circles, crashing into each other. As the grumble of the plane engines faded, our fathers were already loading our gear on the mules. We had to move fast. The Chinese Army would be coming over the hill to finish us off.

Amid the buzz of panicked conversations and the restless stomping and grunting of the yaks, no one noticed that I'd stopped talking. The boy who had grabbed the leg of the stampeding bighorn sheep was gone. My mind swirled with horrible images of the Walking Dead in Mao's uniforms taking me to a Chinese living hell. While the projected fears of grownups are limited to their factual experiences, I was still a twelve-year-old child, and the sky wasn't even my limit. It was no longer the zombie soldiers of nightmares that had me frozen with terror. Our battle with the Evil Empire was with faceless machines. Instead of brave warriors fighting with guns and swords face-to-face—the only kind of battle Khampas were trained for—we were in a war with men we couldn't see who were pushing buttons and sitting behind boxes.

My pony was the first saddled.

While traveling the whole night and the rest of the next day, as we crossed the Nyenchen Thangla pass, this time from the opposite direction, I could count on only one thing. When the Chinese found us again, I would be with my family. My brother Dupa and I would be together.

IN THE OPEN FIELDS, where our conversations couldn't be overheard, Dupa and I listened as our fathers and uncles continued their fiery debate. This couldn't be happening. I felt sick to my stomach. Our families were going to split up.

Although to fight the Chinese, all Tibetans were willing to band together and forget old wounds, that didn't mean Tibetans agreed on *how* to band together, especially Dupa's father and my Uncle Chopak. The issue was size. And safety. Instead of the eighteen people in our two families, our group now included hundreds. As we headed out of Central Tibet to fight the Chinese in Western Tibet, our families were soon joined by dozens of noncombatant Khampa groups who were fleeing Central Tibet, many of whom were from Nangchen province and mostly from our district of Drongpa Medma. Very different from traveling with a dozen well-armed lamas, we were now on the run with a group the size of an entire Tibetan village—hundreds of children, elders, women, boys my age. The numbers kept changing every week, but usually our group swelled from 300 to 500 people.

To avoid being easier targets for the Chinese to surround us in the open fields of no-man's land, we purposely created a city of tents spread out thinly in a disorderly design rather than camping in close circles. Instead of keeping all our eggs in one basket, we made it more difficult for the egg hunters. Even though we had no time to construct pens, with more space between tents, there was room for the goats, yaks, and sheep to roam freely during the day. Tired from the day's travel and following their instincts, when it was time to sleep, each herd stayed with their own kind and followed their leader.

Among the human leaders, however, there was less consensus. As Dupa and I held our breath, my Uncle Chopak and Dupa's father slashed their hands across their jugulars, made chopping movements, and waved both hands at the same time. Arguing that the Chinese "could show up any time," Uncle Chopak wanted our two families to break away and head west by ourselves, claiming, "We're too vulnerable with so many people." Because larger groups had "more manpower and guns," Dupa's father argued that staying with a large refugee community "was safer." A smaller group, he said, would make us "easier targets for bandits and enemies." As when witnessing a dog fight, no one intervened.

When the noisy arguing finally ended, the decision to part was final. Dupa's Khurutsang family would stay in the Nyenchen Thangla mountain ranges to wait for relatives to join them, and my family, Gonatsang, would head toward Western Tibet in hopes of reaching Nepal or India. Both schools of thought were right to a certain degree. What we couldn't know is that both arguments were moot. Neither group would escape the PLA.

Whispering together late that night, Dupa and I vowed we'd find each other again, and live and die together. We were both remembering the mighty dragon of freezing water, blood-red with mud and swollen with hailstones the size of apples, sucking us under the icy surface. It happened back in Kham when Dupa and I were crossing a small river on our property—one which flowed into the great Chedchu River bordering our territory—to rescue a baby horse caught in a hailstorm.

The roar began like a distant cannon shot, then swelled into the sound of an avalanche. Within seconds, a flash flood from the upper valley, pulled us under. No one knew where we were. Battered by hailstones and river rocks, minutes from being swallowed by Tibet's largest river and disappearing forever, we were both thinking about the same thing—each other. When we woke, spit up onto the earth, fifty yards from the raging water, almost unconscious, we'd been holding each other's hands, our fingers interlocking, blood brothers.

On the morning my family was to head west alone, Dupa and I held hands at breakfast, not looking at one another, not speaking, slowly intertwining our fingers.

Glancing over my shoulder one last time, hiding the fact that I was crying—Khampas didn't cry—I kicked my pony forward. This was wrong. In the flash flood, Dupa and I had suffered the rage of Lucifer together and lived. When we became old enough to join our fathers fighting the Chinese, we should be riding side by side, guarding each other, forever.

However, a whole new reality was waiting. Fighting the Red Army separately and alone, far from one another, in different regions of Tibet, we two sheltered nomad boys were about to become trained killers at age twelve.

The Chinese found Dupa's family first.

CHAPTER FOUR

THE SMALL REACTIONARY GROUP AND FISH IN A NET

MARCH 1959 TO WINTER 1960: WESTERN TIBET

JUST FIVE MEN—and one of them Dupa—against an entire company of Red Army soldiers? When, within days of our families parting, the Chinese reconnaissance planes found the group that stayed behind and offered heavy fire—both from the air and the ground—there were only five able fighters with guns left, including Dupa and his father, Khuru Ngajam.

Because the Chinese had to come up the hills on narrow paths through rough terrain and had no place to hide except behind scattered boulders, Khuru Ngajam was killing them off ten at a time. On the order of their commanders, the Chinese soldiers kept pushing ahead, ten soldiers at a time, each of whom had a captain who'd shoot to kill a soldier who turned back or was not firing his weapon. So that they wouldn't be killed by their own leader, some soldiers were firing in the air behind the boulders. They knew that the Chinese government wouldn't pay financial compensation to the families of dead soldiers who were found guilty of turning back or not shooting at the enemy.

On Dupa's side of the battle lines, to save limited bullets, the five men made one shot, one kill. Each time Dupa's father killed ten Chinese, the next ten moved into their place, a scenario repeated the whole day. When the Chinese moved in so close that Dupa's father didn't have time to reload his rifle, he fought with a sword. Later in the battle, after Khuru Ngajam's submachine gun jammed, one Chinese soldier, who was better trained in hand-to-hand combat, challenged Dupa's father to a wrestling match. Although Khuru Ngajam was a strong man, the Chinese almost knocked him down before Dupa's cousin, Lhodur, pulled out a dagger and stabbed the Red Army soldier.

When the battle was over, not one of our five men was injured, but seventy-six Chinese were gunned down or stabbed, and unknown numbers were wounded. Prizes from the battle included a trove of guns and stacks of ammunition. This was a great victory for Dupa's family and far greater for the Tibetan cause. One less Chinese in Tibet would help ten Tibetans survive.

And Dupa, a twelve-year-old in his first gunfight, was the hero. The battle against the Chinese devils took its final turn when Dupa shot the Red Army commander who was giving the orders. That was enough for the remaining Chinese to flee.

While Dupa was proving himself a great warrior for the cause, in another setting, months later, far from Dupa, I, too, would be killing Chinese soldiers at twelve, but, for me, there would be no victory. It started with my stealing 200 sheep.

WHEN THE SHEPHERD REFUSED our request a second time, Uncle Chopak pointed a gun at the old man's head. All we wanted was some yogurt.

The two of us had come asking for food at the camp of a wealthy Western Tibetan nomad family with a large tent in the distance and several thousand sheep milling about. No one would miss two bowls of yogurt. My mother would have given food to any pilgrims or beggars who asked. However, this old shepherd guarding the flock was no gentleman.

On the other hand, Uncle Chopak, by waving a gun, was going far beyond my father's approach—"never flatter or beguile people for a favor."

But we needed food. With no maps or local intelligence to guide us through untraveled territories on unknown terrain, we'd made it to Western Tibet without encountering the Red Army. But our supplies were depleted. For one thing, there were more of us. As preplanned by my father, we'd joined with a new family related to us through my grandmother's side—Namre Geden, his brother, and three sons—who were trained fighters. They had temporarily replaced Dupa's Khurutsang family as our traveling partners.

So, when the shepherd refused to help us, Uncle Chopak pulled out a gun. My granduncle was furious because he understood the underlying source of the old man's insult. Prejudice. In Western Tibet, due in part to the Chinese propaganda against us, Khampas were called *Kuma Jakpas* meaning "thieves and robbers." Many Tibetans in the West believed we Khampas were trouble-makers who were out to sabotage their future dealings with the Chinese. And that was the other problem for my uncle. Instead of standing by our homeland and the Dalai Lama, many greedy and naïve families like this one were choosing to stay behind under Chinese rule. That's what really enraged him. This Tibetan family would give up the Dalai Lama rather than their land and livestock. Of course, they were being tricked. They wouldn't own their possessions for long. They didn't know as much about the Chinese as we Khampas did.

Glaring at us, the old shepherd said, "Go ahead if you want to rob my master, but I can't give you what isn't mine." Even if we'd told him his master's new master would soon be a Chinese commander and his old master would own nothing, he wouldn't have listened. That old man was stubborn.

Lowering his gun, Uncle Chopak spat at the man. *"Pharuzaju tukgen"* or, to translate, "Eat your own dead father's flesh, you old man of Western Tibet."

As we couldn't kill a man over two bowls of yogurt, we left empty-handed.

Well, not exactly empty-handed. And this is where the trouble really started. Never imagining that my action would result in the slaughter of hundreds of Tibetan refugees, I stole some of the wealthy Tibetan's best sheep as revenge for the old man's insult. With a few shots in the air from horseback and without telling anyone, I herded 200 of their milking sheep to a valley near our camp, far from the travel route. That afternoon, one of the families traveling with us got 20 buckets of milk from my stolen animals. When everyone asked how those sheep ended up at our camp, I just looked baffled. I only wished Dupa had been here to see my rendition of frontier justice. For refusing us two bowls of yogurt, the rich nomad's family lost two days of milk from 200 healthy mother sheep—or, over 400 bowls of yogurt.

When, at milking time, the rich nomad found his animals missing and suspected we were the thieves, the owner and his men followed my pony's tracks to our camp. However, when they couldn't find the hidden sheep, it was their turn for frontier justice. When I woke the next morning, my pony Blue Bird was gone.

Then things went from bad to worse. When my father finally handed over the stolen herd, the owner didn't, as expected, return my pony. Now it was war. In Tibet, many lives were lost over the theft of a horse. When I admitted to my father that I'd been the one to steal the sheep, that didn't help. Whatever started all this, we now had to finish it. And that meant getting back my pony from the thieves.

Sending our families and the rest of our group ahead, my father, me, and four of our men stayed behind and, armed to the teeth, found the chieftain of the rich nomad's district. When we arrived in the village ready to demand that the chieftain order the sheep owner's men to return my horse, there were only six of us against an entire village, so force was not an option. Time for plan B.

Convincing the chieftain with a little duress instead of weapons was what my father had in mind. As we'd hoped, when we entered the chieftain's tent, we caught the *ponpo* by surprise surrounded by only a few armed men. Our threat was obvious; we didn't have to say anything. If the chieftain didn't cooperate in finding my stolen pony, my father could hold him hostage until Blue Bird was returned.

Failing to have a Plan B himself, the chieftain offered us tea, promised to send his men looking for my pony, and then explained that his region was large. "You just must give me enough time to investigate." Smiling, he invited us to spend the night and ordered a sheep slaughtered for a feast.

My father glanced at me. Although we couldn't argue with logistics, Western Tibetans were sometimes known to be deceptively smart in the old rivalry between East and West. Was it possible that the chieftain was giving himself time to protect the thief—who might be his relative—or to gather his men to arrest us?

When, at the end of a two-day wait, the chieftain's subordinates brought back my pony—but not the horse thief—we'd had enough of the Wild West. As we saddled up for the two-day trip to catch up with our group, I was just happy to be riding again.

Neither my father nor I understood the terrible consequences of my robbing those sheep or what had actually happened during the two days while we waited for the return of my pony. It appears that the chieftain—whom we were essentially holding hostage for the pony—was actually using the delay to hold us hostage until he could notify his real masters, the Chinese, that we were in the area. Like the rich sheep owner and other families in his district, the chieftain had chosen not to follow the Dalai Lama but to remain under Mao's rule. To appease his new masters, the chieftain, it soon became clear, sent messengers to the Chinese army base reporting our presence in his district.

Looking back, it appears that my impulsive theft of 200 sheep over a bowl of yogurt may have brought on my first gunfight with the enemy and, horribly, the deaths of hundreds of my fellow Tibetans.

WHEN THE CAMP WAS JOLTED AWAKE in the middle of the night—the sky suddenly lit with flares followed by the ceaseless firing of machine-guns—we were more prepared than the 500 panicking refugees in the randomly formed settlement with whom we were spending the night. When we'd stopped at this camp for one night on the way to catch up with our group, my father had remarked that the treacherous narrow ravine—sandwiched between two rocky hills with no way out but east or west—was a "perilous place" to camp. None of the camp's leaders listened. A well-trained fighter, my father had insisted that the six of us sleep with all our clothes on, guns loaded and ready.

Now, surrounded by Chinese troops who'd blocked both ends of the ravine, the camp became a valley of death. The sounds of gunfire were so deafening it caused heart attacks to small birds, rodents, and all the other living creatures fated to be there in the wrong place due to their karmic propensities in past lifetimes. The bullets hitting the rocks created so many sparks that it felt like we were being fired on from all directions.

As people came rushing and rolling out of the tents, the yaks, who were chained with short ropes, were running in circles and dragging along ten or more yaks tied to them by longer ones. The weaker, older people and small children who weren't shot became tangled in the animal tethers and strangled or stomped to death. The screams made me hold my breath.

When my father commanded our men to push through, we gathered control of our frightened mounts, and, in my first battle ever, galloping through the chaos on my rescued pony, I didn't have time to be afraid. Because pistols didn't require reloading with two hands and were better at short range, we aimed them at the oncoming muzzle-flashes, carrying our rifles on our backs. In face-to-face combat, we didn't have time to fix on a target through the rear and front gun-sights, so we had to "point-shoot" from the hip at the flashes of the Red Army gunfire. At such close range this was as deadly as aiming.

Even though the dark shapes attacking us were faceless shapes like the zombies in my nightmares, shooting my way through the Chinese human blockade in the pitch dark at twelve years old, I felt invincible like King

Gesar's uncle Pa Jatsa with his famous magic sword *Yyazukaten*. I was forced to grow up too fast and too furiously—from innocent kid to lethal killer.

Thanks to my father's quick thinking—coupled with gunsmoke, the darkness of the night, and the dust rising from the running animals—the six of us killed dozens of Chinese and rode away unharmed. However, as we would learn, less than half of the approximately five hundred Tibetans survived the attack, and, most of those who weren't slaughtered in the ravine—women, children, and weak elderly people who weren't able to grab important items, such as warm clothes, shoes, bullet-belts, and food—froze to death or died of starvation. Meanwhile, the Red Army soldiers suffered as many casualties as the Tibetans, but most of the Chinese deaths were due to friendly fire. By firing machine-guns indiscriminately from two opposite directions on a level plain with the Tibetans in the middle, they killed themselves.

There are certain things in life that one can't understand and can't ever transcend. My first gun battle at twelve was one of them for me. When it was kill or to be killed, I became a fighting machine. However, in contrast to the five men in Dupa's group single-handedly holding off a battalion of Chinese militia and Dupa's victory killing the Chinese commander, my first gun battle with the Chinese didn't make me feel victorious. Instead of killing a commander as Dupa had, or aiming my rifle at Mao and his Gang of Four, I had killed common Chinese who had been forced into the Red Army. To me, the Chinese leaders resembled animals behaving according to primitive pack dynamics. Rather than working for the benefit of the China, a country of 1.3 billion people starving for freedom, democracy, and universal human rights, the individuals in the Communist Party Politburo had forced their citizens into the Red Army.

Aside from the murderous men at the top, common Tibetans had a lot in common with the common Chinese. They considered each other uncles and cousins for many generations. On the stone pillar in Lhasa that can be seen today, written in both Chinese and Tibetan, is historical evidence of the formerly peaceful coexistence between the people of China and the people of Tibet, mutually accepting each other with equal respect and equal rights.

Long before my first encounter with the Chinese, I used to pray for the courage to fight an enemy and to prove myself. Now, as I'd seen my father and uncles do, after my battle with the enemy, I prayed for the souls of the Chinese soldiers I'd killed, praying for them to rest in peace and have better future lives.

But I didn't pray for myself. From this point forward, whatever came to me, good or bad, I accepted it as my karmic propensities unfolding as a result of my past deeds in many lifetimes before. Now as I looked at the sky and mountains, I believed it was not my choice but my karma that placed me in these situations. This is how a Buddhist looks at things. If I killed to protect my family or country, that was my karma. I didn't create the Chinese invasion. Realizing how fragile human life is and how the nature of impermanence dominates everything that exists, I was coming to believe in karma, the law of cause and effect. The war came to me, and I had no choice but to act accordingly. As part of our duty, we human beings do things we hate. No soldiers like to go to war, but they do it to protect their country. I was growing up.

Meanwhile, I was growing up without my brother. I felt as if I'd left the other half of me behind.

Then—another miracle. A traveler brought the news that the Khurutsang family was only a half-day's ride away from our current campsite in Western Tibet.

In the chilly night, running my hand down the warm fur on my pony's neck, I felt myself let out the breath I'd been holding for months. Within days, Dupa and I, now battle-hardened twelve-year-olds, would be together again.

What I couldn't know was that we'd no longer be evading attacks from the Chinese. Instead, we'd be attacking them. Our families were about to become the only rebels battling the Chinese on our home soil, the lone voice of the resistance in the Tibetan wilderness.

WHISKEY FOR BREAKFAST? When Dupa and I left our tent that morning, my father's oldest brother, Uncle Chebudok, was sitting around a fire with some of our young fighters, passing around a bottle of Chinese whiskey. Our base camp looked like an open market, showcasing guns, hand-grenades, and bullets. Also on display were Chinese army shoes, fresh food, canned food, more bottles of Chinese whiskey, and cigarettes. And tethered about were also many new animals—horses, mules, and, most importantly, yaks.

When, after a six-month separation, we'd reunited with Dupa's family at Bawa Zabdong near the Nepalese border and a half-day's ride from Namla Gon monastery, what we found was not a refugee camp or a makeshift nomadic homestead. We were about to become part of a military encampment, a highly functional guerrilla operation led by Dupa's father, and now mine. While my family still had over half of our original animals and were still nomads who became fighters out of necessity, the group assembled with Dupa's father were fighters who no longer lived as nomads. All their food, like the new yaks in the yard, came from robbing the Chinese.

As was typical, without warning or explanation, the men drinking whiskey for breakfast had left our base camp in the middle of the night three weeks earlier. To avoid any spies for the Chinese or travelers learning about their secret missions, it was not uncommon for our men to disappear for days or weeks without telling anyone whether they had left on a hunting trip for wild sheep or a pleasure trip to play Mahjong and dice. Of course, we knew.

Although most of Tibet was under Chinese occupation, it was along the Nepalese border that the Chinese were still vulnerable in the summer of 1959, and our group, led by our fathers, was ambushing Red Army convoys and camps in the dark of night, attacking the PLA with their own weapons, and killing the ruthless Chinese with Chinese bullets. Coming to recognize and fear our band of a few dozen guerrillas as much as they had Tashi's Chushi Gangdruk fighting force with its army of thousands, the Red Army leaders took our group seriously. So fierce and successful was our small band of fighters that the Chinese sometimes mistook our smaller group for the Chushi Gangdruk, which they called the "Big Reactionary Group." The Chinese gave us our own name—"The Small Reactionary Group."

Although I'm not sure if the whiskey had any impact on the authenticity of the tale, this is the story they told us about the latest mission. From two Chinese poachers on a hunting trip for the famous Tibetan antelope—whose wool was as highly priced as gold—our men had learned about a major Chinese caravan. Based on ten days of reconnaissance behind the enemy lines, our scouts had discovered that the convoy would be coming through a long gorge—a narrow, steep-walled canyon with no way out except two directions, retreat backward or move forward. Taking another swig of whiskey, Uncle Cheboduk started to laugh. "This was a God-given chance to kill Chinese, by either shooting them or leaping from the boulders and slashing the throats of the soldiers on horseback. It was the perfect terrain for an ambush."

With the horses hidden nearby, Dupa's father, Khuru Ngajam, had our men take positions behind boulders for several hundred paces on either side of the gorge. Because of the narrow and windy path, about 150 Chinese soldiers on horseback and a caravan of 100 yaks and 35 pack mules were travelling in single file in a very long line. Ten soldiers headed the procession and another ten protected the end.

Although there was no playbook for the heat of battle when fighting took on its own life, that's where Khampas had the advantage over the Red Army forces. To avoid the sound of gunshots, Dupa's father and a few of his men killed the first five Chinese in hand-to-hand combat with swords and daggers. Then, when the Chinese were quick to fire, a full-blown gun battle, lasting nearly half a day, raged throughout the gorge. The battle ended with fifty-seven confirmed kills and several wounded on the Chinese side and three killed and two wounded on our side. The remaining Chinese simply ran away. Except for two mules and a yak that were killed in the crossfire, our men captured all the weapons, supplies, and animals, including the yaks, from a Red Army convoy, displaying them at our camp.

Dupa's uncle—who always volunteered to slaughter an animal when we needed the meat—was now butchering one of the stolen yaks, cutting the meat into small chunks to make blood sausages. Because we were Buddhists, most of our men wouldn't kill even a large animal.

Of course, our men had no hesitation about killing a large animal if it was a Chinese soldier who was plundering our country, destroying our culture, and murdering our citizens. Despite the Dalai Lama's personal endorsement of the Buddhists' belief in the sanctity of all life, when fighting broke out with the murderous Chinese, the Dalai Lama's Middle Way was left in the middle of the road. For our fathers, the Middle Way could also be interpreted as not using measures that are extreme but doing the right thing as called for in the moment. This may imply killing a few to save many more. The Small Reactionary Group was fine with that.

Based on travelers' exaggerated or distorted reports, legends about our group had been spreading all along the Tibetan-Nepalese border among the Tibetans and the Chinese. Our three families—Gonatsang, Khurutsang, and now Namrutsang—along with some newly distinguished Khampa warriors, were making Tibetan history as the most successful guerrilla operation fighting on Tibetan soil. With no communications systems in Tibet, we couldn't know that we were the only one. While we were escaping from the Chinese ambush in the spring of 1959, Gompo Tashi and his army of Chushi Gangdruk soldiers had ceased operations and fled over the border to India.

One reason for our success was the group of distinguished individuals—self-made, self-taught, experienced killers and legendary Khampa figures, most of them already famous in Kham—who had the joined the Small Reactionary Group looking for a chance to fight alongside Khuru Ngajam, whose growing celebrity as a true hero was spreading throughout Western Tibet.

Especially interesting to Dupa and me was Dadhue Nayue, or Dadhue the Black Face, who had a notorious history as a killer in his early twenties when he'd worked as a *Dhub-dhub* (monk police) for the Ganden Monastery in Lhasa, and later, in Kham, where he'd been a famous bandit. If he was in a good mood, Dadhue would show us his weapons and tell us about his past. As the most infamous story went, while Dadhue was policing in the famous Jokhang Temple, a quarrel with a fellow Khampa turned into a fearsome battle in which Dadhue killed the other man with his bare hands. Although he was expelled for breaking monastic rules, Dadhue wasn't jailed because he was from a powerful monastery. Soon after, while Dadhue was crossing a narrow bridge near the Summer Palace, an arrogant captain in the Tibetan Army pushed Dadhue out of his way saying, *"Pangok pharjuk"* (beggar, you run that way), and Dadhue, who took no insult, drew his dagger and stabbed the captain to death.

Because killing a soldier meant capital punishment, Dadhue couldn't stay in Lhasa and fled to Kham, where he joined the famous bandit leader, Ngubam, the Robin Hood of Kham, who, with his forty notorious bandit militants, robbed the rich and gave to the poor. As children, we'd been thrilled by the lore of the bandit, and I loved my father's stories of when he'd joined bandits for excitement when he was a restless young Khampa. But the stories about Ngubam, who had once actually taken refuge in our district under the leadership of our legendary Chieftain Drongpa Pon Trigyal, filled our heads with romantic images, something like those of bank robbers in the Wild West. When Ngubam and his forty men were surrounded by thousands of Red Army soldiers and everyone was massacred except Dadhue the Black Face, Dadhue came west and became one of the heroic warriors in our encampment, a voluntary freedom fighter robbing the Chinese and helping the Tibetans—the Robin Hood of Western Tibet.

But we loved all the fighters. Like Dadhue, many of the men who joined us had personal nicknames given as forms of praise. Sometimes even a fighter's weapons and horses had names. One fighter, Changtse Zejan, who was nicknamed, *Changtse Zejan mema tsen*—-Changtse Zejan the superman—had a dragon-headed Mauser rifle called *Pame drolgo namkye thok* (thunderbolt) and a horse nicknamed *duwa ngojak jachung dai* (blue horse like Garuda), a reference to Garuda, the mythical King of Birds.

With these men, who were courageous, brave, fearless, and all accomplish-ing—or *Pawo*, or *Pama*, as depicted in the Tibetan Legends of the King Gesar and his Thirty Legendary Heroes—the Small Reactionary Group had become a small but legendary resistance force fighting to liberate Tibet.

At twelve, Dupa and I weren't about to be legendary yet, however. There was no chance we'd be invited on one of these raids. Even though we'd just proved ourselves in battles—Dupa's killing a Red Army commander and my shooting Chinese in the pitch dark from my galloping pony—we weren't in-cluded. It wasn't that our fathers thought we were too young to fight. No. We were precious to our parents. They thought we were too young to die.

Quoting the Khampa saying, "We will live to see each other or die to-gether," Dupa and I argued very eloquently that we should ride with the group. We didn't want to stay back waiting for the news that our fathers weren't coming home.

After our fathers reminded us that we were the only sons to carry on the legacies in both families, they very politely turned us down. "Don't you think it's better to stay home to take care of your mothers?"

Because it wasn't possible to guarantee another fighter's safety on a raid, the legendary heroes didn't want us along either. They were afraid to deliver to our parents the news we wouldn't be coming home. They didn't want any-one asking, "Didn't you protect our sons?"

So, while the men were busy liberating our homeland, Dupa and I were col-lecting dry yak dung for our mothers, taking care of the horses, and staying home with the growing number of noncombatants in the camp.

When we had joined Dupa's family, we brought dozens of refugees from Drongpa Medma who had joined our entourage during the months we were separated, among them the four lamas from my monk uncle's monastery, in-cluding our root lama Serze Tulku and our childhood friend who saw through a vision that we'd killed a rat, the reincarnated lama, Bhayu Tulku.

In part because of the fame of the previous reincarnation of Bhayu Tulku, more and more civilian and religious groups arrived with us at the military encampment in Bawa Zabdong. Bhayu Rinpoche was also said to have per-formed many miracles, such as leaving footprints on rocks and putting his finger in melting silver without getting burned. A famous story claimed that after the child Bhayu shot a monk with a pistol, the bullet disappeared and the monk wasn't injured.

Because our guerrilla operation's success was infamous along the Western border, Tibetan refugees also arrived seeking protection.

My favorite job was cleaning the guns our men had taken off the dead Chinese. In our families, I became the only expert in all aspects of how to operate any type of machine-gun. First, I studied the mechanism of each part in detail through careful examination and analysis of how it functioned and what happened if it was missing or broken. When I took a gun apart, I placed all the parts in numerical order, so as not to get mixed up. After cleaning each piece, I put them together as before. Dirty machine-guns often jammed. Then, I repeated the assembling and disassembling of each gun many times so I wouldn't forget. Even if I wasn't using a machine-gun against an enemy yet, at least I knew how to operate one. Most Tibetans only knew how to cock a rifle and pull the trigger. When Dupa's uncle tried to hunt down a Blue Sheep with a machine-gun, he emptied the entire magazine of fifty bullets in a few seconds without hitting a single sheep.

And we needed someone to kill a few wild sheep. Except for my family, everyone in the camp depended entirely on the Chinese raids for food, and the number of noncombatant Tibetan fugitives pouring into our military encampment was growing each week.

TASHI DROLKAR, the wife of our young chieftain, Pon Gyalpo, began to weep as she wrapped herself in my mother's silk and fur overcoat. After escaping a night attack by the Red Army with only the clothes they were wearing, Pon Gyalpo, his wife, and his two younger brothers had arrived at our door cold and tired, having lost everything, including their personal jewelry, valuable family items, and necessities like shoes, hats, blankets, and even their eating-bowls. As half the refugees from Eastern Tibet died on the way to the border—many from starvation or freezing, not just Chinese bullets—in no man's land, far away from our fatherland and so many years later, we were full of joy that our chieftain and most of his family had made it out of Kham. The last story we had heard of Pon Gyalpo's family was about his uncle Thupten Nyangpo, the lama whose torture wounds healed every night in prison.

It was no surprise that Pon Gyalpo's wife looked like a queen in my mother's coat. As the daughter of another important chieftain from another district within Nangchen Nyer-nga, Tashi Drolkar was actually a princess in her own right. Loved for her good nature, the people of Drongpa Medma treated this wife of our commander–in–chief as the people's princess, much in the same way the British later regarded Lady Diana.

Now, thanks to our having escaped Kham with all our animals and to our "banditry" revolution, we were far better off than the rest of our fellow countrymen. After giving my fur and silk overcoat to our chieftain Pon Gyalpo, my father shared with each family in Pon Gyalpo's group some clothing and some of our original animals from home. We were in this together. For the last gesture, my father distributed our extra belts, belts being as important as clothes in Tibet. Each person needed three belts—one to tie the clothes and two to tie on shoes, and, without them, nothing stayed on the body. Without belts there would have been six million Tibetans running around naked.

Once everyone was dressed and warm, we celebrated with a feast as we welcomed Pon Gyalpo and his group to travel with us. However, no one in their party was a hunter or a fighter. They would be dependent on us. And that meant all of us.

Maybe our fathers wouldn't let their teenage sons go into the battlefield, but while the men were off hunting Mao's wolves, we could do something heroic for our people.

AS WE PACKED, eagles and ravens hovered above us in the sunny sky. Like all our plans, this one was ambitious and grandiose. We would hunt down enough wild game to feed our families for weeks. On the night before departing on a five-day hunting trip, the five of us—Dupa and I. plus my father's youngest brother Delshik, my cousin Namre Tsedor, and Dupa's cousin Pagya—argued about how to bring the meat home and how many sheep each of our horses could carry. Delshik suggested that if we threw away the heads and the skins, each horse could easily carry two sheep. The weight would be about 400 pounds. Namre Tsedor jumped in to say that each horse could indeed carry three sheep if we walked home beside the horses instead of riding them. Everybody liked his idea because it was a mission for food, and we could share more meat with other families.

As I was a slow walker and a lazy one, I wasn't all that interested in his suggestion, particularly about the idea of walking home. No one was surprised when I made a proposal—"Since my pony is too small to carry three sheep, can I just take two sheep and decide whether I'll walk?" They laughed and agreed. They knew me well. While the others moved like Tibetan wild yaks, fast and hasty, I was a slow and steady walker, usually dragging my feet.

However, I had an important role in the group—the brains of the operation.

After unsaddling our horses a half-day's journey away on a beautiful spot high up in the mountains—close enough to hunt blue sheep—we made a typical fireplace with three stones and prepared to cook dinner. There was one problem. When Delshik asked, "Did anyone bring a flint?" no one said, "Yes." Here we were far from home, with no way to start a fire.

Our first thought was to send Pagyal home for a *mecha*, a leather pouch which contained the materials to light a fire—cotton soaked in gun powder, a steel blade, and a flint. But staring at the unlit fire, we faced reality. A half day to go home and another half day to come back? One whole day wasted. What a bunch of fools we were! When I caught Delshik's eye, we both started to laugh. Soon we were all laughing at ourselves. Some hunting party.

Then, taking a bullet from my gun, I held it in the air. "Wait a minute; I have an idea." Now everybody laughed at me.

Dupa punched my shoulder. "What's this?"

Delshik rolled his eyes. "Are you going to shoot the cooking pot?"

Ignoring them, I took the tip of the bullet from the casing, poured out the gunpowder on a piece of wrapping paper, and made a pile of dried grass and yak dung. "Watch." When I picked up my gun, everyone stopped laughing.

Touching the end of the barrel to the gunpowder, I pulled the trigger. *Bang.* The fire started at once. Sitting back on my heels, I smiled at my friends. "Now you know what I meant." And the empty casing still had enough primer to fire the gun. Crisis averted. After tea and a hot dinner, we slept soundly for the night.

However, when it was time to actually shoot our bullets, we weren't so successful. "Can you hit one from this far away?" was my question when Delshik pulled the rifle from his shoulder, chambered a bullet, and took aim at a herd grazing on the other side of a deep gorge a few hundred yards from us.

"I can, and I will." He fired a shot, and a big sheep fell and started rolling—and didn't stop.

As we stared, astonished, it fell more than a thousand feet off the cliff and landed mangled and crushed on the rocks at the bottom of the gorge. That was impressive. However, when Tsedor and Pagyal climbed down the gorge to fetch the sheep, they came back empty-handed. The animal's meat was inedible, spoiled by the hard landing. Apparently, landing on a solid surface from such a height smashed the insides of the sheep into a soup which included waste from the stomach.

We shrugged. That had to be a fluke—until it happened again the next day.

After we'd sneaked up on a flock without spooking them, I shot and killed a large male. Success. However, we'd forgotten to gut out the stomach and intestines to make the body lighter, so the dead sheep was too heavy to carry. When Dupa gave it a push down the hill toward our camp, it got away from us and rolled fast and furious for over a quarter mile. By the time the rolling sheep came to rest, the meat of this animal was also completed spoiled.

Dupa kicked the dead animal. "Oh, well, we'll get it right next time."

On the third day, however, we realized we hadn't brought something else we badly needed if we were going to make it to a "next time." A tent. It rained the whole day, and we were soaking wet and freezing. We were also without a fire. Not only had the rain killed the fire, but it was impossible to restart the fire because the yak dung was wet. We found ourselves with a more serious concern than feeding our families for the coming weeks. Survival today. Rain caused floods, mudslides, washed-out roads, dangerous lightening, and even dangerous hailstorms. Our half-day journey home could turn into days or weeks requiring rescue crews if we became stranded hunters.

We weren't laughing now. Dripping wet and shivering, we limped home empty-handed. Of course, we never doubted that soon enough we'd have domestic herds again and wouldn't need to be big-game hunters instead of shepherds.

And, even if we couldn't return to Kham after we kicked out the Chinese, we could live as nomads in this enchanting camp at Bawa Zabdong in Western Tibet forever.

The lush landscape around our guerrilla encampment was a nomad's paradise. Although remote, our new home had beautiful grassy meadows full of wildflowers, green grass hills, streams, and small lakes. Roaming everywhere were wild asses and Tibetan antelopes. This area also happened to be the travel route for the famous Tibetan black-neck cranes. These were my favorite. All around us, large flocks of them were flying in V shapes, laying eggs bigger than baseballs and walking graciously on their long legs while extending their exotic black necks. After summering in Tibet, the cranes—an endangered species due to poachers—spent winters in India and Bhutan. As the favorite subjects for Chinese artists, they exist today only as images on Chinese porcelains, plates, vases and wall paintings. But when I was twelve, they were free and plentiful, the soft flapping of hundreds of wings filling the sky as they glided toward the shore of the lake.

Although we would have been happy to try to rebuild our lives in this beautiful valley by the Nepalese border, the locals in Western Tibet would not be all that happy to have Khampas relocating in their backyards. Like the stubborn old shepherd who refused us yogurt and called us "thieves,"

Western Tibetans were prejudiced against Tibetans from the East, especially Khampas. Many prideful and arrogant Tibetan Westerners had aligned with the Chinese, and their hatred for us was also due to the propaganda against us spread by the Red Army.

That's why what happened next—which would play a part in the chain of events leading to our family tragedy—was not entirely a surprise.

WHEN DADHUE THE BLACK FACE slapped the Western sub-chieftain in a double tap—pop, pop—first with the palm and next with the back of his hand, the man's teeth fell out. As Dupa's father, Khuru Ngajam, grabbed the toothless man's Russian-made rifle, Dupa and I smiled at each other. These Western Tibetans hadn't known who they were dealing with. The saying goes, "One Khampa enemy is too many."

This confrontation of East against West had all started the day before when a delegation of men from our camp had asked for meat, cheese, and *tsampa* from the annual community gathering in this nearby Western Tibetan district. Following my father's instructions, our men didn't flatter or beguile the Westerners but asked directly, expecting the Westerners would behave like other Tibetans and help others in need. Instead of generously sharing their food, the whole group—hundreds of men drunk on homemade moonshine—had responded first with insults and then violence.

Offering our men one small piece of meat, the chieftain had called our men "robbers" and retorted, "Don't you see we're busy here? Now get lost," after which, the drunken mob ganged up on our men, beat them, took their guns and horses, and forced them to walk home. Dupa's cousin Lhodur was beaten so badly that he had to be carried.

As the sub-chieftain who had just lost his teeth and his gun was now learning, this had been a mistake.

When our men arrived home injured, humiliated, and insulted, Dupa's father had called an emergency meeting, and, insane with anger, announced, "We're going to teach some unforgettable lessons to those Western Tibetans who beat up our men, lessons they will never forget." As the badly beaten Lhodur was the fighter who'd saved Khuru Ngajam's life by stabbing the Chinese in the neck during the wrestling match, Dupa's father had a special soft spot for him. Patting his sword, Dupa's father nodded in the direction of the rude Tibetans' camp. "These Westerners won't attack Khampas again. Not in the foreseeable future." Then Khuru Ngajam smiled at Dupa and me. "Be here early tomorrow morning ready to go for a nice ride and a raid."

A shiver of dread and exhilaration raced along the back of my arms. Finally. Dupa and I were going on a mission with the legendary heroes.

Because the beating of our men had occurred on the final day of a district gathering, our fathers anticipated there might be about 50 fighters still there. But my father, always cautious, warned us. "But never underestimate the strength, the skill and the ability of people with whom you engage in fighting, no matter how small or big their group. A wounded bear who's cornered is more dangerous than a mighty lion in the field." He took a sip of tea. "Be prepared for the unexpected."

Our fathers arrived at the perfect punishment, one which our new enemies would find very unexpected. In the Khampa code of conduct, we'd never kill or torture enemies once they were under our control. It was the Chinese who tortured their prisoners. For us, it would be enough to humiliate these rude Tibetans.

Then, as was typical of Khampas, Dupa's father eased the tension by making us laugh, in this case with exaggeration and boasting. "Don't bother to have any breakfast tomorrow morning because our new Western hosts are giving us a big feast at their expense. They just can't wait to welcome us in person. You know what I mean? A real big feast! The best we ever had so far in Western Tibet!"

Trying to sleep that night, I'd imagined several disastrous scenarios. What if all Tibetans at the gathering were still there and they all had rifles? What if they knew more about us than we knew about them? Certainly a bloodbath was a possibility. If they saw us coming, our surprise attack could backfire, and they might kill us instead. Every catastrophe I pictured was within the realm of possibility. Finally, I calmed myself with Buddhist thoughts on impermanence. If things can get worse tomorrow, then they also can get better the day after. Yesterday they had humiliated our men, and tomorrow we would retaliate. But one cannot be one hundred percent certain of anything, I told myself, there was no way of knowing or preventing what was meant to happen, and the one thing we can be sure of is the certainty of uncertainty. I fell asleep.

After everybody had saddled their horses in the early morning, there was a quick head count and strategy session, but we omitted the usual chanting over a Puja Fire before leaving home base. Today it was rush, rush, hurry, hurry. To execute our surprise plan, we needed to catch the Westerners at sunrise while they were in their tents innocently having breakfast.

When we reached the Westerners' camp after two hours on galloping horses, my father posted a few sharp shooters on the hills. Then it was time to go into action. Rushing to the tents, we cut loose all the ropes that held the tents up, and used the tents as nets to trap the men inside—just like catching fish. It worked. Amid screaming, growling, and yelling, all the Western Tibetans were trapped. Then, to make sure they could move but not grab weapons, we tied up all the men with ropes, hands behind their backs.

While our captives looked on, we feasted on all the food and drink they'd refused to share with us the day before. Our men made fun of our prisoners by inviting them to join us in eating their own food. Furious and humiliated, the Westerners could only watch as we also helped ourselves to their possessions.

After Dadhue the Black Face knocked out the teeth of the leader who'd tried to shoot us and Dupa's father confiscated the sub-chieftain's rifle, I "borrowed" something for myself—a small green box which turned into a record player when opened. Requiring hand-winding and a needle, the record player came with several records, including one that had Tara prayers.

After Dupa's father Khuru Ngajam reminded the sub-chieftain how ungenerous they'd been, he added with a sly smile, "We'd also like to borrow some sheep and yaks. We'll pay you for the animals if we meet again." When I woke up the next morning, 52 new sheep and five new yaks were kicking up dust around our tents. Some of our young warriors along with some of the legendary heroes had "borrowed" these animals from the arrogant Westerners. Dupa's family, who no longer had livestock, took the Westerners' animals for themselves.

We had no way to predict that catching the drunken Westerners like fish in a net and helping ourselves to their animals, a gun, and one record player would play a role in the mass murder of our family. For us, the incident represented not just payback for an insult but fresh supplies and, more importantly, food. Our fighters needed to stay strong to defeat the real enemy—the Chinese.

The problem was that we weren't just running out of food. We were running out of fighters. Each time the Small Reactionary Group went out on an ambush, we lost a few good men. And several of our best fighters, including several legendary heroes, had left for Mustang.

Since August, 1959, we'd been hearing the rumors. Gompo Tashi, the founder of the Chushi Gangdruk who had led the battle we witnessed from a cave at Lake Nyimo, was in India working on a plan to revitalize the Chushi Gangdruk. Because the Indian government had refused the Chushi Gangdruk refugees permission to attack the Chinese across the Indian border, Gompo Tashi and the Dalai Lama's older brother Gyalo Thondup had negotiated CIA backing to establish an operational base along the Nepalese border, the central command post to be in the Kingdom of Mustang in north central Nepal.

Once an independent Buddhist kingdom bordering the Tibetan plateau, when Mustang was annexed by Nepal at the end of the 18th century, the remoteness of Mustang helped preserve its ancient culture, which was more closely tied to Tibet than Nepal. Populated by ethnic Tibetans who spoke Tibetan and practiced Buddhism with a monarch sympathetic to the Tibetan cause, our soldiers would feel less alienated. At the same time, the isolation of this Nepalese territory close to Tibet made Mustang an ideal location for the Chushi Gangdruk to operate secret guerrilla warfare.

Despite the great efforts—by both the Tibetan leaders and the CIA—to keep the operation top secret, wildfire rumors that the CIA was sponsoring Gompo Tashi's reborn undercover operation had reached even the most remote outposts in Tibet. Instead of the 300 hand-picked fighters who were to secretly assemble in Mustang, 2000 fighters—over 70 percent of them from Kham—had been pouring into the tiny Himalayan Kingdom, including several of our legendary heroes.

Everyone also knew that dozens of Khampas—some of whom were now in Mustang—had been trained at secret CIA locations by the best guerrilla-warfare experts in America. To their natural skills as battle-tested warriors, Tibetan freedom fighters were adding parachuting, crawling, rock-climbing with ropes, communication, signaling messages in sunlight using a mirror with a hole in the center, and shooting while lying down (as opposed to the Khampa's typical sitting position). In addition to high-tech modern weapons from the Americans, the Khampas were bringing back invaluable detailed maps of Tibet and the border areas, radio equipment, and compasses.

Most importantly, the Tibetan leaders behind the Mustang operation were Gompo Tashi, the founder of the Chushi Gangdruk, and Gyalo Thondup, the Dalai Lama's older brother.

By the fall of 1959, with no more Khampas arriving to join the Small Reactionary Group, our fighting force was almost back to where we started, just the three families. Of the many refugees that stumbled into our camp, very few were trained fighters. All we had left were our guns, our horses, and Dadhue the Black Face.

It was time to leave, and there was only one place to go. Mustang.

CHAPTER FIVE

THE CAT AND HIS DOGS

WINTER 1960 TO SPRING 1961: MUSTANG, NEPAL

DUPA AND I STOOD AT ATTENTION, our eyes shining, as my monk uncle, a professional tailor, measured us for Chushi Gangdruk uniforms. It was so enticing, almost irresistible. The most powerful country in the world was now our ally.

Although I'd have joined any group fighting the Chinese to win back my old life, the CIA-backed Chushi Gangdruk seemed to have the perfect recipe for a reckless Khampa boy. In my secret dreams, General George Patton was now a Khampa warrior reborn into my body, and I was the young General Patton of Tibet. Except I would be wearing a khaki *chuba* the color of sand and dirt for camouflage, a style already worn by Khampas—loose enough to tack up, creating a pocket around the waist for carrying an eating bowl, a pistol, or a prayer book. While my uncle finished our uniforms, we bought Nepalese army boots—woolen with leather soles—and new hats made of fox fur. Then, Dupa and I checked our guns, sharpened our swords, and made our backpacks.

Not yet thirteen years old, Dupa and I were armed and ready to gallop across the Tibetan border with thousands of other Chushi Gangdruk fighters and bring down the barbarous invaders.

Except, as we would discover, no one was galloping anywhere.

WHAT WE FOUND when we arrived in the Mustang area made no sense. Instead of a modern military encampment outfitted by the Americans, in the spring of 1960, the Mustang resistance outpost consisted of two antiquated villages of poorly built mud and stone houses which accommodated locals and their animals under the same roofs. What was going on? The whole world knew the CIA was funding Mustang. Not only were there no American troops (as the rumors promised), but there were no weapons, equipment, or basic supplies from the CIA.

When Dupa and I investigated the villages at the center of the kingdom, we were grateful to be camping two miles away with our families and friends on the outskirts of Mustang, in Lho near the Gar Monastery. Mustang Village— where the dogs barked twenty-four hours a day—felt familiar at first. Although the locals wore different dresses, had different jewelry, and used a different dialect, Mustang's ethnically Tibetan population spoke, read, and wrote in Tibetan. On the surface, everything in Mustang should have reminded us of the good old days in Tibet.

But these weren't the good old days. Wandering the streets, Dupa and I saw freedom fighters, most of them Khampas, struggling to survive in this frozen land without food or shelter. Roaming through the villages and the camps were almost 2000 unarmed and starving Tibetans. And it wasn't just the fighters who were starving. As was typical of Khampas like us, even in battle, men from Kham travelled with their wives, children, and extended families.

Exactly what the Chushi Gangdruk troops and their families were eating depended upon who was telling the story. When we had arrived in the Mustang area, we heard a rumor that Khampas were eating yak hide. One of the freedom fighters, who didn't even have a coat, told us that refugees were boiling their leather shoes and shoelaces for food. Another soldier told us about Khampas eating their saddles.

Smacking the flanks of our ponies, we headed back to our base camp in the countryside, where we didn't have to smell burning cow dung or watch someone eat yak hide.

BUT THEN THERE WAS THE REAL MYSTERY. The fact that the resistance fighters had no basic supplies didn't explain why 2000 battle-hardened Khampas weren't doing what they came here to do—coordinating with guerrilla bands still fighting in Tibet and slaughtering the Chinese. As we listened in, our fathers questioned why the huge Mustang resistance force had yet to engage the enemy. Even without CIA weapons and supplies, there were still many well-maintained and armed bands of fighters, like ours, expecting at any minute to load their rifles and head into battle. Self-trained and self-taught in basic battle tactics, Khampas were natural born "guerrillas"—a Western term we only learned in Mustang.

But there had been no missions, no raids, which made no sense. Gompo Tashi, a fearless leader—with whom many of the current Chushi Gangdruk had fought in Central Tibet—would have immediately used groups like ours to attack the Red Army, especially now, as the Chinese were in the final stages of closing Tibet's Western border.

Of course, no one had actually seen Gompo Tashi. Or Gyalo Thondup.

That's because the two Tibetan leaders weren't in Mustang. The mission was still in the planning stages, and Gompo Tashi and Gyalo Thondup were in India negotiating with the CIA over the basic blueprint for the Nepalese operation. While Mustang had been teeming with armed warriors waiting for orders to raid Chinese convoys, the operation wasn't scheduled to officially begin until June of 1960. Even worse news for all Tibetan refugees in Nepal, because of unexpected policy conflicts back in Washington, all U.S. support was on hold, and the promised CIA airdrops of weapons and supplies were a full year away. Although, from the first wave of fighters arriving in this barren outpost, everyone assumed that someone was running the operation—either Gompo Tashi or Gyalo Thondup—in fact, no one was. The architects of the Mustang operation hadn't yet even chosen a commander for Mustang. That explained why the freedom fighters weren't fighting. As our Khampa battle code called for strict discipline and complete obedience, Khampas honored the chain of command and followed orders. But there was no commander to give any orders.

No one in Mustang knew this, however. In fact, no one knew that, since January 1960, there were no longer any resistance operations on Tibetan soil with which the Mustang fighters could—as planned—coordinate. In January 1960, the last CIA-supported guerrilla camp, Camp Pembar, was destroyed by Chinese jet bombers, and, with no communication with one another and diminishing resources and men, the few pockets of independent resistance fighters were wiped out by spring. And with the Small Reactionary Force now inactive, the fighting force established by the CIA in this remote and barren Himalayan kingdom would be the only Tibetan freedom operation left. But it wasn't in Tibet.

Camping with our three extended families, our chieftain's entourage, several holy men, including Bhayu Tulku and the other lamas from our monk uncle's monastery, and two dozen other families, mostly from our district in Kham, Dupa and I spent the winter of 1960 watching our fathers' growing confusion at the failure to take any military action.

Further troubling to my father was that the secret resistance movement was no secret. At the first gathering of Gompo Tashi's newly formed resistance movement in 1957, all members took an oath of silence. And secrecy was a condition of CIA involvement. The intelligence agency went so far as to give the CIA-trained operatives gold coins instead of recognizable U.S. currency, in case a fighter was captured by the Chinese or stranded in a foreign country. Although the freedom fighters were forbidden to call themselves by any name, many identified themselves as "Chushi Gangdruk," the secret name first popularized in 1958 for Tashi's operation in Central Tibet. My father shook his head. "The last thing the secret resistance movement needs is a popular name." Of course, with the number of Khampas crowding into Mustang having doubled, 4000 Tibetans were hard to miss. And the locals certainly knew the Chushi Gangdruk were in town. Many Nepalese housewives became girlfriends of the guerrillas, carrying half-Khampa babies in their arms. Everyone, including the press in many countries, knew about the CIA-sponsored mission. The Chushi Gangdruk's clandestine bases on the Nepal border, like Dolpo, which were supposed to be top secret, were common knowledge.

The only secret was why the secret fighting force wasn't fighting.

Instead of liberating Tibet, we spent our time struggling to survive in this frozen landscape. Although our group had the best-stocked camp in Mustang with plenty of weapons and supplies, especially my family's herd, the Mustang landscape—which stretched out, hill after sandy, dusty, gray hill, with only scattered green patches of grass, barley, and mustard—was too barren to support livestock. Keeping just enough for ourselves, we were forced to sell most of our animals to the Chushi Gangdruk soldiers.

But this was the nature of war, wasn't it? For us, it was worth it to stay in this wasteland and subsist on a fraction of our original herds if it meant we were going to fight with a well-armed force of thousands, kill our enemies, and free Tibet.

In our two years in Mustang, we never saw any Chinese soldiers, much less killed them.

My fight with a mastiff was the closest any of our group came to combat.

BECAUSE BHAYU TULKU LOVED HIS DOGS, I didn't want to kill his mastiff. I just needed to stop the dog from killing me. This was not a small puppy. It was a Tibetan *dhugche*—a killer.

The battle occurred the day my father had me take a gift—a quarter of a yak—on my back five miles to Bhayu's camp. As an average yak weighs 500 to 600 pounds, when I arrived at the doorsteps of Bhayu's tent, I was ready for a rest. At the entrance were two mastiffs chained to posts, one about 50 feet away. Because the other mastiff was growling on a chain only three feet from the entrance, visitors had to bend to the side to avoid being bitten. No other Tibetan would put a dog that close to the entrance, but this was the young lama's idea of a joke.

However, that wasn't the dog that worried me. The mastiff tethered furthest away was waggling its post free from the ground. "That dog is coming loose," I told the main attendant monk. And I was right.

Yanking the stake from the ground, the mastiff rushed me. Dropping the meat, I hit the dog on the head with the back of my sword, but that didn't stop him. When the mastiff sank his teeth into my chest, I threw aside my sword, grabbed the dog's ears, and wrestled the bucking and snarling animal to the ground. Once on top of the lama's dog, I smashed the mastiff's nose against the rocky earth until it was bleeding. The dog never bothered me again.

I picked up the yak meat and entered the tent, unhurt.

When Bhayu, who'd been off on a walk, came upon the commotion, he was impressed. "Bravo. You wrestled down my dog."

"Aren't you happy I didn't kill him?" I joked.

But there wasn't much to laugh about.

I may have defeated the lama's *dhugche*, but we weren't prepared for the worst kind of killer dogs—human ones.

DUPA'S FATHER, Khuru Ngajam, stopped cleaning his gun when a visitor confirmed the rumor. The entire Mustang operation was now under the command of Gyen Bawa Yeshi, a former monk. Khuru Ngajam asked the question on everyone's mind. "Who the hell is he? Does anyone know anything about his background?" At first, in June 1960, when the Mustang fighters heard that the "leader of the Chushi Gangdruk" had arrived, everyone in Mustang assumed that at last either Gompo Tashi himself or Gyalo Thondup were here to head the mission.

However, to the puzzlement of historians even today, Yeshi, a Buddhist monk with no formal training in guerrilla warfare nor any experience as a leader, was chosen to lead the CIA-backed resistance movement. Yeshi had no experience as a commander, and the monks who came from India with him had no experience in armed conflict. However it occurred, Yeshi's appointment was as mysterious and unexpected as his eventual treason against Tibet.

Although some of the fighters, like us, were surprised and disappointed that an unknown former monk and not Gompo Tashi was at the command post, no one was suspicious. Initially, when Yeshi arrived in Mustang and said, "I come to Mustang as a simple monk, and I will leave Mustang as a simple monk with no money of my own," no one had reason to doubt him. An inspiring orator, a devoted Buddhist, a fellow Khampa, and a charismatic personality, Yeshi, by all appearances, was the shining star of the resistance movement, the right leader for the job.

And, in truth, most of the Mustang force didn't care who was in charge. The Chushi Gangdruk only cared that Khampas would finally be retaking Tibet. And weren't our real leaders, Gompo Tashi and Gyalo Thondup, behind the scenes? And hadn't they handpicked Yeshi? Crucial to the stability of the nomadic societies of Eastern Tibet, our chieftains ruled absolutely. Khampas were trained to never question a leader.

But it soon became difficult *not* to question this new leader. After Yeshi was installed, nothing changed. While the Mustang forces waited to demolish the Red Army, Yeshi only ordered minimal military actions. Rarely meeting with his generals, our new commander was almost never seen in public and spent the large percentage of his time in seclusion praying instead of commanding a resistance operation.

For the next decade, no one in the outside world knew any of this, however. The remoteness and inaccessibility of the Kingdom of Mustang made any legitimate oversight by Tibetan leaders, who were in India, or CIA officials from the U.S. impossible. In addition, an astonishing stroke of luck had left Yeshi free from scrutiny and quite untouchable. In October, 1961, one of the few raids Yeshi ordered—led by his CIA-trained top commander Rara—unexpectedly netted from a Chinese convoy enough highly important Chinese military and government documents to convince the CIA that Yeshi's mission was worth backing. It would take another decade to unravel the extent of Yeshi's corruption and treason.

However, the innocent monk in charge of the Mustang operation didn't fool our fathers. Sitting over buttered tea, Dupa's father and mine questioned why Yeshi was taking no steps to fulfill the original mission designed by the Tibetan leaders and the American intelligence agency—establishing base camps in Tibet from which to attack the Chinese. Why was Yeshi delaying? With no resistance against Mao's tidal wave of Red soldiers from inside Tibet and none by the thousands of Chushi Gangdruk gathered on the outside, the Red Army had completed the illegal occupation of all of Tibet and was continuing its program to eradicate our people and our culture.

Where was the war? When were the Chushi Gangdruk going to kill the invaders who had tortured and murdered our people, bombed our religious institutions, and destroyed our ancient civilization? Instead, thousands of our fellow Khampas were exiles in a foreign country without guns, food, or a mission.

But that didn't explain a much more puzzling question. Why hadn't Yeshi included our group in the few and sporadic raiding parties he did authorize, like the famous October raid? Aside from the CIA-trained officers, our fathers, Khuru Ngajam and Gona Gedun Sherab, were two of the best battle-tested and most qualified fighters available to Yeshi. With our arsenal of high-powered weapons taken off dead Chinese, an army of self-trained Khampa guerrillas and battle-proven leaders, we were a valuable and lethal asset. And everyone knew it. Including Yeshi. Yet it appeared that Yeshi's commanders were purposely excluding our fathers from action.

At this point, our fathers registered no sinister motives behind Yeshi's failure to call on the Small Reactionary Group. When we received word from Yeshi's commanders pressuring our group to conduct no raids unless ordered by the Chushi Gangdruk, we complied. An army needs to act as one cohesive unit under a chain of command. But we were simply mystified. Dupa, who was very proud of his legendary father, thought Yeshi must be "jealous" of Khuru Ngajam. I thought Dupa was crazy. No one could have imagined the former monk capable of petty jealousy. Yeshi was the esteemed, hand-picked supreme commander of the famous Chushi Gangdruk operation. With the exception of Dupa, no one understood that we represented a threat to Yeshi's image.

However, as would become clear, Yeshi's decision to bar our group from the action was no oversight. The existence of our infamous guerrilla band was a direct challenge to his power and reputation. The Small Reactionary Group made him look bad. We had already succeeded—attacking the Chinese on Tibetan soil—where he was now failing. So, while other Khampas took part in a few modest campaigns, the only action we saw involved moving our camp from site to site, seeking grazing for our remaining animals. While patiently waiting to liberate Tibet, the only opponents our families were fighting in this alien land were disease, an occasional ghost, and boredom.

ABOUT 4:00 A.M. early one morning, while I was sleeping on the roof of the main monastery in the Mustang area, I was startled awake by monks chant-ing and shouting of "Phat" (a word that means something like "crack" in Ti-betan). This utterance—exploding like hand grenades in my eardrum—was, I believed, only used to subdue demons and reserved exclusively for face-to-face encounters with the devil himself. In this instance, the devil was the high fever and diarrhea of our chieftain, Drongpa Pon Gyalo. Hardly able to move by himself, his family had brought him to the monastery where my father and I, like many people from our district, had gathered to help care for him. In ad-dition to the many doctors called in, lamas and monks volunteered to perform prayers of Medicine Buddha, the Buddha of Longevity, and rituals like shout-ing "Phat" from the ground floor to the roof.

I was already having trouble sleeping. From the top of the monastery we could see the dead body of a woman that—unlike other dead bodies that were immediately eaten by vultures, crows, and wolves—had remained intact for several days, each day getting bigger and brighter as it bloated. According to Tibetan superstitions, a body not properly eaten by vultures in a Sky Cere-mony is protected by evil spirits for their own use as *Rolangs*, the walking dead. Some people claimed to have seen the body moving, and everywhere I went, people had been telling stories about *Rolangs* roaming about. In fear of my leg being pulled by one of these walking dead, I slept curled like a dog for several weeks trying not to stare at the bloating corpse. Was it moving? Between the shouting monks and the walking dead, I was awake for days.

Eventually, when Pon Gyalo recovered fully, an old monk cut the dead woman's body into pieces for a for proper sky burial—feeding it all to the vultures—and we returned to our camp, where we floated through the months, uncertain about what we should be doing. Our time with the high-powered CIA-backed resistance movement—which we'd assumed would be full of bloodshed and heroics—was, well, uneventful.

My solution to boredom was spending several months visiting families who invited me to play the Tara Prayers for them on my stolen record player. When I opened the small green box, wound the handle, and dropped the needle, the air in the tent vibrated with the eerie and soulful chanting of the Tara Prayers. The families I visited in the neighboring camps were speechless. One of the children hid behind his mother. Nomads had never seen a box that could play music and prayers. For them, it was magic, a gift of God fallen from heaven into my lap. The families didn't have to know that I'd "borrowed" the record player from the Western Tibetan sub-chieftain in a raid on his camp. For me, sharing Tara prayers with a family was more of an entertainment rather than a religious practice. My concerts were all free. No donations were collected.

When eventually I tired of that distraction, I traded my "confiscated" record player with Bhayu Tulku Rinpoche—whose dog I'd wrestled to the ground—for a small replica of a Russian rifle.

However, I didn't need a rifle. None of us did. Also stored in a corner of our family tent with all our weapons was the Chushi Gangdruk camouflage uniform my monk uncle had made me.

We'd left Kham with 2000 sheep and 300 yaks. Far from the mountains and rivers of Kham and settled in a foreign land, we were now nomads without animals and fighters who didn't fight.

Then, for a moment, Mustang buzzed with hope.

IN THE PITCH DARK, around 3:00 or 4:00 a.m. on March of 1961, the sound was deafening, the ground shaking with vibrations. Jumping from bed, everybody ran out to see this supernatural phenomenon, the likes of which no Tibetans ever experienced in their lifetime, or perhaps even in many past lifetimes. It seemed like a war between the Gods and the Devils. We knew the sound of planes, but, with their lights turned off on purpose, the roaring military helicopters, flying only a few hundred feet above ground to avoid Chinese radar, shook the earth and the air.

Dropped onto a frozen lake just across the Nepal border in March, 1961, were huge wooden pallets loaded with cardboard boxes packed with ammunition, bazookas, machine-guns, grenades, and different material for making bombs like C3, C4, and TNT. Other supplies and equipment were in duffel bags with handles.

Now life would change. Weapons, clothing, boots, and, mercifully, food had arrived! Mustang was alive. Dupa and I retrieved our khaki *chubas* and army boots. Every fighter in Mustang had the same vision. In a terrifying mass, Chushi Gangdruk troops would gallop into Tibet with their CIA-issued rifles and grenades, sweep back the Red Army from Western Tibet, and, moving east like a hurricane, retake our homeland.

Except that didn't happen. Yeshi still didn't order any raids. Instead, while the freedom fighters continued to eat their saddles and boots, Yeshi held a fire sale. My new camouflage-colored hat with a front shield—which I bought in the open market for a few Nepalese coins—was made from a CIA parachute. Although it was a strict violation of the CIA's demand that all parachutes used in the airdrops were to be destroyed immediately, the camouflage-colored synthetic parachute fabric became shirts, pants, backpacks, and hats like mine.

If the freedom fighters wanted the American supplies intended for them, they had to buy them. From Yeshi's men. During the months after the airdrop, Yeshi's men also sold CIA supplies to local people who in turn sold the goods, like my hat, in the local market. On the backs of small dealers or the backs of their mules or donkeys, these goods and other CIA supplies were also showing up door-to-door.

As their own private business enterprise, some the high-ranking guerrilla fighters were selling CIA-issued bullets. These deals took place one-on-one, like shady street-corner deals in a big city, where fighters, like us, traded our animals for bullets with the men in charge of food procurement. It seemed like a fair exchange. They needed the food, and we wanted the bullets. Much later, we learned that no CIA equipment, including bullets, was permitted to be sold but used only for the guerrilla warfare activities against Red China.

Something even more sinister was occurring. We thought the bullet salesmen were working on their own. However, as we would learn, they were acting on Yeshi's orders and turning over the profits to the former monk. Only years later did it come out that Yeshi was actually pocketing for himself the money meant to pay soldiers—eventually 1.5 million dollars in aid from the CIA. While he said he was setting much of the U.S. cash aside for when American support ended, he was stashing money in trunks and ultimately establishing himself in a well-guarded luxury home on the outskirts of Mustang. As a final insult, while he was embezzling money meant for his own starving troops and selling CIA-issued supplies, Yeshi continued to claim that the limited and intermittent CIA support was impossibly inadequate to feed and arm the huge population in Mustang.

The majority of Chushi Gangdruk under Yeshi's command—good people who were passionate about liberating Tibet—weren't aware of any of this and didn't question Yeshi's leadership.

But our fathers did.

AT NIGHT, in the privacy of our tent, Dupa and I listened as our fathers discussed their growing alarm about Yeshi's commanders. Soldiers were imposing themselves on local women, Chushi Gangdruk commanders were selling to freedom fighters the CIA bullets that should have been theirs for free, and more troubling was Yeshi's inexplicable failure—even though he now had crates of U.S. weapons—to complete his assigned mission. Ordering few if any raids, Yeshi also found excuse after excuse to delay complying with the CIA's expectation that he would establish resistance bases over the border and mount the resistance offensive from inside Tibet. This Yeshi never did. Sequestered in his new headquarters, he became even more invisible as he continued to run his growing military empire through his corrupt sub-commanders and his personal business through his *jugche,* his trained dogs and spies.

Although they didn't know the depth of Yeshi's treason, our fathers began to push back. While, upon arriving in Mustang, most Khampas joined the Chushi Gangdruk immediately, for the two years we were there, our fathers continued to delay the decision. Even though our group didn't insult Yeshi overtly, the snub didn't go unnoticed. Because Yeshi needed our supplies and our well-armed, well-trained men on his side, our hesitation undermined his authority and was a humiliating setback to his emerging leadership.

Even more devastating for Yeshi—who had the ambitions of a small Hitler—was the fact that our fathers were gaining a following among the Chushi

Gangdruk who were supposed to be under Yeshi's command. As Yeshi failed to feed his troops or order military actions, a stream of Khampa freedom fighters—drawn by the reputation of the Small Reactionary Group and our famous fathers—had begun riding the two miles to our camp on the outskirts of Mustang.

For all of this, we would pay.

BEFORE OUR DOGS BEGAN TO BARK, Dupa and I saw three horses crossing the rocky hillside toward our camp. Who was visiting from Mustang this time? As we greeted them, Dupa nodded at the lead soldier's hat. I was impressed.

Heading the group was Gyen Tsewang Dorjee, one of the high-ranking CIA-trained Chushi Gangdruk commanders. Tall and well-built, wearing a Japanese navy hat, U.S. Army shoes, and a Tibetan *chuba*, Tsewang didn't need to tell the Chinese who he was. His equipment confirmed it. The Colt-45 pistol model 1911 and Rolex watch were reserved for the top brass in Mustang's resistance operation. No ordinary freedom fighter in Mustang carried a cyanide capsule to poison himself if the Chinese were to capture him alive.

Moving in closer, Dupa and I examined several hundred rounds of ammunition, a compass, and nine sets of nylon maps with Tibetan letters showing every minute detail of Tibet, all of which were issued by the CIA. If these maps—which were top secret CIA maps and the most sophisticated in the world—were to fall in the hands of the PLA, it could do tremendous damage to the U.S. intelligence agency and the Chushi Gangdruk mission. Even more impressive to Dupa and me was the fact that Tsewang had been hand-picked for CIA training by Amdruk Gompo Tashi himself and by Tsewang's chieftain from Garpa, our neighbor district in Kham.

After Dupa and I inspected Tsewang's A1 grenade rifle and two hand grenades, we turned to the weapons brought by the other two Chushi Gangdruk fighters, one of whom had a CIA-issued M3 submachine-gun also known as a grease-gun. The other soldier had a Ruger 22 with long barrel and a built-in silencer. I'd never seen a .22-caliber bullet; it looked too small to do any damage at all.

When I asked, "What sound does it make if fired?" he replied, "No sound at all."

I had one response. "Wow."

He cradled the Ruger in his hand. "This is a very useful gun for killing guards before you ambush military encampments." Wow.

Dupa, however, spit at the ground. Why hadn't Yeshi issued these CIA guns to our fathers? Why was the leader of the Chushi Gangdruk shunning the best fighters in Mustang? At that point, Dupa was the only one who saw betrayal. It didn't seem possible that one Khampa would have a brewing vendetta against fellow Khampas in the middle of a common war. All the fighters in Mustang had set aside old rivalries and feuds to defeat the murderous invaders. We were in this together. We believed the Chinese were our only enemy.

We were wrong.

Coming in from checking on the horses a few days later, Uncle Chopak, Dupa and I saw our men forming a growing circle around our fathers.

MY FATHER LOOKED UP from his dice game. "Bandits? That's crazy." Because our group arrived in Mustang with lots of livestock to sell and our camp was well-supplied with food and weapons, some of Yeshi's commanders were spreading rumors throughout Mustang that our men were "bandits" who had looted all our supplies from innocent Tibetans.

Listening quietly, Dupa's father closed his fist over the dice and gave them a shake. "Forget about some questionable disgruntled men under Bawa Gyen Yeshi's command." But, as they continued their game, Khuru Ngajam looked pensive. We were all thinking the same thing. Why would Chushi Gangdruk commanders say our group of freedom fighters were bandits? Everyone knew much of our livestock had come from raiding Chinese camps. When we sold yaks to the Chushi Gangdruk, they knew we were no magicians who could pull yaks out of our hats.

In fact, the question of freedom fighters robbing Tibetans was absurd. While it was true that animals and some of the weapons we took from Chinese-occupied Tibetan communes had once belonged to Tibetans, during the Cultural Revolution, Mao and his Red Army had confiscated all Tibetan property, goods, and livestock. We weren't stealing from Tibetans. The Chinese had already done that. Many local Tibetans and, often, former owners of the land and livestock lived on those compounds to work for the Red Army, and not always by choice. We never endangered Tibetans on our raids and, when possible, tried to rescue them.

What was going on? Even though, under the CIA rules of engagement for the Chushi Gangdruk, looting from PLA Tibetan communes "except as part of a military action" was forbidden, we'd only confiscated supplies during raids, and those were before we arrived in Mustang. Under orders from Yeshi's men, we weren't even conducting private raids anymore. And we hadn't even joined the CIA-controlled Chushi Gangdruk.

When I was a growing up, my father and I joked about rumors. His advice? "Never swallow everything anybody says, especially rumors from children and gossips, without doing some fact-checking." Being a child myself, I'd replied, "Aba, don't worry about it. I never listen to myself anyway." Instead of calling me a smart-ass, he laughed. Now his advice about the "bandit" rumor was the same. "Ignore it."

But the scout from Mustang hadn't finished. "Bandits" wasn't the end of it. Because our camp had a well-stocked arsenal of modern weapons, the smear campaign also labeled our fathers as agents of the Taiwanese government. The fact that we'd obviously taken our weapons from the Chinese was apparently irrelevant.

So why were some shadowy men in Mustang making claims that we had "robbed innocent Tibetans?"

Although we didn't understand it at the time, these rumors flooding the Chushi Gangdruk ranks were not random. This was a deliberate smear campaign to discredit our fathers. It would be years before historians and Tibetan officials confirmed the existence of Yeshi's private army of guard dogs under his command—his *jugche*—who floated unseen among the troops spreading the rumors. By not accepting Yeshi as our leader, our fathers had humiliated the corrupt commander whose spies were the real ghosts infiltrating the Mustang forces. Because Yeshi was known to pounce on trouble before it got out of his control, according to Chushi Gangdruk survivors interviewed by historians, one of Yeshi's nicknames was "the Cat."

Our popularity was also undermining the Cat in public opinion. When our wealthy group—whom he needed because we had the best-armed camp and best fighters in Mustang—snubbed him, he wanted to undermine our reputation and encourage the freedom fighters to side with him, not the Small Reactionary Group. No doubt Yeshi's secret agents reported the stream of Chushi Gangdruk who spent days at a time at our camp. Our visitors were mostly from Nangchen Nyer-nga, the 25 districts from Nangchen kingdom, and included some of Yeshi's top commanders like Gyen Tsewang Dorjee, Kartse Tsewang Ngodup,

Panre Pon Dakpa Namgyal, and Amdo Abe. These men were all Yeshi's *japons,* or commanders, who visited us often and appeared to be aligning with our fathers.

While growing up, my father warned me to beware of some who "incites divisions within a community." Purely out of jealousy and political expediency, Yeshi was trying to defame the Small Reactionary Group, and, instead of unity, trying to create rifts in the Mustang community.

He failed. No one took the looting charges seriously.

When rumors didn't do the job, the humiliated Chushi Gangdruk leader made his next move. Arresting our men, he put them on public display as "bandits"—the smear campaign in action.

Except that didn't work either.

WHEN THE ALLEGED BANDIT, Khuru Ngajam, Dupa's popular father, entered the tent courtroom, everyone—including the judge and jury, who were Yeshi's henchmen—rose for a standing ovation. Looking back, it's clear this must have further fueled Yeshi's hatred and fury. Yeshi's own emissaries were starstruck by his rival.

When several of our men, including Dupa's father, had been ordered by Yeshi's commanders to stand trial as "bandits" for looting "innocent" Tibetans, Dupa was outraged. Banging one fist into another, he paced in circles. "This is Yeshi. He wants my father to look bad to everyone."

Although Dupa was suspicious, I wasn't so sure. Weren't we all here in Mustang for the same purpose? Why would Yeshi single out our group?

But he had.

While no one had known that the men spreading the "bandit" rumors about our fathers were Yeshi's men, it was now impossible to miss that the judges, juries, and executioners who had taken over the Nepalese legal system were Yeshi's guard dogs and immediate sub-commanders in the Chushi Gangdruk. My father was furious. "Why were the Chushi Gangdruk presiding over a trial in Nepal?" And he was right. The sole purpose of Mustang's highly trained and disciplined fighting force was to regain Tibet's independence from the Red Army through guerrilla warfare—not to take over the Nepalese courts. We Tibetans were refugees in a foreign country with no such rights. This would be similar to the Chinese setting up courts in the United States to prosecute the people they didn't like.

Aside from the illegality of the proceedings, the trial made no sense. Filed against our group by the Western Tibetans who had refused our men and then assaulted them, the lawsuit sought compensation for the yaks and sheep—which by now had been eaten by Khuru Ngajam's group—that we "borrowed" from their camp when we retaliated. Because at the time of the incident, the Tibetans and the sub-chieftain—whose teeth Dadhue had knocked out—weren't yet under Chinese control, it could appear that "innocent" people from Western Tibet were simply asking the court to make us pay for the loss of their animals. But, of course, the case was much more complicated and, anyway, it had already been resolved in Tibet, in a "quid pro quo." After the Western Tibetans almost killed our men, we retaliated by taking their livestock, a Russian rifle, and a small green record player. The end.

So what was going on? Were the charges just the East/West rivalry against Khampas? Or was the court case the work of the Chinese who had taken over all of Western Tibet by now, including the accusers' district? Was this Red Army payback for the humiliating defeats by the Small Reactionary Group? By bringing the lawsuit against enemies of the PLA, the Western Tibetans may well have been appeasing the Chinese, their future masters, doing what they had to do to survive, as pawns on the Chinese agenda.

On the assumption it was one or the other, our side proceeded with an eloquent defense. Although not trained as lawyers, our men had great oratory skills, especially Dupa's father, famous for his role in legal cases. First, Khuru Ngajam argued that taking the livestock was "justified as compensation and punitive damages for the Westerners starting the conflict, causing our people life-threatening injuries, and creating physical and psychological damage to our group." Our chieftain Pon Gyalpo argued that if any of our men had died as the result of the beating, we would have been "justified in asking the court for capital punishment" for the Westerners. As that was the first time we had heard our young chieftain speak in public, our fathers later praised Pon Gyalpo for his flawless defense of our group.

Everyone in the courtroom, including Yeshi's judges, were clearly impressed with our men. And we won. Or, to put it more accurately, the other side lost.

For 52 sheep and five yaks, our men ended up paying nothing of value. We had to give the Westerners an old horse and one badly used rifle—which happened to be the miniature Russian rifle that I had gotten from Bhayu Tulku in the trade for the green record player. In effect, the group's animals, the sub-chieftain's brand new Russian rifle, his lost animals, and his record player came back to him in the form of an old gun. Case closed.

When our men arrived back at camp, however, they weren't celebrating.

MY FATHER'S VOICE WAS FLINT. "Khampas rewarding Khampas isn't justice." Not only were the Chushi Gangdruk hijacking the Nepali courts, but, my father pointed, "when it comes to legal matters involving Tibetans, justice obviously comes down like heavy rocks favoring other Khampas." Shaking his head, he held a cup of tea to his lips but didn't drink. My father said what everyone was thinking. "If we join the Chushi Gangdruk and ignore the fact that the trial was rigged, we'll be as corrupt as they are."

But then, we had missed the point of the court-rigged case. At first, no one, including our fathers, understood that the trial wasn't about Khampas rewarding Khampas over Westerners. Or stolen yaks. Or a humiliated Chinese general. It was about a humiliated Tibetan.

As Yeshi's final attempt to bring the Small Reactionary Group in line, the trial was both a threat and a bribe disguised as a class-action lawsuit. Because our group was still far better-equipped than the underfed and sparsely armed Mustang troop, this show of force was pressure for us to join Yeshi's operation. Yeshi was surely not happy when his spies described the respect, not scorn, our men had inspired in Yeshi's judges. Undercover at the proceedings had been Yeshi's top secret agent, Rara, the Chushi Gangdruk commander who had led the infamous raid capturing the PLA documents. Allusive and mysterious with little to say, Rara was one of Yeshi's *dhugche*, a killing machine that Yeshi sent to do his real dirty work. A second Yeshi spy watching from the sidelines was Khalap Champa. In a few years, it would be Rara and Khalap Champa, along with several other killer dogs, whom Yeshi would send to attack our family. Typical of Yeshi's network, at the time of the trial, however, these two henchmen may not have known one another. Secrecy was vital—not just to the Chushi Gangdruk—but to Yeshi's personal operation. Over the years, the former monk ordered his secret agents to spy on—and even murder—each other.

Labeling our group as thieves and having us arrested was a demonstration of what Yeshi could do. The message was clear: You better join the Chushi Gangdruk or else.

But that was only half of the message.

After threatening us with his show of power, the clever and cunning former monk let us win the case as a form of bribery. This game fits well with Eastern psychology. One hand was waving slings and arrows while the other was dangling carrots—in effect, saying do or die. By throwing the trial in our favor, Yeshi's judges were trying to lure us with fake camaraderie. Implicitly, the Chushi Gangdruk leaders were saying, "We scratched your back and now it's your turn to scratch ours." The decision hinted that, by accepting their judgment in the case, we had tacitly become their loyal partners in Yeshi's organization.

Now we were being given a choice: accept the bribe or risk more of Yeshi's vengeance.

Soon everyone was talking at once. "Yeshi's men don't act like freedom fighters." "What is this Yeshi plotting and scheming to do?" "What's the real reason Yeshi hasn't ordered any raids?"

When my father concluded the discussion with the comment, "The story is getting worse by the day," everyone agreed. Something was very rotten in the kingdom of Mustang.

Meanwhile, Yeshi and his men waited, their feet on both sides of the river—ready for us to go either way. Would we surrender and add our men and supplies to the Mustang operation? Or would we take our huge weapons arsenal and our party of fighting men and leave Mustang?

They didn't have to wait long.

Tucking his pistol into his *chuba*, Khuru Ngajam nodded at us, one by one. "Looks like we are on our own."

After a frustrating two years waiting for Yeshi to order missions that never happened, we took our fourteen families, the animals we had left, our weapons arsenal, and our party of fighting men, and set up our own guerrilla operation near the resistance outpost at Dolpo. Without yaks to carry them, we had to leave behind many large items, such as our yak-hair tent and copper pots, items which were too heavy for horses. We had just enough horses and mules to carry the most essential things, like small tents, food supplies, weapons, and extra clothes.

In Dolpo, with only the bare essentials, we were ready to do what Yeshi had failed to—liberate our beloved country from the murderous and barbaric Chinese devils who had stolen it. For the Tibetan cause, we would make a real difference through real actions, not through being part of an operation known for its famous name. Our men would be "liberators" like the Chushi Gangdruk were meant to be. The Small Reactionary Group were about to ride again. Our first target was a large Chinese military camp just over the border.

In the raiding party would be Dupa and I, now fourteen. When we two spoiled nomad boys had fought with our fathers before, it was in unplanned and isolated events. On this mission, we would be officially guerrilla fighters heading into battle beside our men.

There was just one problem. Even with Dupa and myself joining the ranks, we didn't have enough fighters—my father's required number was between 25 and 35—to make up a raiding party.

CHAPTER SIX

THE SNAKE WITH TWO HEADS

SPRING 1961 TO SPRING 1963:

DOLPO, NEPAL TO MOGUM, NEPAL

AS MY FATHER SLIPPED OUT of our tent to disappear again for hours, Dupa and I looked up from cleaning our guns. Dupa shrugged. Oh, well. We trusted our fathers. Turning back to make the squeaky sounds of oil rubbing on metal, we could hear the click and chuckle of circling ravens.

When a stream of strangers began wandering into the camp to inspect the rifles and machine-guns in our arsenal, we got it. As the men huddled over tea with our fathers, Dupa and I watched each man closely. Then we watched my father. For the first time, the majority of our fighting force would be made up of men we didn't know, many of them from regions of Tibet other than Kham. While the men from our three families—Gonatsang, Khurutsang, and Namretsang—were still the heart and soul of our group, some of the men in the original Small Reactionary Group had been captured or killed, and only three of the original legendary fighters, including Dadhue the Black Face, were still with us. We no longer had my father's required number of fighters for a raid— 25 to 35 men. Larger groups were easily spotted while smaller groups were easily crushed.

Because our group's reputation had reached the Dolpo region long before we did, there was no shortage of volunteers. While trying to attack the Chinese in unorganized small groups, many fighters in this outpost had ended up captured or killed, so, when we appeared—equipped with weapons and horses and led by well-known battle-hardened fighters—every able man in the area wanted to ride with us. The challenge for my father, the leader of this raid, was selecting the right men.

While trusted friends never leave fellow fighters—dead or alive—on the field, we didn't know any of the new men long enough to know how they behaved under pressure. Although my father had fact-checked our new fighters thoroughly and chosen them with care, the majority of the men we'd be fighting with had no reason to be loyal. That they joined the Small Reactionary Group for the mutual benefit of all was understood by everyone. We were about to trust our lives to strangers. But we needed them.

And we needed this raid. Having sold our dying herds to the Chushi Gangdruk before leaving Mustang, our only source of meat was captured Red Army livestock. Since arriving in Dolpo, we had been feeding our growing group— over a dozen families with about 60 members of all ages and genders—by harvesting wild edible plants or vegetables and chasing down wild game. We Khampas were used to eating lots of meat, maybe too much, but it was necessary to have heavy foods for those of us born at an average of 16,000 feet above sea level.

Telling no one, not even Dupa, I had a secret fantasy. Why steal only enough sheep to feed the camp for a month? Why not take enough animals to start our herds again? The Dolpo region would be paradise for a nomad community.

Like other Khampas, our families loved the area. It was about the same altitude as the Tibetan plateau with high mountains, sparkling rivers, and lush grazing land. The rocky mountain slopes were covered in long grass, wildflowers, and trees waving their leafy arms. As ravens circled in the blue sky, Dupa and I watched families of ducks skim across the streambeds. All around us roamed wild yaks, bighorns, blue sheep, and brown bears. Dupa and I agreed that we could stay forever.

We just needed a herd grazing out the back door. And we would steal it from the Chinese.

OUR AMBUSH SITE wasn't much of a camp. The flat ground was our bed, the blue sky our tent, and the mountains our walls. In the freezing dark, on top of an unprotected hill, twenty-seven of us, including the new recruits, waited for orders from my father.

A strictly disciplined strategist, my father, as usual, had designed our first mission meticulously. After our scouting party reported seventeen army tents, each with ten Red Army soldiers, we knew they outnumbered us by about eight to one. Also at the camp was a monastery which acted as headquarters for PLA top commanders and, at the center of the compound, were thirteen nomad tents housing the Tibetan families who lived in this forced collective system. As always, we would be careful that no Tibetans—who now lived under communism as slaves and often as human shields—were harmed. We were in the area to kill the Chinese Red Army—not our brothers and sisters from Tibet.

"The trick about sneaking up," my father told the new recruits, "is to move very slowly." To plan the raid, my father assessed the strength of the enemy in terms of numbers, arms, terrain, and weather conditions. As always, common sense dictated his decisions. Although usually he took every opportunity to employ deceptions and surprises—preferring to capture the enemy or scare them into running rather than killing them—this camp was too well-protected, and we would be out-manned. Sneaking in at dawn while the Chinese slept, we could pick off the soldiers at close range and ride away with all their animals.

Under the cold Tibetan sky, my father explained he had chosen this spot less than a quarter-mile from the Red Army, because it was "close enough to attack their camp quickly, but not close enough" for the Chinese to hear the stomping of our horses. When one of the new recruits looked puzzled, my father told him that humans can't hear horses further than a few hundred yards away. "In fact," my father added, "humans dragging their feet make more noise than horses walking gently."

When another new fighter wondered about dogs barking at our approach, my father smiled. "You're right. They'll hear us, but the dogs of Tibetan nomads are trained to bark only at wild beasts."

We would be attacking just before dawn because, in war, "soldiers are often alert the whole night, but eventually become tired of waiting and fall asleep."

Which meant we all had to get some sleep before our early morning ambush.

Rechecking to make sure everything was working perfectly, we loaded and chambered bullets in our guns, ready to kill or to be killed, and, using saddles as pillows and saddle-blankets as bedding, we settled down on the hard ground beside our horses and weapons.

Nearby an owl hooted and wolves howled at the moon.

Unable to sleep, Dupa and I leaned close, whispering, and swore to protect each other to the death. We would live meaningful, happy lives together leading our district in Kham or die together leaving behind—like our ancestors—the legacy of bravery and heroism.

While, as always, Dupa was courageous, for weeks I had been quietly reinventing myself as the person my family needed me to be—a fearless guerrilla. As the rest of the party chanted prayers over a Fire Puja to the "dang, dang, dang" beat of drums and cymbals, I wrote my own battle prayer, which I recited out loud but in private: "Almighty and Powerful Spirits of Mountains, Rivers, Trees and Nature's Creations, I invoke you all to remove all the obstacles, hindrances, and intents and purposes of Evil Spirits from our way, protect our endeavors, and guide us to victory."

Just before it grew light, with me still trying to think about victory instead of Chinese zombies and our untested new fighters, Dupa and I finally drifted off to sleep. But not for long.

IN THE PITCH BLACK, my father shook us awake. Like some animals can sense coming threats, such as earthquakes and other natural disasters, my father had a natural gift for detecting danger. In a dream, he had seen the Chinese surrounding our camp on the open hill. Every time my father sensed danger, something terrible always happened. He wasn't taking any chances this time. He ordered us to saddle our horses and attack the Chinese camp in the dark. As I attached my pony's bridle, Blue Bird snorted and shook his head. Although we could barely see each other, I could hear the grunt of Dupa's horse as he tightened the cinch.

Then we saw their outlines in the moonlight. On another hill, Red Army soldiers were mounted and preparing to ambush us while we slept. My father's dream had been accurate. In this case, both sides had been trying to surprise the other. And we did. But not as planned.

While we were racing toward the bottom of the hill, we heard the pounding of hooves as the Chinese ambush party arrived from another direction to the top of the hill where we'd been sleeping a few minutes earlier. While the Chinese were attacking an empty campsite, we dug our heels into our horses, spread out, and charged into the main camp, guns blazing.

And, as predicted, the unexpected was waiting for us.

THE WILD BARKING of their mastiffs collided with the firecracker sounds of gunfire. It was attack, attack, rush, rush—fast, furious, determined, and organized. Following my father's training, instead of riding in one after another in a line, we stayed 150 to 200 feet apart from each other, thus covering a larger area to kill more Chinese and causing the Chinese to waste bullets in the empty spaces between us. Within minutes of our first war cry, the Chinese soldiers poured out of their tents like ants from an anthill. As usual, they never failed to outnumber us. The more we killed, the more of them came. That the Chinese leaders didn't value human lives was their real strength and power. It was different for us Tibetans. When we lost just one man, it meant one less fighter, one less friend, one less father, one less husband, or one less brother in a family. It's impossible to fill in so many emotional vacancies left behind by a single person.

Of course, in the dark chaos, the men in our group could have been accidentally shooting each other. In the fury of the unplanned nighttime gun battle, our horses' hooves pounding, firing at close range, Dupa and I had had no idea where each other was or if we were alive.

Suddenly an explosion rocked the atmosphere, and, for a moment, the PLA camp was bathed in bright light. In the confusion and the dark, one of our stray bullets had hit the ammunition depot through a window of the monastery, accidentally turning the building into a fireball, killing the PLA commanders sleeping there, and turning the camp into a lighted amphitheater. In the glow, I could see the bodies of the Chinese beneath me, the faces of the dead contorted in shock and pain, and those still alive clutching their wounds or crawling for the tents. All around us the soldiers were groaning in pain and making baby sounds as they died. Listening to them created itchy sensations and a hair-raising strangeness in my body. They were only humans like us.

But where were the yaks?

Killing all the Chinese, including the Red Army high command, couldn't compensate for the vacant pens we found when the gunfire stopped. Where the animals should have been, the grounds were empty. Clearly, the Chinese had spotted us moving into position the night before and removed all their herds.

At a shout from my father—"Let's get out!"—we grabbed all the guns lying beside the Chinese we had just killed, taking some out of the hands of the dead. As we galloped past our abandoned campsite, we saw a few Red Army soldiers still milling about on the exposed hill, their shadows crisscrossing against the backdrop of an early morning sky.

Much of this raid had been unexpected for both sides.

But we were alive. And victorious. *Wow*. As Dupa pulled his horse beside mine, he raised his rifle in the air. Tugging on Blue Bird's reins, I raised my weapon too.

Back at camp six hours later, the young children in our group, whom I encouraged to listen to the stories of our battles, were peeking around the entrance of the tent or from behind their mothers' legs. Everyone had gathered to hear the reborn Small Reactionary Group brag about outsmarting the Chinese. In our first raid in over two years, our party of twenty-seven men had gone up against 200 Chinese troops—blowing up their munitions, killing off their high command, and leaving dozens of Red Army soldiers dead and dying—without losing one of our own men. With this first victory, our men become famous heroes in Dolpo overnight, and all the fighters in the area wanted to ride under our protection.

Everyone was impressed, that is, except the architect and leader of the mission, my father, Gona Gedun Sherab. Taking a sip of tea, he surprised everyone by describing the raid as "a failure."

The tent was suddenly quiet. The new recruits stared at him. Several children looked up at me. What did he mean? Then everyone began talking at once. How could the destruction of a major command post be a failure? Wasn't it a victory that our two dozen fighters had done so much damage and lost no men? Everyone understood killing the Tibetan was an accident. When Dupa's cousin, who became separated from the group after his horse was attacked by two mastiffs, had unintentionally killed a Tibetan woman, the woman had been with her Chinese soldier boyfriend and just a dark form in the night. Nobody in our group would ever intentionally kill a Tibetan woman or even a Chinese woman. Wasn't this the first and only time a Tibetan was ever injured in one of our raids? Even though the raid didn't go exactly as planned, it was still a victory, wasn't it?

My father's voice was quiet. "Maybe we killed a lot of Chinese, but we failed because we came back with no animals." In my father's version of the raid, returning with no yaks—dead or alive—was no victory. He tapped tobacco unto his thumbnail. Our main objective on this first raid, he reminded us, had been to "replenish our depleted food supply." I'd never seen my pragmatic and confident father deflated. Even my mother looked worried. Sensing the shift in mood, one of the children started to cry.

I wanted to cry too. I'd been as disappointed as my father when I saw the empty pens. My dreams of a new nomad camp in Dolpo depended on those animals.

As my father went on to praise our new recruits, "who performed courageously and skillfully," he shrugged. "At least none of us was hurt."

"I'm fine except for this stupid hole in my stomach." Shifting awkwardly on his mat, and holding his stomach, Namre Geden—the father of the Namretsang family, our third family—nodded at his belly. We all gaped. Usually talkative, enjoying singing, joking, and telling stories of our raids, Namre Geden had been unusually silent. Neither during nor after the attack had he given any indication he had been wounded. Luckily the bullet had missed his vital organs, and his injury would heal. Although he was brave, Namre Geden was a very stubborn man, and his silence was typical of Khampas, who tried to keep things to themselves without complaining.

After stating his initial disappointment, my father also didn't waste any more time talking about what went wrong or right. And, although he wouldn't agree, everyone throughout the entire community of Dolpo and all along the border considered our first raid to be a remarkable victory.

Including the Chinese.

This raid put the Small Reactionary Group back on the Red Army's "most wanted" list. By killing their commanders and blowing up their ammunition, we'd done enough damage to the supply lines and fought with such ferocity that the raid was an embarrassment to the Chinese leaders. To cover up the fact that such a small group of Tibetans on the loose was out of the PLA's control, the Red Army spread the rumor that the Large Reactionary Group—the Chushi Gangdruk from Mustang—had conducted the raid. But soon enough everyone knew that the group destroying Chinese camps was the Red Army's old enemy from two years earlier, the Small Reactionary Group.

After two years languishing in Mustang, we were back, infamous heroes to our people and dreaded enemies to the Chinese.

But we still had no food.

Which is why Dupa and I found ourselves at an elevation of about 19,000 feet above sea level in below-freezing temperatures risking our lives for dinner.

The forces of nature, it would turn out, were much more terrifying than the Chinese.

WE NEEDED THIS KILL. High up on a rock cliff above our new camp in Dolpo, Dupa and I spotted the wounded blue sheep Dupa's father had shot the day before. Dragging one leg, the thick fur on its shoulder pink with blood, the animal refused to die.

Skidding on the ice, the echo of our feet sounding like elephants trampling on a sheet of glass, we got into position. Ice crystals clung to my eyelashes. When we finally managed to come close enough to take a shot at the blue sheep, I fired and missed. The strong wind and fresh snow on the sandy surface had made it difficult to take a good steady aim at the target, even though I was carrying an Enfield rifle, known for its accuracy.

The sheep, unable to run, swiveled its head toward us and jerked at its broken leg.

Suddenly, one of Dupa's cousins, who happened to be nearby looking for the same animal, hit the sheep with a rock and sent it dropping about 1,000 feet off a high cliff. The thump on the animal's skull was followed by a grunt and quick scramble of its feet before it tumbled over the side.

I stared at my gun. This was embarrassing and humiliating. A man with an Enfield rifle couldn't hit his target within 100 yards, whereas a man with a rock got the job done. Dupa shrugged, but we were happy. The meat in this sheep would be good after a soft landing in the snow. We would be returning to camp with food.

As the three of us climbed down the mountain slope toward the sheep, we slipped on a mixture of fresh snow, loose gravel, and sand. In the freezing snowdrifts, my breath was raspy from the icy air, my eyes burned, and I could only see the corner of Dupa's shoulder through the dense snow.

Then, it happened. Halfway to the bottom, we felt the mountain suddenly begin to tremble, a deep rumble somewhere in its belly. In less than a minute, amidst a roaring flood of snow, we were well on our way to the valley of death ourselves, riding on the avalanche with Enfield rifles in our hands, making us look like witches flying through dust clouds, brooms in our hands.

As happened sometimes, like now, our religion put us in danger. Even though every lake and river in Tibet was full of fish with ducks and geese floating along the surface and rabbits hopping along the bank, as my Uncle Chopak kept reminding us, for Buddhists, this buffet of small wild game was off limits.

We had to rely on large animals—like this wild sheep—for food. The Chinese, of course, were better able to endure a food shortage because they ate everything that moved. In Dolpo, living in two different worlds, the human world where we were hungry and the Buddhist world where we observed our beliefs, we had been very hungry. And now, because of those same beliefs, we were going to die.

We Tibetans also believed in the existence of spirits that dwelled in the mountains, rivers, and lakes. They were especially protective of mountain dwellers like this sheep, and natural disasters were their weapons of mass destruction. After surviving a gunfight with the murderous Chinese, here Dupa and I were trying to survive drowning, but this time under thousands of pounds of snow. Mother Nature gave me a baby body, but now she wanted my adult body. Because we couldn't fight back, we were finding the forces of nature were much more daunting than 200 Chinese soldiers.

Somehow, as the snow roared over us, instead of being dragged into the middle of the avalanche, Dupa managed to get hold of a tree branch, and I found myself stuck between two boulders, leaving us—as we had been on the river bank in Kham—nearly dead, but alive. Had we fallen fifteen feet more, we would have been shoved by the snow over the same 1000-foot drop as the blue sheep.

When the two of us scrambled down the slope to join Dupa's cousin—who had arrived at the sheep before the avalanche—amazingly, the animal, cushioned by the snow, was still alive and struggling to stand up, its front feet weakly churning at the air. As our ears were filled with snow and sand, we couldn't hear each other, but I knew what to do. Making a cut in its chest and pulling out the heart, I put the sheep out of its misery in the way I knew best.

Once we had removed the sheep's intestines and stomach to make it lighter, Dupa's cousin carried the carcass on his back. We returned to camp covered in ice and snow, lucky to be alive, and certain that it would much easier to snatch animals from a human enemy.

And for the next year we did. But we never stole enough Chinese yaks to start my new nomad community. That was just my homesick fantasy. We were actually in no place long enough to maintain a herd—including Dolpo.

With so many spies for the Chinese milling about the region, hiding our camp of sixty people in a secure site became impossible after a year.

Our fathers determined it was time to move on. And this time we'd be leaving Nepal. On our way to relocate in Ladakh, a Tibetan region of India, our last stop in Nepal would be Mogum, a remote mountainous Nepali outpost at

19,000 feet on the Tibetan/Indian border, a treacherous three-week journey north of Dolpo.

Thinking about the nature of impermanence once again, I took a last look at the ducks on the pond. Although we were highly skilled warriors, at heart we were still herders who just wanted to live unmolested, tending our sheep and yaks on grassy hillsides, listening to birdcalls instead of gunfire. As nomads, our animals had given us everything we needed without leaving home, but now, forced to defend our country as guerrilla fighters, we had no home and no livestock.

As I gave Bluebird extra grain for the trip, I remembered my father's prediction about the future. Even if we found a perfect place—as we had at Lake Nyimo, then the military encampment at Bawa Zabdong, and now Dolpo—we could not return to our bucolic life as nomads.

This was war. And we were on the run again.

At least we would be traveling on Tibetan soil for most of the journey. Because most of the Red Army troops were concentrated in more strategic locations on the China-India border in preparation for the coming war between India and China, our fathers felt confident traveling to Mogum on the Tibetan side of the border. When we stopped for the night, we would camp far away from any travel routes and not stay long at any one place.

As we headed along the frozen Tibetan plateau, however, I wasn't concerned about an ambush by the Chinese. Riding beside me was my grandmother, her face creased with terrible pain. Tied onto a horse with an inflatable airbed between her and the saddle, her eyes closed, she groaned and shivered. Although we had wrapped her in blankets against the freezing cold, we had no medication for her pain. We all loved this kind and gentle soul, who was always there with tender loving care for her family, but it was I who would miss her the most. When I was a child, she was my second mother, and when I wasn't sleeping with Uncle Chopak in the pasture with the horses, I had always slept with her. Now, for fear of the Chinese, there was nothing we could do for her—not even stop to let her rest.

We could barely care for those who weren't ill. Every day on this remote and desolate mountain route was a struggle to find enough wild game to feed sixty men, women, and children.

Then, again—a miracle.

While we were well hidden in the deserted upper side of a valley along a remote river bank, one of our men out hunting spotted a party of armed men leading a large herd of yaks. Dupa and I ran for our horses. Dinner! Because this travel route wasn't used by Western Tibetans, it had to be bandits out looting or a Chinese supply convoy. Had we actually been lucky enough to have a Chinese supply train deliver yaks to our doorstep? And at a location where we could ambush them before they reached for their rifles?

Naively, we assumed the Red Army was our only enemy.

We were about to discover something that would send our families down the road to hell.

SPEEDING AFTER OUR FATHERS with about twenty other men, Dupa and I headed out to ambush what appeared to be a platoon of Red Army soldiers. Even though none of the men were wearing Red Army uniforms, from a distance we recognized their guns. While most Tibetan fighters had bipods on their rifle—which looked like the horns of Tibetan antelopes and made the guns appear longer—the guns the yak thieves carried, like all Chinese rifles, had no bipods.

Assuming these were PLA soldiers, my father motioned for us all to draw our weapons. When we rounded a small hill, we were right in the path of the looters, blocking them. Dismounting, we prepared to shoot to kill. Raising their rifles, the men leading the yaks assumed that we were the Chinese military. Only when we were staring into their rifle barrels a few hundred yards away and one of the yak thieves waved in a friendly gesture did we recognize our mistake and lower our guns.

Both parties had it wrong. Neither side was Chinese. We were all Tibetans. And this band of eighteen men weren't just Tibetans. They were Khampas.

To the confusion of my pony—who snorted and danced in place wanting to know why we were we coming to a halt during a heated ambush—both groups advanced until we were close enough to shake hands. Running my hand along Blue Bird's furry neck, I whispered, *"gali gali"* (easy).

That was when our fathers recognized the yak thieves as Chushi Gangdruk from Mustang, four of them sub-commanders. The mystery of the "Chinese" guns was solved. Like the Red Army rifles, the ones issued to the Chushi Gangdruk by the CIA also had no bipods, so, from far away, they looked like Chinese weapons. Luckily the few shots fired from the rifles from both sides had missed.

After a brief but friendly exchange, Yeshi's men gave us a yak, and we said goodbye. What we didn't understand was that the yak wasn't a gift. It was a bribe. Under the mandates established by the CIA and the Tibetan government-in-exile, the Chushi Gangdruk resistance fighters were only permitted to "raid," not loot, the Chinese-controlled Tibetan communes. The distinction was critical. Raiding involved killing the enemy, taking prisoners, and capturing supplies, which included animals, weapons, and food. Looting was actually theft—quietly stealing animals and supplies from a camp.

Although everyone in Mustang had heard vague rumors that Yeshi, against CIA rules, was sending his men over the border to steal animals, there had been no proof. By an accident of fate in a remote section of Western Tibet where no one travelled, we had become the only people in the world—in the fall of 1962—who had caught Yeshi's men red-handed. A case of a black kettle calling a crow black, this was the crime for which Yeshi's judges had tried our men back in Mustang—a pack of wolves blaming another pack for eating sheep in their neighborhood.

On the Tibetan plateau with our hungry families feasting on yak, we were alert for whom we assumed was our only enemy, Communist China. Even though our fathers had humiliated the ego-driven Yeshi a year earlier by rejecting his inactive resistance operation, once we left Mustang, we had assumed we were done for good with Bawa Gyen Yeshi and the Chushi Gangdruk. We were wrong.

Unbeknownst to us, the Cat and his dogs were more determined than ever to bring down the Small Reactionary Group. They were just looking for an excuse. News of our celebrity and ongoing victories over the PLA had been reaching Mustang and Dharamsala. Our success made Yeshi look bad. Really bad. Smaller in size, with fewer good fighters than when we first rode into Western Tibet, the Small Reactionary Group, singlehandedly, so to speak, was doing with our few dozen men what Yeshi never accomplished with his 4000 fighters and their pockets full of the CIA's dollars and gold coins. Hypothetically speaking, if our group had been as large as Yeshi's, trained in guerrilla warfare by the CIA, fighting with U.S. military weapons and other sophisticated equipment, and supported by CIA funds, we would have freed Tibet. As it would turn out, every time we took down another Chinese compound, we had fueled Yeshi's determination to wipe the Small Reactionary Group from the earth.

We also knew too much. Although we didn't know Yeshi was pocketing for himself all the money the CIA had airdropped to feed the Chushi Gangdruk troops—no one did—having lived in Mustang for two years, we knew enough. We had witnessed the starving men, Yeshi's failure to order raids, the pregnant Nepalese women, the usurpation of the Nepalese judicial system, and the illegal appropriation and sale of CIA goods meant for the fighters. I'd bought a hat made out of a CIA parachute, and our fathers had bought CIA bullets on the street.

Now that we'd caught Yeshi's men looting, we represented a much more serious threat, one the Cat couldn't afford at the moment. He was already under scrutiny. Responding to rumors and complaints about Yeshi, the U.S. had finally sent representatives to the field in Mustang. Meeting in Nepal with Yeshi and five of his commanders, including Rara, the CIA officials demanded that—before they'd send more supplies—the guerrillas had to relocate the entire Mustang operation inside Tibet. Yeshi made promises he couldn't keep and made new demands, creating a vicious circle that was never resolved. It would still be years before the CIA, Tibetan leaders in India, and most of the troops in Mustang learned the extent of the Chushi Gangdruk commander's dirty tricks and treason. It would also come out that to augment the lack of food, Yeshi had been regularly sending secret teams—like the one we had encountered—across the Tibetan border to liberate yaks, not Tibetans. Even though the thieves had given us a yak as a bribe, Yeshi and his men feared we weren't going to keep quiet about catching the looters red-handed.

We knew far too much. We had to be stopped.

That same night, while we were feasting on the yak, a raiding party—publically denouncing us for attacking Chushi Gangdruk's innocent men—was gathering to attack us.

By a stroke of luck, Yeshi finally had the excuse he needed to order an attack on our camp. While our group had been miles way, another group of Khampas—also mistaking the yak thieves for Chinese—had also attacked Yeshi's looters, and one of Yeshi's henchmen had been wounded in the neck. Back in Mustang, Yeshi's men told everyone that they had been attacked by our group, and this was the chance for which Yeshi had been waiting.

Then we had some luck. Before Yeshi's men mounted their attack on us, the actual culprits admitted their mistake. This was an inconvenient truth for Yeshi. There went his reason to hunt us down. Because any further discussions about this incident might raise questions about what four of Yeshi's lieutenants and a platoon of his fighters were doing in Tibet in the first place, the Chushi Gangdruk went silent on the subject. While his men could claim they were checking out suspicious Red Army activities along the border when they were attacked, that still didn't explain why they returned with a string of 100 yaks and no head count of dead Chinese and no rifles. Naturally, Yeshi's men didn't bother to correct the initial impression that our group attacked our fellow freedom fighters.

Meanwhile, we knew nothing about this and were only concerned about evading the Chinese until we made it to Mogum.

When my grandmother passed away a few days after we encountered the looters, we buried her quickly and moved on. After we were safely back in Nepal, our monks and lamas would pray for the consciousness of my grandmother to reincarnate into higher realms, but the physical body was immaterial now. We had to live in the moment. But that didn't mean we didn't all feel her absence. While my mother and I watched, our dogs didn't gobble down their food right away as they had when my grandmother fed them. My mother wondered if they were waiting for grandmother to fill their bowls. I wondered if they were sad. Did they know? At least she had died on Tibetan soil.

As we decamped and moved on alone along the Tibetan Plateau, we couldn't have predicted that since leaving our homeland in Kham, my grandmother would be our only family member to die of natural causes.

Continuing on our way through the Tibetan wilderness—with icicles forming in our hair and eyelashes and listening to the howls of wolves—our fathers still didn't fully understand that we were fleeing from two sets of enemies, Chinese and Tibetan.

We were in the devil's sights and didn't know it.

Although Yeshi's men had to back off any physical attack on our group after the looting incident, the hatred and fear brewing against us in Mustang was escalating. The Cat was increasingly desperate for an excuse to pounce.

And, although it can be open to interpretation, once we had set up camp near the Mogum area, Yeshi appeared to have found the means.

WHEN THE GUNFIRE ENDED. Dupa's mother stumbled the 100 yards from her tent to the body of Dupa's father, ripped out her headdress, and flung her necklaces to the ground. Jewels and beads which had been tied into her hair and intricately woven into braids to her waist forming the elaborate headdress—which, signified, like a wedding ring, that she was a wife—were scattered on the ground. So violently had she yanked out her headdress— showing that she was no longer a queen, but a grieving widow—that patches of hair and scalp lay about on the ground. Two large amber beads, each one the size of a fist, which had hung at the sides of her head, lay near the body of her husband.

The assassination of Dupa's father, Khuru Ngajam, March 11, 1962, was, at this point in our family history, the darkest moment of our lives.

And it wasn't the Chinese who killed him. It was rogue Khampa bandits. And these killers, as we would discover, had questionable ties to Yeshi.

The tragedy was set in motion when we learned that a family from our district in Kham had been robbed by a band of rogue Khampas. The bandits had robbed the family of the most important possessions of people on the run— their animals and food. Even though the robbery occurred two years earlier and even though we were 1,000 miles from Kham, observing Khampa tribal codes, our fathers decided to seek compensation from the robbers. It made no difference that the robbed family was now in India. The victims had always treated our people well, and our fathers were the kind of *gyenpos* who would seek justice for anyone from our district. That the robbery had happened at gunpoint in broad daylight was enough for our fathers. The difference between sneaking in to steal at night and armed robbery was day and night. While our life mission was to defeat the Communist Chinese, it was also always to protect fellow countrymen. It was a matter of obligation and honor.

When the Nepalese traders came to us with the story, the robbers had just reappeared in the area. Assuring us that the rogue Khampas were so "hated" that they had no friends who might warn them, the Nepalese brought us to a location within rifle range of the robbers. Two hundred feet from their camp, where the women, elders, and children would be out of danger, we set up our tents.

After much discussion and sniffing of tobacco, our fathers decided to try exacting restitution without force, a plan which required a skilled third-party negotiator. Dupa's father dispatched scouts to bring back Lherap—a popular Khampa from our district who was well-known for his diplomatic skills in dealing with the Nepalese border officials and now lived nearby. Dupa and I were excited by the next news. We would get to meet this popular Khampa, who was also famous for his skills as a fighter and a storyteller.

Meanwhile, the bandits, who were below us on a riverbank, had no idea we were there. As we tried to keep warm while waiting for daylight and our negotiator, we took turns sleeping.

Then, the unexpected. In the morning, when our raiding party peered into the robbers' campsite below, we found a surprise. Everyone turned to our fathers. The robbers were breaking camp, taking down their tents, packing their belongings, and saddling their horses. What did we do now? Lhawa Lherap and his men hadn't arrived yet, and we had to act quickly. By a fatal miscalculation in timing and distance, we had thought Lhawa Lherap was only a few hours' ride away, but the distance would turn out to be nearly half a day.

Then it all went to hell. One of the robbers spotted us, and they began loading their weapons.

In desperation, still hoping to resolve the issue without force, our fathers chose a stand-in negotiator, the only man available, a Khampa named Khawu Pendrup, who was neither skilled nor prepared for the job.

After Khawu Pendrup rode into their camp and delivered our message, the robbers began waving their arms in violent mudras and yelling at him. When he rode up the hill with the bandit's response—"Go to hell"—he was trembling and sweating. While we watched, they lit a Fire Puja and held their swords over the flames. They were ready for a fight.

Our stand-in third-party negotiator finally admitted the problem. Yes, he had requested a dialogue about compensating the victims for the stolen property, but he had also unnecessarily told the robbers that they were surrounded by our men. Although he meant this piece of information to pressure them into meeting, the bandits obviously interpreted this news to mean we would kill them anyway. Even though they were outnumbered and surrounded, the robbers—in a typical example of Khampa stubbornness and pride—had to save themselves from the embarrassment of submission. They were going to fight.

To give the bandits one more chance to surrender without violence, Dupa's father Khuru Ngajam sent the terrified Pendrup back with a final ultimatum. Meanwhile, Dupa's father ordered our men to take positions for an ambush. While several of us remained with Khuru Ngajam, my father led another group to the second hill. Then we settled in and waited for our mediator to return with the bandits' final words.

That's when it happened. While we were standing three paces away from Dupa's father, Dupa and I heard a single shot and saw a splash of blood burst into the air from Khuru Ngajam's neck, killing him instantly. For a moment, we couldn't comprehend what we were seeing. What had just happened? We had still been in negotiations. This was an assassination, not death in battle.

Then, hell broke loose. As bullets crashed and sparked against the rocks and our mastiffs began barking, Dupa shot his father's killer in the head. When my father arrived to find his closest friend and brother-in-law had been murdered, he yelled, "Kill them all!" and rushed at the enemy across an open field. While this would normally be a crazy and dangerous move, driven by rage, Khampas do the unthinkable and the impossible. During a battle which lasted almost an hour, we killed all the men at the other ends of our gun barrels.

Once the gunfire stopped, except for the raspy breathing of our men and the snorting of the enemy's terrified horses, there was a terrible silence. Our loose dogs had run away, and the chained ones had stopped barking.

When Dupa knelt beside his trembling mother, clumps of hair still in her hands, her face was covered with dirt and tears, and blood was running from her nose. Through her tear-streaked face, she stared at Dupa as if she didn't know who he was. She looked as if she had been buried under the earth and was risen from a grave. I trembled at this horrific sight. Nobody had ever seen her like this. To remember it even now gives me shivers. In an instant, at the hand of fellow Khampas, Dupa's mother had gone from empress to grieving widow. Although she lived for many more decades, for the rest of her life the wife of Khuru Ngajam never again wove beads into her hair as a headdress.

Looking at the body of Khuru Ngajam, every single soul in our camp began to cry, even the babies. Although Khuru Ngajam always fought like Denma, King Gesar's famous warrior who couldn't be killed but faded into a rainbow, before us was the body of a real man, not a Rainbow Body.

We'll never know if a skilled mediator could have changed the course of history that day.

When Lhawa Lherap arrived two hours after the gunfight was over and saw Khuru Ngajam's body, he was furious. "I would have killed them all, these *pharu Zaju* (dead-father eaters), but unfortunately I came too late." Although he was capable of taking such measures in his own hands and was a well-known fighter who killed many Chinese single-handedly, I wasn't sure I bought the notion that he would fight our fight and kill all the dead-father-eaters.

As our men carried the body of Dupa's father into camp, Dupa and I couldn't watch. While our monks and lamas conducted rituals and prayers, Dupa and I wouldn't leave our tent. We didn't want to see Khuru Ngajam's body disappear under the dirt. By tradition, since Dupa's father died a violent death, he had to be buried within two days. During peacetime, a funeral for a death from natural causes could last weeks. We were glad this required such a short time.

Until the burial, Lhawa stayed on with us, and I spent two days being impressed—too impressed—sitting next to this charming, talkative, boastful storyteller. He could have made a fortune in the West as a TV show host.

Noticing my particular fascination with him, he pulled me aside before he left. "Come here, son. Do you know how many dead-father Chinese I killed?"

"No."

He bent down and whispered in my ear, "Come closer and I'll tell you my secret. I killed 1,000 per minute."

Wow. Was that possible?

When he added, "But when I woke up, there were no dead Chinese around," I jumped back, furious. "You liar. That all happened in a dream."

He shrugged.

I had no time for a fake hero. Bye-bye, Uncle Lherab.

We were burying a real hero.

As Dupa's father had lived through so many dangerous battles in his lifetime, both with Tibetans and Chinese, no one ever imagined Dupa's famous father would die at the hands of a few rogue Khampas. Not only was Khuru Ngajam one of the fifteen who had fought off an enemy force of 500 back in Kham, but, leading the Small Reactionary Group—even when outnumbered on the ground and outgunned from the air—he was the Red Army's nemesis. Now, instead of dying at the hand of the Evil Empire while fighting to liberate his country, Dupa's father was felled by petty criminals. One high lama in our group asked, "How so, a man of such greatness died in the hands of so few men of lesser dignity?"

WHEN WE GATHERED UP the robbers' guns, the story became more sinister. At first, we told ourselves that the robbers shot Dupa's father because he was sitting at the front of our group and they could easily assume he was in charge. When the bandits, who were outnumbered and outgunned, knew they were going to die anyway, they took down our leader with them and cut off the head of the snake.

But were the rogue bandits really acting independently when they eliminated one of Yeshi's key enemies? By killing one of the leaders of the Small Reactionary Group, the bandits had done Yeshi a significant favor. While it might appear that stupid Khampa pride led to this day of sadness, shock, and disbelief, was assassination of Khuru Ngajam just an ironic accident of fate, only two weeks after our men caught Yeshi's men looting yaks and violating CIA rules?

The evidence pointed in another direction. The weapons of these bandit Khampas were Chinese submachine-guns and Springfield rifles, exactly like the ones that the CIA issued to Yeshi and the Chushi Gangdruk. How did these men, who had just returned to the Mogum area from India, get CIA–issued guns? Although the bandits were camped in Mogum, not Mustang, Yeshi's reach was far. I would also learn that one of the robbers came from the same district as Bawa Gyen Yeshi, and the others came from Yeshi's neighboring districts.

Had the looters been another band of Yeshi's *jugche* increasing Yeshi's coffers by stealing from Tibetans? Although at the time, no one could have imagined that Yeshi would send men to steal from Tibetans, years later, it would surface that Yeshi had been robbing from fellow Tibetans by having his commanders collect a tariff of jewels and other valuables from all refugees attempting to cross the border from Tibet into Mustang.

Although we never had concrete proof of Yeshi's involvement in the death of Dupa's father, as history would reveal, when the ego-driven, jealous, and devious commander stood to benefit, he was inventive and resourceful. With no legitimate reason to attack us overtly himself, was the wily Cat capable of something more subtle, something that appeared completely disconnected from him and the Chushi Gangdruk?

With Yeshi, it was easy to see conspiracies everywhere. Had the Nepalese traders who took us to the bandits' camp been Yeshi's operatives setting us up for a gunfight with a band of Yeshi's secret operatives? Had they worked together to lure our fathers into a trap—a gun battle where the objective was to assassinate both our leaders?

If so, Yeshi's plot was only partially successful. Whether by accident or design, the bandits had severed only one head of the snake.

My father was still alive.

In the same moment that Dupa lost his father and Dupa's mother became a widow, my father, Gona Gedun Sherab, now the sole leader of the Small Reactionary Group, abandoned our plans to head for India. From our base camp in the Mogum area, my father recommitted our group to fighting the barbarous Red Army.

We weren't going anywhere.

CHAPTER SEVEN

2,000 SHEEP AND A DEAD YAK

SPRING 1963 TO WINTER 1964: MOGUM, NEPAL

 E ALL HEARD the *"Wow! What! Wow! What!"* and looked up to see the two shiny black ravens, appearing in their usual magical way, sounding an alarm. What was this?

As always, my father's plan had been meticulous—cross the border, attack our target—a PLA fortress, kill the enemy, take their weapons, and steal enough animals to feed the camp for a month. However, in the first of many raids during our next year in Mogum, while thirty-six of us were on reconnaissance for the mission, we encountered what father always told us to expect, "the unexpected." Having split off from our group to track an antelope, five of us had found ourselves alone in uncharted territory staring at the darting black streaks.

Sure enough, through my binoculars, I spotted a hunter dressed in a Tibetan *chuba* carrying what looked like a rifle.

Thinking maybe he could lead us to the Chinese camp, my father called out, "Let's get him!" and the five of us kicked our horses into full gallop. At first, because we were still in the shadows of the morning sun rising behind the high mountains, the man with the long gun, which turned out to be a musket, didn't see us coming. When he did, he took off in the other direction. If he were an innocent ordinary Tibetan hunter, he would have no reason to flee; he was behaving like a PLA spy running to sound the alarm.

Then it happened. In his panic, the hunter abandoned his gun, and then all his clothes.

At first, we saw a man fleeing in a dark chuba. Dropping his heavy dark overcoat to run faster, he appeared, from a distance, to be riding on a small white pony—his white pants. Then, having dropped his belt, he lost his pants, and, too scared to stop for them, he now appeared to be riding a brown pony—his bare skin. He was running naked. From my perspective, I saw a man change color three times within a few seconds. It was like a magic trick.

Although I only meant to scare him, when I jumped from my horse and fired a shot above the hunter's head, my bullet scratched his scalp. Falling into a sitting position on the ground, the man, who, as it turned out, was half-Tibetan and half-Chinese, raised his hands. Immediately, the terrified man told us the location of a nearby Chinese fortress. I smiled. Yes. As usual, the ravens were right. When my father handed the hunter his clothes, one of our men started laughing. "Why on earth were you running naked?"

The hunter's face was apple-red from embarrassment.

At the point that the hunter dropped his pants, we were still within shouting distance from our group, so my father gathered the whole reconnaissance party, and, taking the hunter with us, we galloped to the hill overlooking the camp.

Then the next surprise. Suddenly, swirling about the legs of our horses, were a few thousand sheep busily grazing. As I listened to the soft clicking and thudding of their hooves and a chorus of "*Mahh, mahh, mahh,*" I thought what we Tibetans all thought these days when we saw a herd of animals. Food. Kidnaping this flock could feed our families for a year.

But first we had to defeat their Chinese owners.

Below us, a half-mile down a hillside, were at least twenty Chinese tents encircling the Tibetans' larger yak tents. Placing the Tibetans in the center allowed the Chinese—who never trusted Tibetans even when they were working for them—to keep eyes on their captives. I watched my father. How would he handle this? Twenty Chinese tents meant 200 Chinese soldiers.

Always organizing our raids with great precision, my father preferred to surprise the enemy and send them running rather than killing them. But that wasn't an option here. Well prepared for any possible ambushes, the Red Army had barricaded themselves behind trenches and sandbags from which the soldiers could hide and shoot. Never choosing to engage in a losing fight because of anger or pride, my father knew when to attack and when to flee.

Riding down the hill for half a mile and attacking the Red Army soldiers in broad daylight would have been suicidal.

Choosing the smart path, my father didn't call for an attack, but elected to steal the 2,000 sheep. We were freedom fighters who needed food to survive—not a bunch of bandits. Dead men couldn't fight.

But nothing goes smoothly in battle. Just as my father was turning us away from an uneven fight, a boaster named Khetsa Jamdak, who was riding with us for the first time—and, as it would turn out, was a coward—refused to retreat. Declaring his own personal war against the Chinese, he kept yelling, "We've come this far to fight the Chinese. Now's the time. Let's do some real fighting. I want to get my hands dirty with Chinese blood."

We all stared at the first-time fighter. Was he a fool?

Unfortunately, this delay gave the shepherds on the opposite hill time to see us and start shouting to the Chinese soldiers, "The reactionaries are coming, the reactionaries are coming!" And then, "The reactionaries are here!" As we watched amazed, the entire camp of 200 Chinese soldiers mounted their horses and started speeding in the opposite direction toward the shepherds. When they had heard, "The reactionaries are here," the Chinese thought we were on the hill with the shepherds.

At this lucky break, my father sent the men with weaker horses heading back to camp with 2,000 sheep. His revised plan was simple. If the Chinese caught on and came for us, the seventeen men with the herd were to butcher a few sheep, leave the rest, and head home. Meanwhile, my father motioned nineteen of us to dismount and head for cover behind a riverbank, where we could monitor the enemy.

We didn't have to wait long. Within minutes, the Chinese realized they were going in the wrong direction and headed back toward us. As was typical when Tibetans were up against the Chinese army, the odds were now eleven to one.

However, the battle began one-on-one as my father and the Chinese commander arrived at the riverbank at the same moment, both firing their rifles, the Red Army commander yelling he would kill us all and "take back the sheep." When my father's shot hit the target, we discovered the commander was half-Tibetan. However, this soldier didn't die like a Tibetan warrior, but a Chinese mad dog. As he fell, he started firing his submachine-gun. After Namre Geden shot the soldier in the head, the half-Tibetan Red Army leader's gun was still raised in a shooting position. When another shot from

Namre Geden hit the gun's magazine—causing a small blaze—the gun fell out of the soldier's hand. But he wasn't dead yet. Even though the mad dog wasn't moving, he was still breathing hard. Finally, Delshik chopped off his head with a sword. Not nice, but it did the job.

Crawling to the bank, I grabbed the dead man's damaged submachine-gun, replaced the exploded magazine, and began firing. Delshik drew his sword and shouted the Khampa war cry, *"Kee hee hee, kee hee hee heee, duo ahe thee!"* (Got you!). As often happened, the Chinese were more afraid of this war cry than of gunshots, and some of them stopped advancing. Others even crawled backward. Later in the gunfight, as the remaining Chinese began advancing toward us again, I found myself next to Khetsa Jamdak, the boaster who had declared a personal "war against the Chinese." As I maneuvered forward to set up a better shot, the self-declared avenger pulled back my legs, his face pale. "Son, please don't go any farther. They'll get you."

"I'll get them first," I told him, shaking my leg loose.

As he inched backwards, Khetsa Jamdak began shooting from behind me, hitting a stone next to my head. This man, who looked and talked tough, was going to kill me.

"Shoot the damned Chinese—not me!" I yelled over the roar of the gunfire.

Toward the end of the two-hour battle, due to our limited ammunition, we used the "one-shot, one-kill" tactic, alternating shots, with each gunman calling out, *"Nga yen!"* (My turn!). At one point, when one of our men cried, *"Nga yen,"* his shot only made a Chinese soldier's hat fly off his head. After touching his head, the soldier threw what I thought was his weapon at us to surrender, but it was a grenade. Behind the small cloud of dust and smoke, the man turned and ran until my father shot him dead. At that point, one by one, the Chinese jumped up and fled for their lives, showing their backs to us, making them easy targets. Without one serious injury on our side, we killed sixteen Chinese, and the rest of the 200 ran away. Later we learned from the locals that the Chinese soldiers didn't even stop at their base camp. Instead, they headed all the way to the main Chinese garrison, a day and half's journey.

For all of us, it was "mission accomplished." Purely by accident, we had destroyed our target, the enemy fortress, weeks before we had intended. No need now to find an ambush site from which to launch the attack. And we also wouldn't need to shoot an antelope for a while, not when we had unexpectedly stumbled on 2,000 sheep and would be heading back to Mogum with enough food for many months.

That night each unit—the thirty-six of us had divided up into four campsites— butchered a sheep and celebrated. Around my family's campfire, we relived the operation, often pausing to tease the only man who had sustained an injury. In exactly the same place where one would put an earring, his ear had been pierced by a bullet, and everyone congratulated him on a free ear-piercing from his Chinese uncles. Then, without mentioning his name, I pointed to Khetsa Jamdak. "That man with a beard is a coward, and he almost shot me." He shrugged and gave up boasting forever.

On another note, we all laughed about the hunter dropping his pants. Luckily, due to my good karma, I had barely wounded the hunter. I didn't want to kill a man who was half-Tibetan. Had my bullet struck him an inch lower, I would have sent him to Chinese hell with Madam Mao. Then I thought about the mad dog Chinese commander whom we had sent to hell. For us, his being half-Tibetan was far worse than if he had been a full-blooded Chinese. Being attacked by our enemies was the way of the world. Being betrayed by our own people—like the Khampa bandits who killed Dupa's father—was devastating.

When we arrived home and distributed some of the 2,000 sheep among allies, friends, and the less fortunate, we became immediately famous in Mogum, in the same way our group had after our first raid in Dolpo. Everyone in the area wanted to ride with the Small Reactionary Group.

Apparently, this bloody raid—occurring even as it did, without my father's usual meticulous planning—was so devastating that the Chinese who escaped, like many of our previous Chinese victims, again spread rumors that the attack came from Yeshi's organized and CIA–armed "Big Reactionary Group" from Mustang and not our small band of nineteen guerillas. Certainly when this news reached Mustang, Yeshi's failure to actually send the official Chushi Gangdruk troops to attack the Chinese became even more difficult to dismiss. Or explain.

Meanwhile, here was my fantasy come true. We actually had enough sheep to support our families, the same number we had at our homestead in Kham, and, here, protected by high rocky mountain walls on three sides, our lives took on some of the old nomad rhythms.

To honor my grandmother who died on the way from Dolpo to Mogum, my Uncle Chopak, Delshik, and I spent almost six weeks carving the mantra *Om Mani Padme Hum* on the flat rock face of the mountain behind our camp. Using ropes for climbing and special hammers and picks, it took us four to five days to carve each letter, seven Tibetan letters in all. Each letter was as big as two elephants put together.

But our sense that we could resume our old lives was always fleeting. Even though we now had a herd of 2,000 sheep, we couldn't simply stop fighting and live as nomads again. We were in a war zone.

At the same time, my parents, more than anyone, understood that our families couldn't live forever as guerrilla fighters, risking our lives, losing loved ones, and living off stolen animals.

With no country, no land, and, eventually, no animals again, our future was unscripted. So it was time to write it.

THE TRANSITION WAS SLOW, but now at the age of fifteen, I began taking the first steps in what would be my metamorphosis from nomad herder and trained killer to businessman in the West, one who would fight for Tibet with politics and words instead of a gun. When I had befriended the commanders of the border security post—which was jointly operated by the Nepalese and Indian armies to provide physical protection and border security—and had an opportunity to spend a month living in the town of Mogum learning Nepalese, I left my family for the first time. Although they missed me, my parents encouraged me to find a world beyond herding yaks and certainly one beyond the life of a guerrilla warrior. From the Nepalese commander-in-chief of the Nepalese army I soon learned to speak a few sentences in Nepali, and to say "yes" and "no" in English. This was too much knowledge of English for a nomadic boy. "Yes" and "no" became my daily mantras. I said, "yes" for "no" and "no" for "yes," and I didn't even know the difference. But it didn't matter. Not many Tibetans knew their mantras' meanings either, even though they kept repeating them ceaselessly.

Also in exchange for yak meat, the man in charge of the Indian division—which was largely responsible for intelligence-gathering and communication—offered me room and board. My Indian host, Namgyal Lhapcha—who was of Sikkimese origin and spoke some Tibetan in the Lhasa dialect—and I became good friends. From him, I learned many things about Indian politics—its democratic form of government; leaders like Mahatma Gandhi and Jawaharlal Nehru; and India's winning of independence from British colonization. In their home, I was introduced to Indian culture as I ate small animals—chicken, pigeons, fish, and pheasants—for the first time, and listened to his recordings of Indian songs that sounded to me like sweet screaming.

And, listening to the radio at the Indian military outpost—where I heard news about the brief war between India and China in October 1962, and about the assassination of President Kennedy on November 22nd, 1963—it was an eye-opener for me to become aware of the world outside. What would become my lifelong interest in politics surfaced very quickly.

Because I introduced the local Tibetans living near the border to radio broadcasts for the first time in their lives, I soon became the local Tibetan public-relations and international information officer. Almost every night Tibetans in the area were coming to hear the news in the Tibetan language on All-India Radio. Occasionally, there were mentions of the words "Dalai Lama" on the radio, but the Tibetans didn't recognize it, as they only knew His Holiness by his Tibetan names. Dalai Lama sounded to them like *"da da la la ma ma mia."* The little children climbed behind the radio to see who was talking.

Sitting in my small room in the Indian official's home, I remembered my father's words: "As a successful businessman, you'll be free to travel and enjoy a life of prosperity and fame." I was applying my father's advice to seek a different life. In fact, when he wasn't raiding Chinese camps, my father himself was becoming more of a businessman.

Unfortunately, at fifteen, when I returned to our base camp in Mogum, I wasn't quite reliable enough to join him in the world of commerce.

WHEN MY FATHER'S NEPALESE BUSINESS FRIEND appeared to complain about the yak we had sold him a week earlier, my father was surprised. Apparently the yak, for which the friend had paid 975 rupees, had suddenly dropped dead.

My father frowned. "Really?"

The yak buyer accepted a cup of tea. "Really."

Sipping buttered tea, they pondered the mystery. There was no suspect and not a single shred of evidence, and no weapons left on the scene of the mysterious death of the yak in question.

But this yak had it coming. When I had shot the animal in its left horn the day before it was sold, I had intended to scare the yak into submission. To me, yak horns looked like plastic ornaments on a yak hat, like the horns on Vikings' hats. My job had been to bring sixteen yaks safely to our camp, not to kill one of them. But I had never seen a yak this crazy.

The sixteen yaks I was trying to herd back to our camp had been running madly in all directions following one hare-brained yak. Because the animals were born on the open plains of the Tibetan plateau, they were spooked by the narrow paths of the Nepal forest with the bushes and trees rustling in the wind on either side. When the crazy yak in question bolted and kept running around madly in every direction but the right one, the rest of the herd, already skittish, followed. Yaks don't move gracefully like horses or gazelles.

And when it came to yaks, I had assumed I knew what I was talking about. I slept with baby yaks in yak tents. I ate and drank everything that came from yaks. I had watched yak races where the clumsy animals took off back to the starting line. But this situation was beyond my experience. After trying for hours to control the animal, I pulled my British Enfield rifle off my shoulder and shot the yak in the left horn, never imagining this could be fatal. After shaking its head a couple of times, the crazy yak now became calm and led the whole herd home.

The next day, my father sold the one-horned yak to the Nepalese man sitting in our tent.

I said nothing. And I felt no guilt. Guilt may be a special gift of God for Westerners. Not only would volunteering the real story have gotten me in one hell of a lot of trouble, but my silence helped things to subside in their proper way, without further conflict. In the end, my family got the money for the soon-to-be-dead yak, and the Nepalese businessman had to butcher extra yak meat sooner than he planned.

Maybe my father would have laughed like he did when I admitted I was the one who stole the 200 sheep from the wealthy Westerner. I never bothered to tell him. We weren't dependent on buying and selling for our livelihood. Leading guerrilla raids against the enemy was how my father fed our families.

That is, until the fall of 1963. It shouldn't have happened—and wouldn't have—had my father led the raid. In the worst bloodbath in our group's history, one third of our men were killed or wounded, irremediably devastating our forces, and ending our five-year guerrilla operation.

And it wasn't the Red Army or Yeshi the Cat that ended the career of the Small Reactionary Group. We did it to ourselves.

AS MY FATHER'S OLDEST BROTHER, Uncle Chebudok, rushed into our tent, his eyes were filmy with tears, his body trembling. "Delshik was killed. Our brother now dead, dead and gone!" Turning his back on my parents and me, Uncle Chebudok covered his face with both hands and sobbed.

Saying to me, "Care for your mother," my father and Uncle Chebudok left to bury the body of their youngest brother. And Delshik wasn't the only dead fighter in our camp. A third of our men were gone. Throughout the community, stunned voices rended the air, the dogs began howling, and people were crying, choking, gasping, and holding each other. A woman screamed.

I closed my eyes. Delshik? Dead? I turned to my mother, who cried the whole day.

Unfortunately for our families and our guerrilla operation, as there were no recruits to oversee, my father and I had stayed home from that mission. At first it all went smoothly—even without my father. My father's careful plan at first resulted in a successful mission, our men killing a number of Chinese and confiscating several AK-47s and SKS semiautomatic rifles as well as over 300 yaks.

Sometimes, karma takes over and makes smart people do stupid things. If the party had returned home without stopping, they would have made it safely. However, even though it was the group's decision, working as a team without selecting a new leader for the raid, Namre Geden—our stubborn relative, the one who had said he was "fine" except for the "stupid hole" in his stomach—selected himself.

In his self-appointed role, Namre Geden, who had never lead a raid before, insisted on stopping for a day to split up the spoils—something my father never would have done. Because Namre Geden was a respected senior who had a vague role as my father's right-hand man after the death of Khuru Ngajam, the men didn't challenge him. But they should have. This delay gave the remaining Chinese soldiers—who outnumbered and outgunned our men—time to catch up with our group.

As the Chinese came galloping over the hill, one of Dupa's uncles mounted his horse ready to flee, urging the others to follow. However, Namre Geden stopped him at gunpoint and made his next bad decision—to stay and fight. He threatened he would shoot to kill anyone who attempted to leave. "No one here is to run; we are here to fight and kill the freaking Chinese!"

As the uneven battle raged, our small group thought magicians were pulling Chinese soldiers out of hats. When our soldiers killed one Chinese, ten more showed up, and after killing ten, a hundred more rushed in with bullets and swords.

When the blade of his sword fell to the ground, leaving his son Namre Kalsang holding only the handle during his attack on a Chinese soldier, Namre Geden shot the Red Army soldier with his AK-47 at point-blank range. But Namre Geden couldn't save his youngest son Tsedor—my close friend and other hunting pal. As they saw Tsedor fall, Namre Geden and Namre Kalsang rushed forward and fought hand-to-hand combat with the killer. But it was too late. When, in the confusion of the battle, Kalsang told his wounded brother, "Go help our father and I'll take down these Chinese," he didn't realize Tsedor couldn't move. His backbone was severed, and he was dying.

A misunderstanding was the last twist of fate that left our small band of guerrilla fighters decimated. Those who were in a good position on a hill and downrange from the Chinese abandoned their posts when a man from our party waved his hands. Not able to hear what he was saying, our fighters thought he was signaling them to come down the hill, so they abandoned safe cover. When the Chinese fired a hail of semiautomatic bullets at our exposed men, they killed a great many of them, including Namre Geden, who had made another mistake by placing himself, the leader, on the front line. As the men who survived described the scene, while the Red Army soldiers were screaming for help, our wounded men made no sounds, silently accepting their karma and death.

Then more bad luck occurred in the form of a snowstorm which covered the battlefield as it became too dark and cold to continue. After both sides retreated and went in circles in the stormy, snow-blown darkness, only to face each other the next day, all of the men were too exhausted and battered to fight again.

Although the casualties on the Chinese side were ten times higher, we now had many broken hearts, and many less friends with whom to share experiences, far too few good fighters on whom to depend.

When my father returned to our tent, where my mother was still crying, I learned what happened to Delshik, my father's youngest brother and my hunting buddy. As the surviving fighters told the story, in the final stage of the Small Reactionary Group's final battle, after Delshik had been shot in the head—the bullet going through his brain and knocking him momentarily unconscious—he got up and fought the rest of the day. He had lived for the five days it took for our men to make the journey home before he died.

For Dupa and me, it was a day of deep sadness. Two of our hunting partners and fighting comrades, Delshik and Namre Tsedor, were dead. Sitting alone in our tent, Dupa and I remembered our grand hunting trip when we forgot a flint and a tent and limped home in a rainstorm, soaking wet and empty-handed. Now my great childhood friends were gone.

It was clear to all of us. If my father had been there as leader, none of this would have happened. But things happened for reasons beyond our comprehension.

For over a year, our group had launched armed attacks against the Chinese occupiers of Tibet from our new camp in Mogum. But now it was over. This bloody fight marked the end of the only systematic and ongoing campaign to attack the Chinese on Tibetan soil—the Small Reactionary Group's battle against the People's Liberation Army of the People's Republic of China. For the same reason that my father and I were absent on that raid, what was karmically destined to happen, happened. Ending where it all started—like dreams and nightmares—this fatal raid was our last. There were no longer enough men alive to continue the fight.

But that didn't stop the devil from Mustang from coming after what was left of us. Even if the Chushi Gangdruk commander knew that our ranks had been devastated, the accumulated fame and accomplishments of our small fighting force still cast a shadow over his failures. Possibly as much about exacting vengeance as removing the competition, Yeshi wasn't about to rest until he found a reason to kill off what little was left of the Small Reactionary Group. And, of course—knowing what he did about Yeshi—my father still posed a great threat. However, because my father was a well-known hero, Yeshi would need a good reason to cut off the other head of the snake.

And then he found one.

COMING OUT OF THE SNOW FLURRIES was a man riding one horse and leading another. Calming the mad barking of our mastiff Tajama, I squinted into the white blur. Who was coming to our camp in the middle of winter? As the figure came closer, I recognized Gyen Tsewang Dorjee, the CIA–trained Chushi Gangdruk commander—the one with the Rolex watch, Colt .45 pistol, and top-secret CIA maps—who had spent nights reciting the tales of King Gesar with our fathers in Mustang. Covering Tsewang as well as half of his mount was a strange light green coat with a hood, which I recognized as a U.S. Army raincoat. Tying down the four corners and using a rifle in the middle as a pole, it could be pitched as a tent. I wanted one.

Feeling the air in our quiet camp change, I hurried to greet him. Was this the good news I thought it was? A trained CIA guerrilla fighter coming to fight the Chinese with us?

When he recognized me, Tsewang dismounted and smiled. "Is your father at home?"

I smiled back. Tibetans don't shake hands.

As I took the halter of his second horse and led him to my father's tent, I glanced sideways. Yes. He was wearing his Japanese navy hat and U.S. Army shoes. I wondered if he still had the cyanide pills.

When I called out, "Aba, Tsewang is here" and my father pushed aside the tent flap to greet Tsewang, my father was feeling what I was. This was much more than a friendly visit. Just at the moment when our operation no longer had enough men to fight for Tibet, here was a seasoned commander.

Somewhere a *bubo bubo* (an eagle-owl) was hooting during the day.

As I unsaddled Tsewang's horses and took his belongings to my tent, I grunted under the weight of the saddlebags. Ammunition. Lots of it. When Dupa returned from feeding the horses, I tossed him a bag and blurted out the news.

After Dupa and I prepared Tsewang a bed in our tent, we hurried to join the crowd that was gathering. As my mother served Tsewang tsampa, buttered tea, and a large chunk of cooked meat, the Chushi Gangdruk commander settled comfortably, sitting cross-legged on a carpet.

When my father described the fatal raid and our decimated forces, Dupa and I fixed our eyes on Tsewang and waited.

Tsewang took a sip and set down his bowl of tea. Conversations stopped.

The only sound was the rattle of wind rippling the tent and a sharp utterance from the animal pens as our shepherdess scolded the sheep.

Looking at my father, Tsewang's eyes were almost twinkling. "I'm here to do something I'm not able to do under the Chushi Gangdruk—fight the PLA. I'm here to join your group and attack our enemies."

My father was smiling. Dupa and I poked each other.

Describing how impressed he was with our victories, even though we had been under-equipped and had so few men, Gyen Tsewang Dorjee looked at each of us in turn, including Dupa and me. "Your group has demonstrated what we Khampas can do and who we really are—the few, the proud, and the brave!"

The air in the tent became charged. I could feel my stomach flip-flop. With a senior official from the Chushi Gangdruk—trained as a guerrilla fighter by the CIA in Colorado, and a fighter from our homeland in the Kingdom of Nangchen—as my father's co-leader, we wouldn't have to give up the fight to liberate Tibet. I breathed in the mingled smell of buttered tea and snow.

As the tent swirled with chatter, I realized Dupa was staring at the ground. I knew what he was thinking. Dupa's father and Tsewang had spent hours in our tent in Mustang together sniffing tobacco and strategizing about the fate of Tibet. Our fathers and Tsewang had formed a close bond as comrades and friends. If Khuru Ngajam had lived, the three of them riding together could wipe out the entire Red Army.

Unfortunately, no one was going to do any liberating right away. All the passes were blocked by snow, so crossing the border to attack the Red Army couldn't happen until April. It was astonishing that Tsewang had survived the freezing snowstorms on his long, treacherously dangerous journey from Mustang to Mogum on the Tibet side of the border. Not weary, however, Tsewang was animated, and he brushed away my father's suggestion that he rest.

With Dupa and myself sitting in on the sessions, for the next five months, my father and Tsewang spent part of each day planning their strategy for a spring offensive, once the snow melted. If both had lived long enough, Tsewang would have been my father's new co-leader, and the Small Reactionary Group would have yet another life.

As Tsewang, a soldier with CIA training, became well integrated into our camp and our family, he introduced Dupa, me, and our remaining men to an array of guerrilla-warfare tactics. He even let me shoot his M1 Garand rifle and a Colt M1911 semi-automatic pistol. When they weren't strategizing, my father and Tsewang played dice, recited the tales of King Gesar, and, on a few occasions, Tsewang went hunting with Dupa and me. Each night, after eating dinner, he slept in the tent with Dupa, Dupa's grandfather, and me.

When they weren't talking about how to defeat the Chinese, Tsewang and my father were concerned about the huge numbers of Tibetan refugees who were returning to Chinese-ruled Tibet. To Tsewang's mind, it was not only an embarrassment that our countrymen were willing to live under Chinese occupation, but also a betrayal of His Holiness the Dalai Lama. Tsewang and my father discussed ways to stop them from returning, even if it took the use of force. But, of course, this was unrealistic. Most Tibetans who went back to live in servitude under the Communists were returning because they had no means to survive. In fact, the majority of the people going back were the weakest Tibetans—widows, orphans, and old, sick people who had lost their caretakers to Chinese bullets.

No matter how persuasive my father was when he talked to the returning refugees who stopped by our camp, my father and Tsewang were also battling the Chinese propaganda machine. Back in Mustang, Tsewang had heard on the radio the same Chinese promises that I had heard while I was living at the border. In their broadcasts, the Chinese enticed the Tibetans to return with promises of forgiveness and good employment. The wolves were promising the sheep safety and prosperity. I heard their pitch so many times I could repeat it exactly:

> You, our Tibetan brothers and sisters who left for foreign countries, come back home. In foreign lands, you will find nothing like your own homes. Here at home, you all will be treated with respect and equal rights and have good jobs. Those who killed our soldiers will be forgiven and even will be promoted to better positions and given special rewards. In gun battles, people kill people and bullets have no eyes. We can understand that and therefore we will forgive you. You cannot trust the Reactionary Indians and the Capitalistic Imperialist Americans. They train your men to kill you. Chairman Mao is your own father and the Communist Party is your caretaker, and you don't need these untrustworthy foreigners in your life.

Of course, as my father and Tsewang understood, most of the thousands of Tibetans returning to be second-class citizens under their Chinese masters didn't believe the Chinese lies, but couldn't survive outside the Land of Snows.

One of those forced to return was Lhawa Lherap—whom we had wanted to mediate for us with the rogue Khampas who killed Dupa's father. When Lherap's son-in-law—who was the caretaker of Lherap's entire family—was captured by the Chinese during a looting raid in Western Tibet, Lherap's family was left without food. Lhawa Lherap then became one of the vulnerable Tibetans the Chinese enlisted in their propaganda program. The great showman and storyteller was repeating the PLA's false promises on Chinese radio. However, rather than feel angry about Lherap's working for the Chinese, my father and Tsewang came to understand that Lherap was doing this out of necessity. There was no Red Cross assistance available to Tibetan refugees. For us to convince Tibetans to remain in exile would require our providing all their basic necessities, which we ourselves had in very limited supply.

Another reason my father and Tsewang accepted the inevitability of the reverse migration was that many Tibetans believed that exile to India might be "much worse than living in their own country under Communism." More than they feared the barbaric Chinese, my father explained, many were wary of a different culture, language, religion, altitude, and food. These fears about India were fueled by the Chinese. Tsewang described Chinese broadcasters claiming, "Indian politicians are as cunning as monkeys, soldiers as cowardly as chickens, and the Indians as lazy as pigs doing nothing except making more and more babies," leaving some ignorant Tibetans wondering why His Holiness the Dalai Lama went into exile in such a country. Although the Chinese lies were obvious and shallow, they told them so often that many gullible Tibetans swallowed them and abandoned plans to join His Holiness.

Well, we weren't going to India. Although I was curious about India and the rest of the world after my time with the Indian family at the border, for us, home right now was Mogum in Nepal, until we could liberate our homeland and return to a free Tibet.

About the time Tsewang had a falling-out with the Chushi Gangdruk and sought refuge with us, officials back in India, including the Dalai Lama's older brother Gyalo Thondup, were hearing that Yeshi was embezzling CIA funds. However, because all this was occurring in a place too remote and far away to control, Yeshi continued operating without any oversight, still stealing from his fighters and still promising to set up Chushi Gangdruk bases in Tibet, which he never did. Eventually, the world would learn that the majority of the freedom fighters in Mustang—who were honest Khampas devoted to the cause of liberating Tibet—were actually Yeshi's unknowing victims. He was keeping the CIA–issued food money and rations from his nearly starving soldiers. Killing the enemy and freeing Tibet was incidental to Yeshi's men as they made occasional raids across the border to steal food and animals from the Chinese.

How much Tsewang knew of Yeshi's corruption and treachery, he didn't say. Although it's possible Tsewang confided more details to my father, Tsewang was a gentleman and didn't condemn anyone or seem to hold any grudges, only telling our group he had abandoned his post as top commander in Yeshi's operation because of ongoing "disputes with his fellow top commanders." Tsewang did mention disliking Yeshi's famous killer accomplice Rara, but Tsewang never explained. Perhaps his dispute with Rara started as early as their CIA training together in Colorado.

All we knew was that the air in our camp was electric again. In the winter of 1964, only our small group—as well as the fighters in Mustang waiting for Yeshi's orders that never came—still believed in the fight to liberate our beloved homeland. Once the snow receded, with Tsewang at my father's side, we could resume attacking the Red Army outposts. Sitting there in the afternoons talking for hours about what a small band of guerrillas would be able to do against a nation of barbarians, our men reserved a particular place in Tibetan hell for the treasonous Tibetans who were sleeping with the enemy. Speaking about the Tibetans like those in Lhasa who chose to collaborate with the Chinese and leak secrets to the Red Army, my father would become animated. Dupa and I fantasized about killing these traitors ourselves.

At that point we still believed that it was only the Chinese or their Tibetan collaborators who were the real enemy.

So when a dozen Chushi Gangdruk—two of whom, Kartse Tsewang Ngodup and Amdo Abe, both *Japons* or commanders of a Chushi Gangdruk unit who had visited us often in Mustang—arrived at our camp wanting to speak to Tsewang, we were curious, but not alarmed. I went looking for Dupa. These were comrades from the same region and the same resistance movement. Even when they didn't know each other well, Khampas trusted each other and were all united as brothers, fighting for a common cause against the Chinese invaders, committed to die for our people, our country, and our religion.

As they explained before setting up camp at the periphery of our site, they had come from Mustang to negotiate a mutually acceptable deal in which Gyen Tsewang could set aside his dispute with Yeshi's other commanders and rejoin the Chushi Gangdruk without retribution or embarrassment.

Even the ravens failed to appear at the approach of these comrades.

YAK HERD IN
MOUNTAIN VALLEY OF
TIBETAN HIMALAYA
COURTESY OF
PALJOR THONDUP

NYENCHEN TANGLHA
MOUNTAIN RANGE
AND LAKE NAMTSO
COURTESY OF TIBET
HOUSE US, NYC

GENERAL GOMPO
TASHI ANDRUTSANG,
COMMANDER OF THE
CHUSHI GANGDRUK,
FROM *BUDDHA'S
WARRIORS* (2004)
BY MIKEL DUNHAM
COLLECTION OF
KALSANG GYATOTSANG

KHAMPA RESISTANCE
FIGHTERS ARRIVE
AT GREAT PRAYER
FESTIVAL (*MONLAM
CHENMO*), LHASA.
COURTESY OF TIBET
HOUSE US, NYC

CHUSHI GANGDRUK
REBELS RIDE
IN LHOKA,
FROM *BUDDHA'S
WARRIORS* (2004)
BY MIKEL DUNHAM
COLLECTION OF
ATHAR LITHANG

CHUSHI GANGDRUK
WARRIORS
ON PATROL,
FROM *BUDDHA'S*
WARRIORS (2004)
BY MIKEL DUNHAM
FRONT JACKET
PHOTO COURTESY
OF THE AUTHOR

PALJOR THONDUP,
IN SANTA FE,
NEW MEXICO
1977
COURTESY OF
PALJOR THONDUP

TOBTSANG ZODA, DUPA AND PALJOR'S CARPET FACTORY AND HANDICRAFTS CENTER IN KATHMANDU
1978
COURTESY OF PALJOR THONDUP

DUPA AND PALJOR AT PROJECT TIBET, SANTA FE, NEW MEXICO
1989
COURTESY OF PALJOR THONDUP

↗
THE DALAI LAMA
ARRIVES IN SANTA FE.
1991
COURTESY OF
PALJOR THONDUP

↘
THE DALAI LAMA
TAKES A CHAIR-LIFT
TO SKI BASIN.
1991
COURTESY OF
PALJOR THONDUP

PALJOR IN SANTA FE
1989
COURTESY OF
PALJOR THONDUP

THE DEVIL SENDS HIS DHUGCHE

APRIL 1964: MOGUM, NEPAL

IN THE DEAD SILENCE of the early morning in April 1964, I woke to my father's whispering next to my pillow. "We're surrounded by Chushi Gangdruk men." I rubbed my eyes. Why would our friends "surround" us? And where were the usual sounds of morning? Why weren't our mastiffs barking? But there was no time to think about any of that. While Dupa's grandfather remained in bed performing his usual morning prayers, Dupa and I quickly dressed. I glanced at my pistol in a holster tied to the tent pole, but left it. I didn't need a gun to meet friends. Most of our other guns were in a cave wrapped in blankets, hidden from the Nepalese border guards.

As we watched my father and Gyen Tsewang Dorjee walk unarmed toward the trees where the negotiators were waiting, we didn't notice anything out of the ordinary.

Then Dupa touched my arm. "Paljor, I don't see Amdo Abe. Where are the negotiators? Where is everyone?"

Suddenly, loud shouting shattered the air, and, as if thunder and lightning were striking at the same time, the whole valley shook and crackled, as the blasts of semiautomatic submachine-guns bounced off the rocky mountain-side. In the volley of gunfire coming from every direction, I leapt behind a large boulder with Namre Kalsang, while Dupa, my Uncle Chopak, and my monk uncle crouched behind a flimsy pile of firewood opposite us.

From my hiding place, I could see a woman running for cover to the riverbank, carrying a baby in one arm and a holy book in the other. At the rattle of a machine-gun, the mother collapsed to the ground on her belly, the baby tumbling to the earth. Clawing at the dirt, the woman tried to crawl the few feet to her child, but she couldn't. Her backbone had been shattered. After a second fiery burst, mother and child lay motionless only a few feet away from shelter, the mother's arms still reaching for her baby. The new wife and baby of Dadhue the Black Face were dead.

The men killing a woman and a baby were not the Chinese invaders we had been fighting for six years. Was this real or was I dreaming? This was a slaughter of Tibetans by Tibetans.

When I stepped out into the open to head back for my pistol, my Uncle Chopak stood from behind the woodpile, shouting and waving his hands in the air. As I thought he was saying "ja-ja," which meant "Chinese, Chinese," I hesitated. By the time I realized he was actually yelling, "zja-zja"—which meant "hide, hide down"—it was too late. A bullet shot off the back of his left hand, leaving only the skin of his palm holding the fingers together. As I dashed across the open ground back to my hiding place, several machine-guns fired at me, and I felt like I was being tossed about in a strong windy hailstorm, the hail coming at me horizontally. When I dropped behind the boulder, there were eight bullet holes in my chuba.

For the next half-hour, streams of gunfire riddled our tents and flashed across the open ground. After a twenty-second pause in the shooting, three shots rang out from the direction of our tent, and, for nearly another hour, the killers poured another volley of intense, continuous gunfire into our camp. As if it were happening in slow motion, we watched my father's oldest brother— my monk uncle who helped teach me Tibetan and was our tailor—fall to the ground, shot dead. And what was happening in the rest of the camp? We couldn't see. Crouching lower behind the rock, I closed my eyes. This couldn't be real. But it was.

When the gunfire stopped, there was dead silence, and the entire world seemed to momentarily stop. No one moved. As Kalsang, Dupa, and I stepped out from our hiding places, we saw bodies everywhere, men and women of all ages, and the baby. I wasn't sure even I was alive. What had just happened? Why? How? In our bullet-shattered camp strewn with bodies, it was difficult to tell who was dead and who wasn't. The dead only seemed sleeping. Then, my ears still ringing from the sound of gunfire echoing off the mountain ranges, I ran, sidestepping the dead.

Only a few paces from the body of my dead mother, I dropped to my knees. My father, barely breathing and riddled with multiple gunshot wounds, was still alive. It was a true nightmare in broad daylight. He lived long enough to utter two cryptic phrases: *"Gyalwa Yeshen Norbu"* (Victorious Wish Fulfilling Jewel)—the name my father always used for the Dalai Lama—and "you two sons." Although he died before he could finish all that he wished to say, I understood. My father wanted Dupa and me to seek wisdom and acceptance by telling the story of the massacre to His Holiness.

In that moment, the notion of being enlightened by the Dalai Lama was the last thing on my mind. I couldn't feel a thing beyond a blind, searing anger. Someone was going to pay for this.

From my monk cousin—whom the killers didn't shoot no doubt because he was wearing monk's robes—we learned the story. As my father and Gyen Tsewang were heading toward the trees where the official negotiators waited, Rara and a few other killer dogs sent by Yeshi—who had broken ranks with the negotiating party and had been hiding behind rocks and bushes camouflaged under long grasses and leaves—stepped into the path with machine-guns raised. Although my father always took the extra time before a raid to make sure our horses were sound and that we packed extra bullets to "prepare for the unexpected," an attack by fellow Khampas was something he would never have expected.

When Gyen Tsewang realized that he had been set up and he ran back for his M1 Garand rifle, the ambushers shot him in the thigh, breaking the bone, leaving him to crawl to our tent. Three shots from our tent told the killers that Tsewang was still alive. This sparked another hour of slaughter. When the massacre ended, Gyen Tsewang Dorjee had 27 bullet holes in his body. Then, in a show of contempt against their own comrade, Rara put a rope around the neck of Gyen Tsewang Dorjee and dragged his dead body around behind a horse while a photographer took a series of pictures from all angles.

According to my monk cousin, it was also Rara who killed my father. When Tsewang was shot, my father pulled his pistol, but Rara, who was fifteen paces away and holding a fully automatic submachine-gun, was already firing. A burst of machine-gun fire literally tore my father apart.

The murder of my mother was more horrible. As she ran across the open field to her dying husband, two men who had been hiding behind a boulder stepped out with their guns raised. But even a machine-gun round to her foot from one of them didn't stop my mother. However, a CIA–issued Colt-.45 semiautomatic pistol did. As she grabbed the rifle from one of the attackers,

Khalap Champa—a Khampa who had trained with the CIA in the U.S. and who had been one of Yeshi's spies at the trial in Mustang—shot my mother three times in the head with his pistol at point-blank range. No one can survive one shot with that weapon, but Khalap Champa kept firing.

In my shock and disbelief—with everyone crying out, *"So many are killed— so many are killed!!!"*—I wasn't capable of taking a body count. I just knew that very few of us out of sixty were still alive, and that every dead body had more than one bullet wound, many more than a dozen.

We found Dupa's grandfather dead in his bed of multiple gunshots, murdered during his morning prayers. Dadhue's baby—who was chubby like a fat little puppy or kitten and who, as the only baby in in our camp, had become everybody's little pet, including mine—was shot twice, once in the stomach and once in the head, and the mother was shot five times all over her body. Uncle Chopak, clutching the wrist of his missing hand and moaning in terrible pain, was losing blood.

Dupa, Kalsang, and I were the only able men alive in this ghost town of bullet-ripped tents—all shredded into fishing nets with our cooking utensils looking like filters—where now the weakest of weak people lived. Once upon a time, we were the toughest and strongest freedom fighters, a well-organized resistance unit. Now we were reduced to a beleaguered group of orphans, widows, a physically wounded man, and four mentally tormented freedom fighters.

Standing beside me, looking at my murdered parents and the silent camp strewn with bodies, Namre Kalsang, who had fought hand-to-hand combat with the Chinese, started to sob. *"Cheda seshag, cheda seshag, Kun-chuk-chen"* (All are killed, all are killed, my Lord!).

I gripped his arm. *"Shanye Kalsang, ngu-mayong. Khongtso ngatso dagchag sung"* (My brother Kalsang, stop crying in front of the people who just became our enemies). No Khampa man cries in the presence of enemies, even though the unthinkable has just happened.

My head was pounding. My body was shaking. These baby-killers had defamed the character of the good people in the Tibetan resistance organization and its very name, *Chushi Gangdruk*. As we knew from our time in Mustang, and history would eventually reveal, no one in the Chushi Gangdruk acted without the knowledge and direct orders of the former monk whose loyal trained dogs did the dirty jobs for him. The massacre of our families had been ordered by the leader of Chushi Gangdruk, Bawa Gyen Yeshi. The slaughter of our loved ones had been Yeshi's vengeance not only against Tsewang but another man—my father—who had humiliated the Mustang leader by rejecting his command. Gyen Tsewang's departure from the Chushi Gangdruk had finally given Yeshi the excuse to pounce and finish what he had been trying to do for four years—destroy the Small Reactionary Group.

Above us, vultures were hovering in figure eights, emitting eerie squawks as we pulled and pushed the dead bodies of our relatives to the riverbank. Because we didn't have shovels and there were few small stones at our campsite, we had to surrender our loved ones to the river. At the smell of death everywhere, the mastiffs were whimpering and the horses were stomping and tugging at their halters. It took several hours.

Dupa and I knew what we had to do. By tradition, it would be up to the survivors to avenge the deaths of our families. It was our job to kill these thugs and butchers.

From the day I stepped away from my birthplace in Kham and became a refugee on the run, my greatest fear had been of losing my parents. Now the jewel of our family, my mother, and my beloved father, who, far beyond his worth as a fearless and respected fighter and leader, kept promises at the cost of his own life, had died by the bullets of Yeshi's traitorous brutes. Now that my parents were gone, even while feeling the pain of seeing my dear ones caught in the current, their bodies leaving me forever, I couldn't think of them as dead. For me, my mother and father were still alive and high in spirits and warm in their hearts. I imagined them in some beautiful place like the Buddhafield, where they would live happily ever after.

At the same time, I was about to push the killers over a cliff into a fiery hell.

WHEN I HEARD SOMEBODY SAY, "They want to talk to us," I looked around. "What? Who?" Wasn't everybody dead? Dupa, who was standing behind me, placed his hand on my arm. "We have to go."

When men with guns said, "Come with us," you went.

As Dupa, Namre Kalsang, and I walked in the same direction as the killers toward the official negotiators, who were waiting 100 paces outside our camp, how did we know they weren't going to kill us? We didn't. Training guns on us when we arrived at the meeting site were the men who had just massacred our family. Two of them—my mother's killer Khalap Champa, and Rara, who shot my father—introduced themselves by name.

What was going on? As it turned out, we weren't the only ones being held at gunpoint. Rara's rogue group had also surprised the four negotiators who had come to mediate—not to murder. One of the mediators whispered to me, "We weren't here to kill anyone. We came to negotiate with Gyen Tsewang Dorjee for his peaceful return to his base-camp in Mustang. We wanted him to continue his leadership role there." They were like most of the freedom fighters—dedicated men who had had been grossly misled by Yeshi and his corrupt *jugche*—not the few murderous brutes training rifles on the rest of us now.

With the armed killers standing nearby, the negotiators—not one of whom had fired a single shot while Yeshi's mad dogs were ambushing my father and Tsewang and killing a camp full of innocent Tibetans—were now expected to whitewash the murders and put us, the survivors, on trial. The charge? We had instigated the slaughter by firing first.

In the new version of events, which the negotiators were required to spin, our men fired first on Yeshi's men. When the killers were forced to return fire, the tragic deaths of women and babies were due to "terrible mistakes made by their bullets." "Bullets have no eyes" was also the official excuse used by the Chinese propagandists in the border areas at the time.

The killers' one piece of evidence that we had fired first—my granduncle's blood on his AK-47—was ludicrous. This, the negotiators and commanders alleged, proved that Uncle Chopak had attempted to fire his weapon. They failed to take into account that it was after they shot off his hand that my granduncle's blood spilled everywhere, including on his gun. In effect, they were suggesting it was my granduncle's fault that he was bleeding. By blaming the victims for their own deaths, Yeshi's henchmen were licensing themselves to kill.

To compound the illogical proceedings, the kangaroo court of the Chushi Gangdruk generously found Dupa, Kalsang, and myself "not guilty" for the crimes they themselves had committed. Case closed.

After the "meeting," the killers gave us our guns back, but not all of them. To our surprise, Yeshi's men knew that most of our weapons were hidden in a nearby cave. Not only did they know the hiding place, but they knew exactly which guns were ours. While the guerrillas left our weapons, they confiscated the rifles and machine-guns we had seized from the Red Army and—to compound my questions about the assassination of Dupa's father—they took the CIA-issued guns we had taken from the killers of Khuru Ngajam. How did they know these were the guns of the robbers and not ours?

Then I saw him, and I understood why the dogs didn't bark and the killers knew which guns weren't ours and where they were hidden. The negotiators weren't the only ones being threatened and bullied by Rara and his killer dogs. Standing at the edge of the killers' camp was the homeless orphan from Western Tibet who had lived with us for several months and left our camp the day before the Chushi Gangdruk arrived.

Months earlier, when I found the boy in Mogum and brought him to stay with us, he had been wandering door-to-door begging. Unlike most beggars in Tibet, who recite prayers to attract attention, he had played a flute, sang, and danced. When he lived with us, he slept in our tent, and my mother treated him like a family member. Our dogs knew him and he knew everything about our camp, including where we kept the guns.

Now a hostage of these brutal thugs, he looked sad. During the massacre, the killers had kept him hidden, and I'm certain that he never knew I saw him. Many years later when he would seek me out while I was in Kathmandu, I didn't mention I had seen him with Yeshi's men at the massacre. No one could stand up to Yeshi's killer dogs, certainly not a young boy.

But we would. Standing at the entrance to the bullet-riddled family tent, I clenched my fists and stared at their camp. The guerrillas had underestimated us. We might be sixteen-year-old orphans, but Dupa and I were trained guerrillas, and they had just turned us into deadly wounded animals with nothing to lose.

But we had to move quickly. The baby-killers were camped within walking distance—and unsuspecting—but soon they would be heading back to Mustang.

Two days later, when the last surviving able male, my Uncle Chebudok, came down from the remote mountain area where he had been taking care of our horses, I outlined my plan. There were now four of us—Chebudok, Dupa, Kalsang, and I. Although Uncle Chebudok was eleven years older than I, he was a man of few words, and I took charge. My strategy was simple: "Let's kill as many as we can before they kill us." To use my father's words, we were going to "teach our enemies lessons they would never forget," and we would fight to the death. No one hesitated.

That afternoon, as we huddled in our bullet-shredded tent, it didn't take long to decide on the best tactics. Their location was perfect for an ambush. Because there was a big river in front of their camp with the rest surrounded by forested hills, we would easily sneak into close range after dark without being detected. Taking our positions, we would attack in the morning. Because they were on flat ground in plain view, they would have no place to hide and nothing with which to barricade themselves. Based on our extensive experience of such maneuvers, we knew we could easily kill a large number of the guerrillas before they even spotted us hiding among the trees and bushes.

As we were assembling what weapons we could find, my mastiff lifted his head. Someone was here.

WITH DUPA'S MOTHER IN THE LEAD, all the surviving widows and orphans, including Ostok our shepherdess, burst in, sobbing and beating their fists against their chests. The mistress of Kalsang's father overheard us planning our kamikaze mission and reported us to Dupa's mother and Kalsang's sister.

Weeping and yelling at the same time, Dupa's mother, who was still recovering from a gunshot wound to her paralyzed left elbow, now pounded her head with her good hand. "What is the matter with you kids? It's against our Buddhist belief to commit suicide. Are you going to cause us more tears? And what happens to us after you're all dead?" Like the rapid firing of a machine-gun, she said all this in one breath. "Haven't you thought about what your deaths would do to the rest of the group?"

We all stared at her.

She was still talking. "This is no time to be terrified or frustrated or question why things happen in the ways they do."

And here it was—the contradiction that was my heritage—the uneasy coexistence between the Khampa codes for revenge and Buddhist pacifism. By tradition, Khampas are required to take revenge and not let enemies go unpunished. In a Khampa community, the pressure was as psychological as it was cultural. If you didn't get even with your enemies, eye for an eye, then you weren't considered man enough to be respected.

At the same time, the Khampa chieftains who killed their enemies and the Tibetan guerrillas who killed the Chinese were also Buddhists, respectful of the lives of all sentient beings, even enemies. After they were parachuted into Tibet to attack the Chinese with the Chushi Gangdruk, the CIA–trained fighters spent a day performing Puja ceremonies and praying. While the Dalai Lama refused to directly endorse violence in the Tibetan battle against the bloodthirsty Chinese, from 1957 until Mustang's Chushi Gangdruk outpost disbanded in the 1970's, his older brother worked with the CIA and Chushi Gangdruk to support active armed attacks on the Chinese.

These were the competing messages with which I had grown up.

And then there was my father. His final words were those of a Tibetan Buddhist, not a Khampa warrior. Although he had killed many enemies throughout his life, upon his death at the hands of traitors, my father had invoked the path of the Dalai Lama.

And now here were the women with the message of my Buddhist upbringing and my dying father.

And it was my father's wisdom that guided me now. On one of our walks he told me, "*Bu*, I want you to remember these simple words. Think broadly, deeply, and, in the long term, consider the benefit of others."

Although it was still vengeance, not respect for all living things, that filled my heart, I understood. As the only able men left in our group, the four of us couldn't abandon the survivors.

At that moment, a few of the guerrillas wandered over to investigate the wailing women and the commotion. Thinking fast, I told them, "You can't expect people to stop crying. In fact, some have even attempted to commit suicide." It was a lie, but the killers were gullible enough to believe me, and they went back to packing up their camp.

That night, once Rara and his thugs were gone, I stared at the river that had taken my parents. We couldn't remain in this ghost town of shredded tents where our two families had turned into half a family in one tent that had more than a hundred bullet holes and could hardly hold the weather out. It was time to leave behind the past, not anticipate the future, and live in the present. Time to accept the nature of impermanence, the law of karma, and the fragility of all living things. And our present had to occur away from the killing fields.

Before we left for Mogum, I took a last look at the giant mantra, *Om Mani Padme Hum,* which I had carved for my grandmother on the mountain with Delshik, now dead, and Uncle Chopak, who now had only one hand. The huge letters were chipped and riddled with bullet holes. Picking up my father's rifle from the dirt next to where he was killed, I called out to my father's other living brother. I knew I had to destroy this deadly means of taking lives. As Uncle Chebudok and I took turns smashing the gun against a boulder, cracking and hammering sounds echoed off the mountain walls.

AT A TEMPORARY CAMP we set up a few hours from the place of the massacre site, while we were conducting a death watch over Uncle Chopak and still trying to grasp the horror of the massacre, Dadhue the Black Face arrived. Intent on vengeance, he expected us to join him hunting down the killers of his wife and baby. Even though he was slightly injured from a Chinese hand grenade when his group was ambushed by the Red Army, he was ready to load a machine-gun and find the killers. I still often wonder, "What if?" What would my life be like if we had agreed and joined him to hunt down Yeshi right then?

Disappointed with my decision, Dadhue Nayue planned to avenge his family by joining the Chushi Gangdruk. Although he never mentioned his specific strategy, as he saddled his horse to leave for Mustang, he told us it would make more sense to be "as close as possible" to his enemies and join the Chushi Gangdruk as a "wolf in sheepskin."

Meanwhile, in our makeshift camp, we suffered along with my terribly wounded granduncle. Even far away from the camp by the river where I went to think, I could hear Uncle Chopak's moaning day and night as he lay dying. I could bear the deaths of my parents, but not my granduncle's horrible pain. He was in a living hell. Although we washed his destroyed hand and put alcohol, salt, and even baking powder on it—anything that came to the mind—nothing worked.

In addition to physical pain, his torment was also coupled with mental agony. When he knew he was dying, he became obsessed with worry about Dupa and me, repeating over and over, "The two kids, the two kids. What's going to happen to them? Oh my Lord Buddha."

Of course, Dupa and I were no longer kids. We had been forced to grow up fast and do men's jobs since the age of twelve. But in my early life, my granduncle had been an important figure. I had spent many nights as a child gazing at the sky and listening to the sound of the silence and the wolves when I had slept under the stars guarding the horses with him. He taught me the Tibetan names of the stars, and even told me star stories, including one about Shercharing, the Milky Way, which, according to Tibetan folk tale, was the wish-fulfilling galaxy.

Supposedly, all of a sudden, once every night, the Milky Way turned direction, and, if one waited up long enough to make a wish when that happened, the wish would come true. In one of his stories, a poor Khampa girl, who wanted some large amber beads for her headdress, waited up, and when she saw the Milky Way turning fast, she said, "I wish this bead here and here," marking the spots for the beads with her fists. But, because she didn't say "amber beads," she only got two big bumps the exact size of her fists on the sides of her head. He also told me the seven stars of the Pleiades were the heart of a giant in the sky, that three vertical stars in the group were the penis of the giant, and a short horizontal line of three stars, his sword. It was Uncle Chopak who had been the last man standing as a young warrior in the famous Killing Field of the Eighteen. He was tough, but no one was tough enough for the living hell he was suffering now.

By the second week, when maggots began eating away the flesh in his wound, in a desperate attempt to find some medical aid for my dying uncle, I lied to our other enemies—the Chinese—and made a deal I had no intention of keeping. As the Chinese had already heard about the massacre and, through Nepalese messengers, were urging us to come back to Tibet, I sent the mistress of Namre Geden along with our shepherdess Ostok on a three-day journey to a Chinese garrison across the Tibet-Nepal border with a letter to the Chinese commander-in-chief, agreeing to return to Tibet if they sent medical supplies for my uncle.

To everyone's surprise, the women returned with a group of Nepalese traders carrying sixteen yak-loads of medical supplies and goods such as shoes, clothes, canned food, tea, cigarettes, and even a case of Chinese whiskey. As I distributed the Chinese gifts among the widows and elderly, I was tempted to keep a pair of shoes. However, I didn't like the idea of walking in Chinese shoes. Nothing, as I would soon discover, ever came from the Chinese without deadly strings attached,

Unfortunately, it was too late for the medicine to save Uncle Chopak. He had been a dead man living with a fatal wound in this remote world far away from modern civilization. After a month in our ragged tent on the outskirts of Mogum waiting for the medicine to work, my Uncle Chopak finally died. Although I had suspected that I would be haunted by his tormented soul forever, that wasn't the case. Glad to see his physical and mental torments ended, I found myself as relieved by his death as he seemed to be. And, although I had feared seeing a dreadful face on his dead body full of pain and agony, on the night he passed away, there was peace and tranquility in the air. The next morning, we found him dead with a serene smile on his face, a sign of what a good religious man he was. He never missed his daily morning prayers and evening meditations. While he suffered during his last days to pay off his past karmic debts, he died at peace and with good karma. It was the first time that I felt comforted and even thankful to see someone dead.

Now that Uncle Chopak's ordeal was finally over, our beleaguered band of survivors was ready to leave for India rather than, like many destitute Tibetans, return to live under Chinese rule in Tibet.

From our group, only our shepherdess Ostok, whom I loved dearly and would miss, went back. Although she had always been ready to kill the Red Army soldiers bare-handed, she was willing to accept Chinese false promises of a good living at home rather than live in Nepal where the Chushi Gangdruk still roamed. This iron lady, with her unwavering determination, hated Yeshi and his dogs more than she hated the Chinese. For her, it was not destitution that drove her back over the border. "I never want to see any of Yeshi's men again in my lifetime," she told us.

As I saw it, the Chushi Gangdruk were no longer a threat. Yeshi had already killed his targets, the men like my father who were a threat to him, and had no reason to go after a tiny band of women and teenagers. The survivors of our three families—Gonatsang, Khurutsang and Namretsang—were united as relatives and best friends to live together anywhere but under the unbearable rule of the murderous Chinese.

Our first stop on the way to India was among a disorganized collection of refugee campsites next to a roaring river in Mogum village. My second oldest uncle, Uncle Chebudok and I—the only two survivors in my family—and Dupa, who only had his mother, together made up two sorts of half-families, and one barely full family. There, the four of us settled in one bullet-ridden tent, and Namre Kalsang, with his family of six, in another. Across a bridge from our tents sat the military post where, in happier times, I had studied Nepalese with the commander-in-chief of the Nepalese Army.

Sitting alone on the riverbank our first night in Mogum, staring at the military compound, thoughts kept pouring through my mind, flowing like the water. How would I fight for Tibet if I left Nepal for India? And what kind of life could I have if it wasn't as a nomad and the son of my parents? I had spent my battle-torn youth fearing the death of my parents, and now they were dead.

After two years living in the Mogum area, the valley of death and destruction, it felt as if everything had ceased to exist. The glorious days of the Gonatsang and Khurutsang families in Kham faded away like rainbows. The battles that were fought, with victories and losses, remained as dreams of the triumph of human spirit and goodwill against the forces of evil's demonic nature. The precious lives of beloved ones were blown away by the karmic winds of cause and effect. The trials and tribulations we endured during the invasion of Tibet by China and the violent years of being chased or chasing the Chinese now were passing like migrating birds. The torturous journeys of life had come to a temporary dead end. Life itself proved to be nothing else but a temporary existence in the physical realm of *samsara*. Nothing was left except the sensation of emptiness. Everything was empty. Our tent was empty. My family was empty. My heart was empty. Even our pockets were empty. Except for my pony, a mule, and a few horses, I had nothing much left of the Gonatsang family.

Not long before he was killed, my father had told me, "*Bu* (son). rise above your enemies to be what you can potentially be, because it's your own world to create." Was my father preparing me to reinvent myself and seek a new life with a new purpose?

I listened to the soft hush of the flowing water for an answer.

Tomorrow, I would talk to the commander, with whom I had become friends, and seek his advice.

CHAPTER NINE

WORDS, NOT RIFLES

SPRING 1964 TO FALL 1965: MOGUM TO KATHMANDU

WHEN I ARRIVED SOAKING WET at the Nepalese military post, the same commander who had taught me Nepalese was surprised. He knew we had set up camp the previous day, but he was puzzled. Why, in such chilly weather, had I swum across the cold, churning river from our camp to the army base to say hello? Why hadn't I taken the bridge?

As I stood dripping icy river water, I was about to find my next purpose in life: teenage lawyer.

Hastily, I reported an incident of assault and battery against a Tibetan widow. He was stunned.

When I had spotted two Nepalese men shoving and kicking a Tibetan widow in front of her nearby tent, I had rushed to the commotion. The woman, whose husband had been killed by the Chinese only a few months earlier, was lying on her side in front of her tent, her hands protecting her face, sobbing.

I clenched my fists. "What are you doing to this poor lady?"

A man grabbing the widow by the hair glanced up at me. "This bitch's husband owed me a bag of rice."

"'This bitch?'" I could feel my pulse speeding up.

"Yes, 'this bitch.'"

"I don't know this bitch you speak about. I only know this poor lady lost her husband just a few months earlier." My voice was steely.

Both men paused in their attack and stared at me.

"If you want that lousy bag of rice, you go and find her dead husband to dig up your rice." I was growling now, but, of course, as a Tibetan teenage orphan up against two grown men, I was easy to ignore.

Tossing me a threatening look, one of the thugs turned back, grabbing the woman's long hair again and yanking at the beads around her throat. Later, I would learn that the greedy Nepalese thugs had refused the woman's offer of her husband's saddle, saddlebags, and saddle blanket, which were valued as at least ten times the price of the rice. These men were thieves. They wanted her jewelry. And they were going to kill her for it.

Diving into the fight, I jumped on the man pulling the widow's hair. Like a tiger's claws, my fingernails punched through his sheepskin overcoat before I grabbed him at both sides of his waist, picked him up, and threw him five feet away to the ground.

When he leapt to his feet and headed for the bridge, I had to act fast. I knew where he was going. According to the Nepalese legal custom, whoever arrived first to report a crime won the case. Although I had once been a spoiled nomadic prince, through circumstances and not by nature, I had had to become tough.

As I explained to the commander, instead of taking the bridge, I dove into the roaring river and swam the hundred yards through the strong currents to arrive first.

The commander was shocked. "Did this man really beat up a woman?" To touch a woman forcefully under any circumstances was illegal in Nepal, and I knew that. Using such emotional buttons as "widow" and "dead husband," I'd made sure the military chief was emotionally charged in favor of my case.

When the Nepalese woman-beater frantically rushed into the court ten minutes later, he clutched at his chest as if he were having a heart attack, horrified to see me drenched and standing next to the military chief. Even though the man rattled on saying, "*bala bala bala*" in Nepali and showed the commander some deep bruises I'd given him in the beating, the commander immediately ordered him arrested.

Although I didn't plan it, at sixteen, I had just won my first legal battle. Even though maybe I wasn't the smartest and brightest young man among the Tibetans in the area, when another Tibetan refugee, my friend Dhondup Charieas, had to appear in court charged with illegal possession of a deadly weapon by a foreigner on Nepalese soil, he turned to me. Why not? With nothing to lose or to fear, I was Billy the Kid from Kham, ready, as my father had taught me, to protect the weak and undefended. It was like the story of the young handsome man who, when asked why he married an ugly old lady, explained, "She's the only eligible woman in town." Like that lady, I was the only eligible person willing to act as a lawyer for the other refugees.

Dhondup had been caught carrying a revolver in the town of Mogum and then escaped from jail, leaving behind his very expensive necklace of coral and *dzi* beads and his gun. To argue that the courts should return the necklace, free my "client," and drop the fines for his criminal charges, I surprised my friend the commander friend, who was also the Nepalese military judge, by producing as a witness, the Tibetan girl with whom he was having an affair. Under my instruction, she also told the judge that Dhondup was "an innocent man caught for his mistakes due to his ignorance of the laws of His Majesty's good government of Nepal." When the judge's mistress asked him to do her "the favor" of pardoning Dhondup and returning the necklace to "the poor Tibetan refugee," the commander sighed and reluctantly agreed.

As I won my second case in the role of master negotiator for my fellow Tibetan refugees, I remembered my fathering telling me—as we prepared to flee Kham—that I could pursue a life different from that of a nomad. He told me, "Dance according to the sound of the drum."

The drum I heard came from India where Dupa and I would not only act on my father's dying request to tell the Dalai Lama our story, we would get an education, and we would file a case in the Tibetan courts and seek justice against the killers of our families. Instead of using a sword or a gun, with the tremendous energy and life still kicking in me, I would overpower our enemies with my new legal savvy and my wits.

And I needed them. My next client was myself.

THE MAYOR'S VOICE WAS STERN. "You're not going anywhere."

On a sunny day, just as we were planning our departure for India, the mayor of Mogum, along with several other "*gyenchens*" (senior officials) and two Nepalese traders, walked the hundred yards over the bridge to our camp and threatened to take us to court if we tried to leave Nepal. The Nepali officials were prepared to block us from going anywhere except back to Tibet.

I took a deep breath. This wasn't good. Although our shepherdess Ostok was safe as a woman, returning to Tibet could easily mean execution for the male survivors of the Small Reactionary Group. Unfortunately, although I had never intended to keep it, I had made a bargain with the Red Menace.

I scrutinized my accusers. It was several of the Nepalese traders who had brought us medicine for my uncle and sixteen yak-loads of goods from the Chinese garrison. The charges were "alleged illegal possession of Chinese goods, refusal to return the goods, and resisting compensatory payment for the goods." Desperate for medicine while my uncle was dying, I had signed a pledge promising that we would return to Tibet in exchange for the goods, a pledge I had no intention of keeping.

As it turned out, the Nepalese traders had also signed contracts with the Red Army promising to return us to our Chinese-occupied homeland. Without considering that entering Tibet could easily mean a Chinese death sentence for us, their goal was to appease the Chinese authorities and maintain good trade relations.

The officials gave us two choices: either our group return all sixteen yak-loads of Chinese goods and medical supplies, or, option two, deliver ourselves up to our Chinese enemies.

When I explained that we no longer had any goods to return—except for cigarettes and whiskey, I had distributed the clothes, food, and medicine among the neediest people in the area—a Nepalese official snarled, "Justice will be done by the military court." Looking directly at me, an angry trader added, "This is our land and not yours."

I took another deep breath. In my mind, I could hear my father's advice, "Be prepared for the unexpected, and teach your enemies a lesson they will never forget."

In that moment, I knew what to do. Smiling at the opposition party, I said, "I guess I'll see you guys in court."

The officials frowned at each other and then at me, an uneducated nomad teenager.

As I began to back away toward my battered tent, I added. "By the way, the commander-in-chief is a friend of mine. I suppose you know that, don't you?"

They looked at each other in disbelief.

When I received the summons to appear in court, I assured Dupa that there was "nothing to worry about." He wasn't so sure. The group suing us consisted of over thirty Nepalese who had a vested interest in dealing with the Chinese, including the district chieftain (mayor), city council members, and the Nepalese traders who had brought the Chinese goods as "gifts" for us. Dupa had a point. We were foreigners in Nepal, and anything bad could happen in this remote border area far away from civilization.

We couldn't go back. We were going to India. I patted my cousin on the shoulder. "I'll handle everything."

That night I dreamed I was cut in half from the head down, and I tied the two halves of my body together with a long woven belt and continued to fight until I killed the enemy, who looked like an ancient soldier in armor. When I picked up the armor, there was no body in it. This was just one more of my recurring nightmares about fighting the Red Army and being attacked by ghostly-looking zombies or animals that were fiercer than real-life Chinese soldiers. Of course, it can only happen like that in dreams. I was fighting the projection of my own mind. And I was going to keep fighting the Chinese in my dreams and real life.

The way I "handled everything" was to invite my friend, the military commander—whose official duties included arresting me, confiscating my guns, and officiating as chief justice at the court proceedings the next day—to my tent for a good meat dinner. Although I was now his prisoner instead of his friend, he accepted and was delighted to discover that good Chinese whiskey was on the menu. In this small remote town, there was no whiskey of any kind available except home brew from local moonshiners. This whiskey, I explained, was one of the items that was the subject of the alleged illegal possession. Then I smiled at him. "It was a birthday gift from my Chinese uncles." I held my breath.

He began to laugh. And, of course, by drinking the whiskey with me, the commander was even perhaps now an accessory and accomplice in the illegal possession of Chinese goods!

As we finished the entire bottle together, I selected just the right words to turn him against my thirty Nepalese accusers in favor of an untrained teenage lawyer. First, I explained to him that the goods were "actually Chinese bribes in the form of gifts" to entice us to return to Tibet, where, in all probability, at least the men in our group would be executed. Thus, I argued, Nepalese traders had signed an illegal contract to deliver us to the Chinese because they were sending us before a firing squad. While I had only my suspicions but no way of knowing whether the Chinese would actually kill us or not, by pushing the commander's emotional buttons with the word "execution," I achieved the right effect. Such a dramatic word as "execution" impressed on the judge that our lives were in great danger if we were forced to return to illegally occupied Tibet. At the same time, such a strong word suggested how ruthless the Nepalese accusers were if they would turn us over to the Chinese only to be slaughtered.

With each glass of whiskey, the commander became more infuriated at my opponents.

When he asked what I wanted him to do, I suggested he dismiss the case and tell his fellow subjects not to block us from leaving Mogum. He agreed to do just that.

Offering him more meat, I offered him the legal grounds on which he could do just that. First, I explained, the sixteen yak-loads of Chinese goods were actually "gifts" to us, not merchandise consigned to the Nepalese traders to be sold to us. Thus, we didn't owe the Chinese anything. It was my word against theirs. More importantly, however, was my explanation that "Because the dispute involves international legal issues, the Nepalese military court has no jurisdiction over this case." I shrugged my shoulders and tipped the last drops of Chinese whiskey into our cups. "As the case involves the exchange of goods or properties between Chinese and Tibetans, it isn't a domestic issue. So," I added, "it's a foreign affairs dispute involving complex international legalities, one in which Kathmandu might not want to be involved."

He understood me perfectly. He had no interest in becoming involved in complex legalities. Now he just had to conduct the court proceedings in my favor the next morning.

BECAUSE THERE WAS NO ROOM or tent in Mogum large enough to accommodate so many "plaintiffs," the "trial" was held in a grassy field, where, from the outside, it looked like a gathering of all of Mogum for a village meeting.

In the middle of the grassy field sat the chief justice, my friend the commander. Barely visible among the crowd, Dupa, Kalsang, and I sat to one side. Opposite us, in a half-circle around the commander, were the thirty-two opposition members sitting in two rows, flexing their muscles like a large pack of fat cats waiting to make a kill of three little mice.

Dupa bumped my shoulder and nodded. Hanging at the sides of each of our Nepalese opponents were Khampa swords and daggers, which, no doubt, the Nepalese had obtained at a fraction of their value by exchanging a few bags of barley and rice with desperate Tibetan refugees. If carrying Khampa swords to testify against a Khampa was meant to intimidate us, it wasn't working. They should have known better. These particular three little mice were armed and deadly, should the mob attack us. Concealed in our chubas were handguns. Standing behind us, the mistress of Namre Geden—who had secured the medical supplies from the Chinese—had a Mauser pistol ready to shoot first.

Like the Chinese military during their barbaric takeover of our country, the Nepalese traders underestimated the indomitable spirit of the Tibetan people. If the Chinese command—with the Nepalese traders bringing the legal case for them—assumed that we would be willing to surrender to the Chinese to avoid potential bloodshed from other Tibetans like Yeshi, they were dead wrong. Although Tibetans were capable of infighting and even, as in our case, killing one another, for us there was no contest between the threat from other Tibetans and the danger waiting for us from the demonic forces of the evil empire.

After the commander opened the court session by demanding all present to speak the truth and nothing but the truth, he didn't even bother to have translated for us whatever truths the officials and traders on the other side were claiming. And all thirty-two of them had something to say, which took several hours. They were desperate to save face by taking my group to the Chinese as they promised, or at least returning the Chinese goods.

When it was my turn, the judge had my statements translated for our accusers, all of whom sat stunned. When I began by thanking the judge and the leaders of the opposing party "for creating a new international legal precedent in which private citizens and government officials alike would allow the return and exchange of properties between two peoples or two countries in the event of war or invasion of one country by another," they all looked at each other. What was this? I went on to argue that such an international legal procedure would allow me to now reclaim my family's eighteen-square-mile property in exchange for the Chinese gift of goods that the Nepalese brought to us, "as well as compensation for my family's loss of lives."

At this point, the judge was hiding a smile, and everyone else was wondering what the hell I was talking about.

Furthermore, I stated, "Our leader the Dalai Lama would highly appreciate the efforts of these Nepalese gentlemen to return Tibet to her rightful Tibetan owners." By now my opponents looked very perplexed and had no idea what I was talking about. To be honest, neither did I. My bold statements were based largely on my personal belief in the fair justice system of good governments in democratic countries (unlike the Chinese), and also things I heard on the radio. Because I had no sound knowledge of these issues and didn't have much confidence in what I was saying, I spoke loudly and clearly. I tried to sound like a man who knew too much, while, in reality, since I did not have any formal education, I was as ignorant as my opponents. It worked. I was the better actor.

As promised, my friend the commander, who was also the chief justice, dismissed the case as "baseless" and sternly warned my opponents against any attempt to block our freedom of movement in the kingdom of Nepal. We could now leave the living hell of Mogum and head for India. As the birthplace of Lord Buddha and the land where his teachings took place before they eventually reached Tibet, India was already a logical and comfortable second home for the majority of the Tibetan refugee population in exile—the holy land of enlightenment and the origin of the Buddha Dharma. There we would tell our story to the Dalai Lama, file a lawsuit against Yeshi and his dogs, and start a new life from scratch.

I was hearing the different drum my father predicted.

But getting there wasn't going to be easy. First we had to negotiate the treacherous paths deeper into Nepal and find a way to get across the border.

WHILE I STOOD ON ONE SIDE of the swinging bridge that hung between two hills several hundred feet over a roaring river, the rest of my family waited with the horses on the other side. With the sounds of the river and people shouting at each other a hundred yards across the bridge, it was difficult to hear, but, when I whistled to my pony Bluebird in the same way I called him at feeding time, he placed a hoof on one of the wooden planks dangling over the ravine and started over the swaying structure towards me. Often the only way forward on the treacherous paths deeper into Nepal was across these swinging bridges that had two long chains on the sides and wooden planks—some of which were missing—to step on. Because the bridge couldn't hold too much weight, we could let only one animal cross at a time.

At the center of the flimsy bridge, where it swung like a pendulum under Bluebird's weight, my pony steadied himself. And I held my breath. We had all heard about the horse traveling with another group that had lost its balance on a swinging bridge and tumbled to its death. When I shouted, "Come here, buddy. Time to eat," he picked his way across the rest of the weathered boards.

Horses don't think like humans or fear like humans. While fear prevents people from doing the impossible and thinking the unthinkable, we should never underestimate animals. They have a better survival instinct than humans. Once my pony had gone first, Dupa and I whistled and called the other horses by name. Like the yaks who had followed the one crazy yak I had shot in the horn for leading the herd in circles—the other horses followed Bluebird, one at a time.

Although we got all our horses to safety over the bridges, traveling hill after hill and valley after valley for the next two weeks on the rough paths to our stop on the way to India—Dorpatan, Nepal—was grueling. We were used to high altitudes, but Nepal was humid and hot in contrast to Eastern Tibet, which was dry. And most areas on our route were infested with mosquitoes and leeches. Like little vampires, leeches sucked our blood, gripping our skin so firmly that we could only get them off us by burning their tails with cigarettes.

Nepal was not such a friendly place for Tibetans.

EVEN IN THE VILLAGES, Nepal was not a friendly place. We were outsiders, what was left of us. Although we were now out of the living hell of Mogum, once we reached Dorpatan, we were reminded that the basic problems of life persisted, no matter where we were. In this small town, the Nepalese villagers smelled to us like wood burning or smoked cow horns. We must have smelled to them like yak shit. Who knows? It was a clash of cultures between high-altitude nomads and lowland farmers from two different countries. None of us smelled good, Nepalese and Tibetans alike, because nobody took showers or bathed.

As we set up camp on the outskirts of Dorpatan, with only our bullet-shattered goods, guns, and a few horses and a mule, we were also destitute. Most of our valuable belongings had been obliterated by the bullets of the Tibetan killers of my family. And what we had left I used to honor my late parents. To conduct prayers for my mother's future rebirths in higher realms, I had given all her belongings, which included mainly priceless pieces of jewelry, to several high lamas. To conduct prayers for my father's higher rebirths, I had offered my father's horse to the high Lama Tarik Tulku Rinpoche. And with the rest of what little money was left, I began a project which, as far I know, no Tibetans in the old country or Tibetans in exile ever undertook.

Dedicated to my beloved parents and all Tibetans who gave their lives for the most civilized nation on the Roof of the World, the Land of Snow, and the Home of Brave Tibetans, I hired a professional stone carver, an old man who had been traveling in our group, to inscribe an entire holy book onto thousands of Mani stones. While it was common in the good old days in Tibet to pay tribute to the dead with one short mantra such as *Om Mani Padme Hum* carved on a rock—as we did on the rock face for my grandmother—I commissioned a stone book of the entire 1000-page ancient text, *Therpa Chenpodo* (The Book of Great Liberation). Tibetans in Dorpatan came to watch Doko Penambeen (*doko* means stone carver) as he inscribed the Tibetan letters on stones of all different sizes from three feet in diameter to round and smooth river rocks. The cost was thousands of Nepalese rupees, a huge sum of money at the time.

Although money meant nothing to me, my religious projects had left us penniless.

Living as we were in samsara is like swimming in an ocean of suffering. The Buddha taught the Four Noble Truths as a means to get out of this ocean. But it seemed the Buddha was no longer with us either. No Buddha and no money. Even though my Uncle Chebudok was older, since the massacre, I had made the major decisions for our little group. Although, at sixteen, I had sometimes walked away with a few metaphorical broken ribs, like a rodeo cowboy falling off a bull, all along the way I had tried to execute my decisions—such as making a dangerous deal with the Chinese for medicine; moving our camp to the town of Mogum; facing the Chinese and Nepalese traders in court; and now moving to Dorpatan—after careful consideration. And everyone was dependent on me to make another decision.

What to do? To travel further into Nepal and on to India, we needed money, and it took money to make money, which we didn't have. What to do? That was the question ringing in my head constantly, day and night. I kept asking myself, "What can I do with the horses? What can I do with the horses?"

When my father told me I would be better off as a trader than a nomad, I had been confused by this idea. My father wasn't. He had seen the future. In Kham, I had been a cowboy and, as a young teenager, I had stolen horses from the Chinese. I would become a horse trader instead of a horse thief.

As there were no roads for trucks, Red Cross supplies to the two large Tibetan refugee communities—which the Red Cross had established and maintained in the area—had to be transported by mules and horses. The next morning, I arrived at the offices of the International Red Cross and signed us up with the manager in charge of deliveries. We were in business.

In our operation, I was the boss behind the scenes. Very much like the dynamic between our fathers, I was the businessman mapping out strategy while my partner Dupa, like his charismatic father, was the front man—the charming womanizer, the public-relations director, and, in the Tibetan refugee community, the most trusted of our group. If Dupa was Churchill, Roosevelt, and the Home Minister all combined, I was his General Montgomery and Secretary of State who did the fieldwork for him. We had a tacit agreement to keep it that way. Uncle Chebudok, who was a good and honest man, kept things to himself and preferred to do all the physical work for our horse-transportation trading enterprise. When necessary, we worked as a team with Kalsang, who had his own horses and was running a similar operation in the area.

Within a few weeks, Dupa and I expanded our enterprise beyond Red Cross deliveries and began trading and delivering goods such as salt and grains throughout the entire area. Because we had more horses and mules than anyone else, in a very short time, we were making more money than most of the Tibetans in the region.

As my father had hoped for me, and, in a reverse of the history of Gompo Tashi and the other businessmen who became Khampa founders of the resistance movement, I was beginning my transition from deadly Khampa guerrilla fighter to freedom fighter turned businessman.

With enough money to live well, life in Dorpatan was easy. Almost every night, we built bonfires and danced. Namre Kalsang and I—he knew many Tibetan folk dances and songs—started a dance group for all the other young girls and men from the Tibetan refugee settlements. At our new home, Dupa's mother became a mother to both Dupa and me, caring for us both equally as her own sons. Despite suffering tremendous physical pain from her stroke and a head injury during the Chinese air raid in 1959 at Nyenchen Thangla range, mentally and morally she upheld her dignity and worked as hard as anyone able-bodied. At ease and happy-go-lucky by nature, she had a tremendous will to live.

And so did I. Eventually, dancing and singing worked like psychotherapy treatments for my battle stress. Slowly, my nostalgia and loneliness began to lift. That's the nature of impermanence.

And the stone book of "the Great Liberation" dedicated to my parents could now be seen for miles away. I was a sixteen-year-old whose parents had just been killed when I used the last of our money to hire a carver. It took a year and half to complete a thousand pages, and the whole display of tens of thousands of stones was stacked in a pile that was visible from miles away. Although some Tibetans might and could have done such undertakings before the invasion, as far as I know, something of this size had not been done by any Tibetan refugees in exile, especially in a poor country like Nepal.

At the same time, having lived such a dangerously active life, ordinary living eventually began to feel a bit boring and meaningless for me. I enjoyed the action in the past, and, now in Nepal I missed the adventures of my early life in Tibet and especially the important work of galloping into a camp and demolishing the Red Army. Having lived in Chinese hell for so long, the Nepalese heaven looked like a fool's paradise. After all, hell was one hell of a lot more exciting than paradise.

However, I told myself, at least we were safe from being shot by anyone—Chinese or Tibetan. We had won our court case and the Chinese couldn't force us back to Tibet, where they would most likely slaughter us, and the murderous Yeshi had already killed the persons who seemed a threat to him like my father. He had no reason to go after a crippled woman and two teenagers.

On the other hand, once I got to India and could file my lawsuit, I was going after him.

When Kalsang arrived in Mustang to retrieve items we had left behind with our Nepalese friends, I had even more reason to seek vengeance. Implicitly acknowledging their wrongdoing for the lost lives in our group, the Chushi Gangdruk leaders offered Kalsang 700 Nepalese rupees—less than 100 U.S. dollars—for each individual they killed in the massacre of our families.

I stared at Kalsang. "Our family members are worth less than a yak?" I looked from Dupa to Kalsang. "This is how they value human lives?"

When Kalsang added that they refused to pay for my dead granduncle, who, they continued to argue, was guilty of attempting to fire an AK-47 because of his bloodstains on the gun, I couldn't swallow. Our uncle had died from the wound he received when they blew his hand off with their bullets. My heart was pounding.

To increase the insult, the items we had left in Mustang—the large yak-hair tent, huge pots, and other large items—had been appropriated by Bawa Gyen Yeshi's men.

That night, I dreamed of punching somebody's face and woke up with a deep bruise on my fingers. Apparently I hit my hand on the sharp edge of the rear sight of my submachine gun, which I kept by my pillow. I was feeling ready to load the gun and head for Mustang.

Physical vengeance against the killers, however, was not realistic. Many of our relatives and friends had begun organizing a revolt after they heard about the slaughter of our families, but, in the end, there had been no retaliation against Rara and his gang by any group. And no one was about to challenge Yeshi, the man who gave the orders. Arguing that those in the Chushi Gangdruk didn't join to start civil war to kill each other but to fight the Chinese invaders together to free Tibet, some cooler heads had convinced our friends and family to abandon their revenge plot and take vengeance on the PLA, who had killed 1.2 million Tibetans. According to stories that came back to us, Dadhue the Black Face never actualized any personal retaliation either. Some intelligent and thoughtful men intervened to stop actions that would have plunged the resistance into a cycle of revenge, causing more needless bloodshed.

No. I would listen to that wisdom. I would avenge the murder of my family, but not with a gun. I would follow my plan, and, once in Dharamsala, India, the seat of the Tibetan government-in-exile, I would avenge the murder of my family by filing a lawsuit with the newly formed Tibetan government. I would tell Tibetans in India about the murderous Yeshi and his followers in the Chushi Gangdruk. Also in India, for my own redemption, I would fulfill my other dream. To honor my father's dying wish, I would find a way to tell the story of the massacre to His Holiness the Dalai Lama.

A few nights later, still awake at midnight, I knew what to do. We would leave for Dharamsala immediately. Even at sixteen, I knew that giving up was the end of a worthwhile existence. No one could afford to do this. I wanted to live a meaningful life. To do that I needed the only means of starting again in foreign countries—an education. There is no such thing as being too late to do anything. Any time is a good time. When one starts doing something for the sake of doing good to others, then good things begin for all, including oneself, if even just the day before one dies. This would become the way of my life. Although it was difficult for Tibetan refugees to cross the border without an Indian residential permit because of the war between India and Pakistan, nothing could stop me. I became a man with a mission who would make things happen, instead of sitting back wondering why the hell things happened to me.

The next morning, when I told Dupa, he wasn't surprised at all. We were shadows of each other, and he agreed to come with me—no matter where. His mother, who never wanted to see us get stuck in this tiny little village for the rest of our lives, was happy for us. She strongly urged us to waste no time.

Then we suddenly found an even better reason to leave. And leave even faster.

WHEN A DOZEN HIGH-RANKING OFFICIALS from the Chushi Gangdruk coincidentally showed up at our camp a few days later claiming they "happened to be in the area" to buy more horses and recruit new members, Dupa and I were suspicious. We were right. They were there to "recruit" us.

Just as Ostok been correct when she understood that the Red Army was invading our camp—not escorting the chieftains—Ostok's intuition that we weren't yet done with the Chushi Gangdruk had proven prophetic.

With his smiles and gentle handshakes, the lead commander told us, "Due to the deaths of your parents, if you join us in Mustang, we'll provide you with preferential treatment. We're making an exception for you." And, while camping next to us for the next three weeks, they continued the sales pitch.

Of course, Gyen Yeshi's people were too nice to believe. And I didn't believe them. Although I had no proof they were spies for Yeshi, since the massacre, I had regarded all Chushi Gangdruk as enemies—not our Khampa friends. In fact, the killing of our people by common enemies like the Chinese felt more acceptable than being killed by our fellow countrymen. We were not about to be intimidated or lured into their den of betrayal and death.

I had to be smart, however. I anticipated that a tentative agreement with them would buy me both some time and a better price for our horses.

"Before we join you," I explained, "Dupa and I are going to make a traditional trip to India on pilgrimage to visit holy places to pray for the departed souls of our parents." I didn't tell them of my hope to tell the Dalai Lama about the Chushi Gangdruk's massacre of our families or my plan to file legal action against them.

The men looked at each other and then at us. "Are you coming back after the pilgrimage?"

Dupa and I exchanged a glance. He was thinking what I was. They didn't want news of the massacre to reach India, or the Dalai Lama. Clearly they would rather see us in Mustang than Dharamsala. I tried to remain calm, but at that moment, I feared for our lives. Anything could happen, and did, with these thugs. Tibetans simply disappeared and nobody questioned the henchmen under Gyen Yeshi. If they wanted to silence Dupa and me, they could do so secretly and nobody would ever find out.

"Oh, yes," I said, "we're coming back."

The commander nodded. "That's good. In Mustang, we'll place you in high posts, pay you well, and take good care of you."

I met his eyes. "But first we might try to find a school in India and pursue an education."

Shaking his head, the commander frowned. "No. No. That's not necessary. If you join us, we'll make special arrangements for your education in Mustang."

Of course they would. I had to be careful here. Smiling again, I said, "That's so nice. We'd appreciate that. We'll join up after our return from India—as soon as our pilgrimage ends." I held my breath. Were they going to believe us? Those killer dogs were capable of anything. Would they return to Mustang without us?

After mumbling among themselves, they settled on a bribe—paying us more for our horses than they paid anyone else. As they headed out of the camp toward Mustang, I took a breath for the first time in three weeks.

When the last Chushi Gangdruk solider glanced one last time over his shoulder at us before they disappeared over the hill, I knew it was time to leave town. Dupa and I weren't going to wait for Yeshi to send his dogs back.

In less than a week, Dupa and I had packed up our dirty clothes, sold our last horses—my Bluebird and Khuru's warhorse, Ta Tongrie—and left for India.

Of course, making it to the border and then crossing into India wasn't all that simple.

THE JOURNEY ON FOOT through the rain forest to our first stop, Pokhara, took three days. When we weren't being eaten by bugs, we were listening to political science lessons from Sonam Wangchuk, our official caretaker and guide to the border, a kind man who did everything possible to get us to Dharamsala in spite of the difficulties created by India's war with Pakistan. Sent by the Tibetan government-in-exile to lecture on the democratic principles of the new Tibetan constitution established by the Dalai Lama, he was our teacher as well as our guide. In all the Tibetan refugee settlements along the way—even to some very small groups in very remote areas—we were his traveling audience as he tried to explain democracy.

When Sonam described them, the democratic principles sounded as sweet as honey and as beautiful as rainbows. However, most Tibetans were rather puzzled by the lectures, which they somehow had thought were going to be Dharma teachings. At least these re-education classes were taught by a representative of the Tibetan government-in-exile, so people were willing to listen. Most of the Tibetan refugees were simple uneducated farmers and nomads who weren't accustomed to listening to daylong lectures. They also thought choosing leaders by election, rather than selection, as had been done in old Tibet, was a strange method. When they were told about the registration of voters and secret ballots, most people—who did not even know how to write their names—thought that putting names in ballot boxes, and their leaders coming out from the same boxes as a result, sounded very funny. They also had some doubts about the age limit for voting, arguing that if you were old enough to fight, you were old enough to vote. Although they didn't know what to do with this knowledge, everybody listened very attentively every day and went home every evening even more confused.

However, everybody seemed to agree that democracy must be good if His Holiness the Dalai Lama chose it. To them, anything His Holiness did was good for all, not only in this life but also the life after. When the honey was eaten and the rainbow faded away, however, the Tibetan refugees in these small towns continued to carry on with their familiar Dharma and old dogma.

In my limited comprehension, I understood that what was at stake was whether one's decisions were made by choice or by force. In democratic societies, people chose their leaders by choice and free will, whereas in China the leaders did the choosing, according to who they can count on doing the best job for the rest of the men in the leadership in Beijing.

I found all this interesting. At the same time, being a Khampa and an heir to my old family position in Kham, the idea of electing leaders rather than the selection of leaders by an interest group did not particularly appeal to me. I just wanted that which was rightfully mine by inheritance as a chieftain. Democracy would cost me my future position in my own district.

At least I understood the difference between the old Tibetan system and the new, and Dupa and I were getting a feeling for what we could expect from the Tibetan government-in-exile when we arrived to start our court case.

While we stayed in Pokhara—a beautiful town with great views of the majestic mountains of the Himalayas and a nice lake—Sonam also prepared us for the future by teaching us to ride bicycles. To practice, we used a small airport where the runway was an open field filled with cows and buffaloes who were cleared out just before landings. Explaining to me that this was how to learn most quickly, Sonam put me on a bike on a steep slope by the airport and pushed. "Just let yourself go down the hill, eyes closed. If you hit something, you'll know it." He was right. I hit a buffalo. Going too fast to stop, I rammed the side of the animal and knocked us both to the ground.

However, by the time Dupa and I were ready to leave for Kathmandu, no more animals had to suffer, and we were prepared to ride the modern iron ponies on wheels.

What we weren't prepared for was how much longer we would have to wait once we made it to Kathmandu.

EVEN WITH THE HELP of a fellow Khampa, Donchuk Serga, the man in charge of the Office of Tibet in Kathmandu, Dupa and I ended up spending another six months waiting for permits to enter India. Due to the India/Pakistan War, we confronted endless obstacles trying to make the right connections and arrangements.

At first, we enjoyed being in the largest city we had ever seen next to Lhasa. Resourceful seventeen-year-olds, we filled the time with holy observances by night and gambling by day. With its big stupas, monasteries and temples, Kathmandu was truly a holy place. With its sense of spiritual calm and bliss, the city was perfect for pilgrimages and circumambulations. As Buddhist tradition required, to honor the departed souls of our parents, Dupa and I circumambulated the stupas every evening.

During the day, however, we gambled. It was actually a useful pastime because we didn't know how to cook. While he was trying to make some tea, Dupa nearly blew up our room by over-pumping the gas stove's pressure tank. His hair caught on fire and his eyebrows vanished. That was the end of our cooking.

We soon discovered a small gambling place where people played mahjong day and night, and the food was free as long as we played the games. Our wins and losses came out to be about the same at the end of the week, and we got free food. Gambling posed no moral dilemma for us. If we were old enough to kill Chinese soldiers at age thirteen, we supposed we should be old enough to play Mahjong for money at age seventeen. But we also didn't want to upset the man who was supposed to help us get to India. When Donchuk Serga and his wife sent people from the Office of Tibet to check whether we were doing okay, we told them everything except the gambling part.

Finally, six months after making the decision to go to India, much of it waiting in Kathmandu, Dupa and I were short on money and short on patience. We could only circumambulate the stupas and break even gambling for so long. Together we decided. Disguised as Nepalese traders, we were going to sneak across the border.

When we told Donchuk Serga that we were willing to take the risk of being arrested rather than wasting both our money and time waiting in Nepal, his office reluctantly sent us a guide who knew how to bypass the border checkpoints. This involved traveling six hours by bus past poor houses over the flat dirty landscape and arriving in the dead of night at the border. There we found the poor man's border security systems on both sides. With no booths or buildings on either side, the border security guards camped in tents. Because the Nepal side didn't care about people going to India, we knew we would pass their checkpoint easily. It was crossing the Indian checkpoint that was a risk because of the war between India and Pakistan.

The plan was simple. On the same schedule every morning, the border officials all had breakfast in their tents. In the morning, timing it just right, while the guards were having their morning tea, we walked quickly past both checkpoints, rushed to the station, and boarded the train to Dharamsala. We were illegal, but we were out of Nepal and out of Yeshi's reach.

On the long train ride across India, we looked at our new country and dreamed. Dirty and exhausted, we got off the train in Pathankot and took a bus to Dharamsala, where our dreams would be realized. With its majestic mountains as a backdrop, tropical forests in the foreground, and a small lake at the side, Dharamsala was beautiful. A small Tibetan village in a foreign land, this was the home of the Dalai Lama and the new Tibetan government. Here we would build new lives and would be able to do as my dying father asked and tell His Holiness our story.

But first, could we accomplish our other goal—justice? I may have succeeded against the Chinese as a lawyer in the Nepalese courts, but could I defeat my Tibetan enemies—Yeshi and the Chushi Gangdruk *jugche*—with fellow Tibetans hearing the case?

As it turned out, none of it was going to happen fast, and it wasn't going to be easy.

CHAPTER TEN

YAKS AMONG SHEEP

1965-73: DHARAMSALA, KULU, AND PONDICHERRY

WHEN WE ARRIVED IN DHARAMSALA, the home of the Tibetan community in exile, everyone knew the story of the massacre, but they didn't know the specifics—including the fact that it was our group which was slaughtered. And Dupa and I didn't tell them. We had to be smart. We soon learned that the Chushi Gangdruk commanders had already sent word to the Tibetan officials in India that the massacre was a "big mistake." This was, of course, a less cynical version of the slaughter than they gave us right after the massacre, when they claimed "accidental and incidental bullets with no eyes" had shot our friends and family.

To Tibetans now exiled in India, Yeshi and the Chushi Gangdruk represented a powerful force still fighting for Tibet. Many members of Parliament took an oath with Yeshi in front of the Tibetan protector deity, putting their hands on a holy book and swearing to be lifetime friends under the leadership of Gompo Tashi Andrugtsang, Gyalo Thondup, and—our enemy—Bawa Gyen Yeshi. It wasn't realistic to bring our complaints against Yeshi to officials in Dharamsala. Not yet.

We soon realized the only support we could get for our lawsuit would come from our chieftain Pon Gyalpo and the people from our home district in Kham, most of whom were working in road construction in Kulu, northern India. And before we could reunite with our people in the Tibetan "tent camps" there, Dupa and I needed residential permits to live in India. This meant more waiting.

Meanwhile, being in Dharamsala was like being in the old Tibet before the Chinese invasion. Here there was a Tibetan Performing Arts Center for the Opera, a Tibetan medical center, several small Tibetan restaurants, and the Tibetan Children's Village, an orphanage headed by the Dalai Lama's elder sister. At the center of everything in this Tibetan city in India was the residence of His Holiness.

Even though we didn't tell anyone in Dharamsala about our connection to the massacre, we wanted to tell the Dalai Lama. Unfortunately, despite our requests, he wasn't available to meet with us. During our months waiting for our permits, our only chances to see His Holiness were at his public audiences. For us, these were very emotional moments. Because Dupa and I had seen him at a distance when His Holiness was cross-examined by the Tibetan scholars during his final religious study examinations at the Jokhang Temple in Lhasa in 1959, it was very different seeing him in India. On the one hand, we were joyful and happy to see His Holiness in person, which had been a very rare opportunity in Tibet. On the other hand, to see him living in an Indian bungalow in exile and not in the Norbulingka palace in Lhasa was sad.

Perhaps it was just as well we weren't able to arrange a meeting at that time. Whenever I saw our spiritual and political leader, I became speechless.

Much of Dharamsala involved the offices for the Dalai Lama's new government. The three most important offices, or departments, operating closely together were the Office of the Dalai Lama, the Kashag (the ministers), and the Parliament, most of whom were the top members of the Chushi Gangdruk headquarters in India. Some of the members of the Tibetan Parliament shared one large room in a small hotel, and, when Dupa and I stayed there for a short time, we befriended many of the officials.

I was inspired by them—their views, conduct, and deeds as good examples for my generation of Tibetans and even younger generations to come. All the officers in the poor refugee government-in-exile worked extremely hard for minimal wages, which were barely enough to meet their basic needs. They worked hard, not for money, but for the Tibetan cause. As they walked to their offices with files in their hands and went home carrying babies on their backs, they had indomitable spirits and unwavering faith, determinedly united under the leadership of His Holiness the Dalai Lama. Even the Home

Minister, Kalon Wangdu Dorjee, with whom we became friends, walked to his office an hour early and left the office one or two hours after closing time, putting in at least ten hours of office work on top of other duties. His job, presiding over all the domestic affairs of the Tibetans in exile, was not an easy one.

Watching the hardworking representatives of the Dalai Lama's new government reaffirmed my own conviction to do everything within my capacity to fight for the Tibetan struggle against the injustices committed by the Communist regime of the so-called People's Republic of China, and to serve our people with everything I had.

But all that was on hold for several months while we waited for our papers.

Meanwhile, being in Dharamsala was like being in a school. As a Khampa and a newcomer, and not so familiar with local customs, protocols, and the proper ways to approach government officials and Tibetan aristocrats, I had both differences in dialect and social problems to contend with in my communications with a certain class of Tibetans from Lhasa.

In Dharamsala, Dupa and I were the Wild East yak-boys confronting the Wild West cowboys. The Lhasa dialect had rich selections of names to call people, depending upon their social status. The high-ranking officials, like the prime minister, home ministers, and foreign ministers were always called "*Kun-ngo*," which roughly means "the real person"—the Tibetan equivalent of "sir"—and the aristocrats were referred to as "*Kudraks*," which seemed to mean "better persons." So my dialectical dilemma was to know who were the real persons and better persons, or whether the real persons were the better persons, or the better persons were the real ones. It was very confusing. One had to be born in Lhasa to know these nuances.

Even to order food in restaurants was not easy. One had to choose between *Shela* and *Khala*; *Shela* was for the better persons or the "*Kudraks*," while *Khala* was for the ordinary ones, even though it was the same dish. I couldn't order *Shela* for myself because the people around me would laugh at me for pretending to be a *Kudrak*; nor could I order *Khala* for a *Kudrak*, or better person, because it would insult him, making him less of a better man. If I were to behave in a typical Khampa manner of asking an aristocrat or a better person to have a lunch with me, I would say something like this: "*Ahro Kudrak*, come here and eat this *Khala* with me." "*Ahro*," means "hey" in Kham. So the "better person" would probably kill me for bringing him to an ordinary level like mine. For him it would mean something like: "Hey you aristocrat, eat this poor man's meal with me."

In Kham, the good guys were called "good" and the bad guys were called "bad." The rich were called rich and the poor were called poor, simple and straightforward. We didn't have any other names to go by. I should have asked the *Kun-ngos* to give me a new name to make myself a better person and a real one, too, but that didn't seem an appropriate thing to do at the time since I did not know anyone that I could trust enough not to give me a name in Lhasa dialect that would make me worse than I was. It was too risky a business. I did not want to be called "the honorable Khampa horse thief."

And because in Tibet, different tribes, regions, and ethnic subgroups have different dialects, we made some comical errors when dealing with Tibetans who were not from our district. After waiting for hours at a Tibetan government office to complete some official paperwork, when we finally got to see the man in charge, a *Kun-ngo*, I was slightly bent backward and had both my hands in my pockets.

The first thing the *Kun-ngo* said was, "*Bu* (boy) what is the matter with you? You don't look so well."

I didn't understand that the *Kun-ngo* thought I was impolite and rude. "My back hurts from waiting here too long," I responded.

Shaking his head, he said, "*alay* (ahem), *alay*." I was embarrassed. I knew what it meant in my own local dialect. When he continued using the phrase, "*ane, ane, alay, alay ane*," after every sentence, I couldn't understand why this "real person" was so interested in a nun's uterus. In my local dialect "*ane*" meant nun and "*alay*" meant uterus. When we returned to our hotel, I noticed everybody was saying, "*alay, ane, ane alay*." It sounded like this famous nun's uterus had taken over the entire town of Dharamsala. Later, I learned that "*ane*" meant "then" in central Tibetan dialect, but was often used as an interjection, in which case it has no meaning, and "*alay*" meant "ahem" or "I see" in Lhasa dialect. The *Kun-ngo* wasn't that interested in a nun's uterus after all.

Although we were now encountering the "wider knowledge" my father urged me to explore, we were also becoming more impatient to get our permits and join people who spoke our dialect.

Finally, for the old time's sake of his father's friendship with our former chieftain, Dhawu Pon Rinchen Tsering, a member of Parliament and rising star in Tibetan politics, came to the rescue. Along with Kalzang Dhadul, another Parliament member, Dhawu Pon helped us secure our permanent residential permits. At last we were on our way to Kulu, where our chieftain Pon

Gyalpo was living with hundreds of people from Drongpa Medma. There, we would be more at home.

And we would have support filing our lawsuit against Yeshi and his butchers. Finally—*justice*.

WHEN WE ARRIVED AT THE CAMPS in Kulu expecting a happy reunion, we saw nobody in the tents. They were all out working on the roads. Although it was sad to see these friends who had enjoyed their lives in Tibet now working as road builders with shovels and picks and getting sunburned with dust all over their faces and clothes, they were energetic and high-spirited and seemed happy to be alive. And they were ready to help us avenge the massacre of their fellow Khampas and my parents.

Over the next month in Kulu, with the help of Pon Gyalpo, we prepared a formal lawsuit, which was several pages long and signed by hundreds of our people from Drongpa Medma. It described in detail the massacre. We named names—Rara, the killer of my father and Tsewang; Khalap Jampa, the man who shot my mother; and everyone else present at the slaughter. Our lawsuit also named Bawa Gyen Yeshi, who, as the leader of the Chushi Gangdruk, ordered the massacre. We argued that the murder of so many innocent Tibetans occurred without any justification, and our suit rejected the Chushi Gangdruk claim that the massacre was "a big mistake." We claimed that the Chushi Gangdruk implicitly admitted responsibility for the slaughter by offering us financial reparations for those killed. Otherwise, they wouldn't have paid anything at all. In our petition, we demanded that the "absolute truth" be determined through "a thorough investigation" and that "justice be done."

Unfortunately, nothing was going to come to light in 1965.

When Pon Gyalpo hand-delivered our lawsuit to Home Minister Wangdu Dorje, who delivered it to the Kashag—the executive branch of the Tibetan government-in-exile—our pleas fell on deaf ears. For one thing, as they were operating from India and had never been in Nepal, the Tibetan officials knew only what Gyen Yeshi's group told them. It may not have been clear to the top officials in India what was happening and whose story was true. Our version was certainly in direct opposition to Yeshi's.

There was also some confusion over who was in charge. Although the newly formed exile government was operating on democratic principles as urged by the Dalai Lama, I don't believe the government even had a written constitution yet. Of the three most important offices or departments operating closely together—the Office of the Dalai Lama, the Kashag, and the Parliament—there was confusion about deciding which of the departments were responsible. Afraid of causing internal conflicts among themselves or being misunderstood as taking sides, nobody wanted to cross the lines and risk stepping on somebody else's toes.

When there was no official response after a few months, Dupa and I had to face the facts. Although the Tibetan officials might claim it wasn't clear what happened and whose story was true, the real truth was that the fall of Bawa Gyen Yeshi wasn't possible at that time. We were up against a strong backing for Bawa Gyen Yeshi from the top leaders of the Chushi Gangdruk headquarters in India, including Gyalo Thondup, the elder brother of His Holiness the Dalai Lama. Although there had always been some questions from CIA officials and some Tibetan leaders about Yeshi, no one was ready at this time to challenge the Cat. As the leader chosen to head the Mustang resistance, the man in charge of taking back Tibet from the Chinese occupation, Yeshi was untouchable. As one official explained to me years later, questioning Yeshi would be a betrayal of their sworn oath to support the Chushi Gangdruk. No one was ready to do that in 1965.

Because Dupa and I admired our new government system and our leaders, we found it easier to face the lack of response. The officials making the decision were not some aristocrats and chieftains recreating the old Tibetan feudalistic and theocratic system; it was a new government of the people, by the people, and for the people of Tibet. Most of the officials, like Home Minister Kalon Wangdu Dorjee, were common Tibetans who had risen to the highest positions in the government to work as the people's servants, not their bosses.

What Dupa and I didn't know was that, at about the same time we filed our lawsuit, the top Tibetan leaders and the CIA were actually hearing about Yeshi's corrupt regime from sources more credible than two teenage orphans. A group of disenchanted Mustang commanders had traveled to India complaining to the CIA and Tibetan officials about Yeshi's lack of accountability for the CIA funds and his failure as a commander. Because no one felt it was possible to remove Yeshi and his large group of supporters by force, Gyalo Thondup sent Wangdu, Gompo Tashi's nephew and a CIA–trained guerrilla, to Mustang to oversee the "financial" aspects of the operation. But none of this was public knowledge. It would be several more years before anyone admitted that Yeshi had been embezzling money and betraying his homeland.

In the end, our lawsuit became useless, and we were seen as some orphaned Khampa babes in the woods, barking up the wrong trees. However, as the only person who ever filed a public complaint against Yeshi, the lawsuit gave me some comfort. At least we had tried to let the officials know what kind of man Yeshi was—a dangerous and corrupt thug.

For the next few months, we remained in Kulu, but this wasn't enough for us. Although we enjoyed staying with our friends at the tent camps, we were homeless Tibetan gypsies wandering in search of a meaningful life. Where Tibetans were gaining respect was in the Indian military, so Dupa and I considered joining the "22"—the Tibetan Army within the Indian Army. The "22" had contributed to the tremendous success of the Indian victory over Pakistan. Without any formal education, the only thing we knew well and were good at was fighting with guns.

But our friends in Kulu talked us out of this, reminding Dupa and me that one of our other reasons we had for coming to India was to seek an education. When Dupa and I were growing up, there were no regular schools in our district, and the monasteries where the monks studied were the only places of learning. When my father and my oldest uncle taught me to read the Tibetan alphabet, I memorized it in three days by rote and could recite the letters in order without looking at the book. But my uncle caught me red-handed. When he picked a letter from the middle of the alphabet with a two-foot stick as a pointer, he discovered that I had simply been reciting the alphabet from memory without actually recognizing the individual letters. Eventually, with the added help of a monk tutor, I learned how to read small prayer books, and, occasionally, the epic Tales of the Legendary King Gesar. But my skills were very basic.

Although Dupa and I couldn't use our skills as guerrilla fighters, a formal education could be a formidable weapon in the struggle for a free Tibet. We were soon disappointed to learn, however, that as seventeen-year-olds without primary-school educations, it was impossible for us to enroll in the school system in India. We were too old.

What we found instead, with the help of our chieftain Pon Gyalpo, was a temporary school for Tibetan refugee lamas and nuns in Dalhousie—an area in northern India. The founder of the Kailash Monastic School for Young Lamas, a British woman named Mrs. Bedi, promised she would find a good school in India who would accept older students. In the meantime, we could study with the reincarnated lamas.

Because we weren't lamas, but killers in desperate need of the lamas' school as a springboard to a real school, we weren't allowed to stay in the school's dormitory rooms. Instead, we stayed with Western volunteers who studied Buddhism while teaching English, math, and history to the lamas. We learned many things about world history, geography, math, and astronomy. We also made good progress in our studies, which included Tibetan handwriting, grammar, and Tibetan-style paintings. With a *geshe* (a degreed teacher), I studied the Elegant Sayings of the Sakya Pandit. Living with Westerners also gave us an opportunity to learn and study English. Our English texts were American standard school textbooks, which covered many things about America, such as its discovery by Christopher Columbus, the Declaration of Independence, the Civil War, the fight against British colonization, and the burning of the White House.

These subjects were very fascinating and educational, excepting the discovery of America by Columbus. I had the impression that Columbus was a poor navigator who got lost on his way to India and ended up landing on American soil purely by mistake. He seemed nothing but a lost man without historical merit. His discovery resulted in the sufferings of the Native Americans, whom he called Red Indians, under foreign domination by the Spanish, the French and the British, much in same the way the Tibetans now suffered under Chinese occupation. The Tibetans and the Native Americans both became powerless minorities in their rightful countries.

The teachers we lived with were quite a diverse group—a German scholar, a Canadian, a Scotsman, an Englishman, an American hippie couple, and two Tibetans. The German scholar, Dr. Lough, was highly educated and knew many languages, including Tibetan, Sanskrit, Pali, and English, in addition to German. The Canadian, Warren, also spoke Tibetan; he had taught English at the Tibetan Performing Arts Center in Dharamsala before he moved to Dalhousie.

While Dupa and I enjoyed Dalhousie—located high up in the hills, with beautiful views and scenic landscapes, with its large Tibetan community, two Tantric colleges, Tibetan restaurants, and several hundred monks—we were frustrated when Mrs. Bedi hadn't found us the promised Indian school after a year. Although we learned a lot and improved our English, we didn't want to be lamas. We wanted to attend real Indian schools, and we weren't getting any younger. She asked us to be patient.

Hoping for better news from Mrs. Bedi when we returned, Dupa and I made our first trip back to Dorpatan to spend two months of summer vacation with Dupa's mother and my uncle. Although we went by train to the border of Nepal, once in Nepal, we had to go on foot along treacherous paths, crossing high and dangerous chain bridges for several days on the way to Dorpatan. We didn't mind. We were just happy to find Dupa's mother and my uncle doing quite well on their own. My uncle still had a few horses, which he used for a small transporting business.

When Dupa and I told our friends there about the solar system and the earth being round, and that there was no water on the moon, they were in disbelief. It would have been the same reaction if we told them that Buddha never existed. They may have suspected that my brain got roasted in the Indian sun's heat waves. They argued that if the earth was round, then how did they see it as flat while traveling all the way from Tibet to Nepal? If we could have water on our planet, why did others not have water on their planets? Weren't all things created equally for everyone in the universe? The Buddha did not mention that the earth was round. And nobody heard him say there was no water on the moon either.

It was a conversation I shouldn't have started, as it almost turned into quarrels. I realized how difficult it must have been for Sonam Wangchuk to introduce the democratic principles to the same people a few years earlier. As the Tibetans say, these "green-brained" (raw or sapling-minded) people didn't like anything new except new clothes. In fact, the Chinese have failed miserably to brainwash them, despite their relentless efforts for decades. According to my friends in Dorpatan, "old is gold." Our old civilization was as good as gold, and even better as far as the Tibetans were concerned, before the Chinese managed to destroy it.

At least I was also responsible for some gold. Standing before the mani-stone book I'd had carved for my parents, I felt inspired and blessed to know that the completed stone book of "the Great Liberation" would spread the holy Dharma repeatedly and countlessly every moment to all the others traveling through Nepal for thousands of years to come, blessed by natural elements—wind, sunlight, and rainwater.

But we lived in India now.

When we returned from the visit, and questioned Mrs. Bedi again about the possibility of transferring to regular or special schools, she continued telling us "not to worry" and that she would find a school for us "sooner or later." Sooner or later dragged on for another year. While our English improved a great deal and we also learned much more about Buddhism by just being with the lamas and watching metaphysical, philosophical, and dialectical debates on a daily basis, we finally confronted Mrs. Bedi and were shocked to discover the truth. She was not going to keep her promise to find us a regular school. Because we were "too old" for primary school, she instead had jobs for us. She had been having us work on our English so we could work as drivers and translators for the Sixteenth Gyalwang Karmapa. She had never intended to help us.

Simply and sadly, we walked away. We had come to India for an education so that we could fight the Chinese for our homeland. Working as drivers for Mrs. Bedi wasn't going to free Tibet.

When we told my Western friends that night, everybody was shocked and disappointed. They knew all about Mrs. Bedi's promise. My hippie American friend William got so angry that he left his dinner unfinished and ran to the nunnery where Mrs. Bedi lived and had a heated argument with her. All that glitters is not always gold and good, even in a Buddhist nunnery.

And it was William, once he returned to America, who actually found us a school that would take us—the Sri Aurobindo International Center of Education, in Pondicherry, South India. Established under the guidance of the Divine Mother of Sri Aurobindo Ashram, this was one of the best and certainly the most famous school in India. And it admitted Tibetan students with similar situations to ours in terms of age and lack of former primary education. It also turned out that Mrs. Bedi had sent other students to the school, but failed to mention it to us.

From America, William sent us the money to enroll, and with the added help of the English teacher at the lama school, Dupa and I were admitted.

This was the greatest moment and the happiest day of our lives since we had left Tibet.

And, with formal educations, we could carry on the fight to take back our stolen homeland.

ON OUR FIRST DAY AT SRI AUROBINDO, Dupa and I were the oldest and biggest students in our second-grade classroom. At eighteen years old, we looked like yaks sitting among little lambs. It was rather embarrassing. However, had we not studied at the lamas' school, we would have been in kindergarten, which would have been even more embarrassing. Since we couldn't shrink ourselves to the others' sizes, we had to be content. And we were.

During our time there, from 1967 to 1973, this fantastic school was far beyond our expectations. Upon our arrival, we were immediately taken under the wing of the head of the school, the Divine Mother. When she heard our story, the Divine Mother wrote to us: "For those who died in a good cause for the benefit of others, death is not misfortune. Dedicate your life to the service of the truth, you will find peace and meaning in your life." In this wonderful place, we began that journey. The teachers were excellent and highly respected by their students, and the school grounds were large and beautiful, with standard Olympic-size facilities. This was our dreamland come true.

In the first couple of years, because of our quick progress, we jumped two grades each year, from second grade to fourth, to sixth and to eighth. While Dupa and I both studied hard, he was more industrious in his studies than I was. He got up earlier and went to bed later than I did. Every morning, as my morning sleep was the sweetest thing that I enjoyed the most, he woke me up. I kept telling myself to sleep "one more minute" and "some more minutes" until I was late for my classes. As I am a fast learner by nature, I caught up, but I was also lucky to have my six-months-younger brother acting as my big older brother, keeping me on a straight and narrow path.

Besides the standard daily curriculum in the school, we had two hours of daily physical education, which included sports such as gymnastics, swimming, martial arts, bodybuilding, and boxing. The physical program in our school was the best known in the country. One year I won the annual boxing competition in my class and Dupa won in wrestling. We were both at brown-belt level in Jujitsu and Judo before we left, and I set a school record for cricket ball-throwing for three consecutive years.

When we visited Nepal during our first winter school holiday, our relatives were happy to hear that we had fallen in love with our school and everyone who worked there. We were also happy to find our mother and uncle resettled in a new refugee camp in Pokhara, where they had a nice stone house built on the edge of a riverbank with a great view of the Himalayan mountain ranges. Life for them in Pokhara—which was a big town compared to Dorpatan—was much better.

With things good at home, and good at our school, life had finally begun to turn around for the better for all of us. And then it got even better. At the end of the first year, I wrote a letter to the Divine Mother to ask her if it was possible for us to study at the school free of charge, as our sponsor was a poor American hippie who only worked six months a year. She was so kind as not only to say "yes" to our humble inquiry, but she also ordered the finance office to refund us the previous year's school fees! That was such a big relief for us, not having to burden our hippie friend William. He was our true American uncle whose heart was as big as Mount Kailash. With the refund money from the school, Dupa and I were able to buy two bicycles, and we no longer had to walk in the rain and on hot Indian summer days.

Over the next five years, when we weren't traveling home together or separately, Dupa and I often spent our school holidays in Dharamsala, where—due to the fame and popularity of His Holiness the Dalai Lama rapidly spreading worldwide—tourists began to crowd into this small Tibetan refuge. Hanging around in little restaurants and drinking *chang* (Tibetan home-brewed rice beer) with some of the English-speaking tourists gave me a chance to practice my English and make a little money selling them Tibetan trinkets. As an evolving entrepreneur, I also learned a new trick in trading. Because my new English-speaking friends were selling their things before they headed home, I was able to buy lots of Western goods—jeans, sleeping bags, down jackets, backpacks, and just about anything else—for a fraction of their value and then resell them to Tibetans. Items like blue jeans were especially very rare and popular among the young Tibetans.

We also spent some school vacations in Delhi, a big city where the wheel of life was prevalent in all the streets. One didn't need to go anywhere else to see all the realms of existence as *samsara* (illusion) in action. Connecting with the Tibetan Bureau in Delhi, Dupa and I participated in demonstrations and public protests against the Chinese official visitors to India; we also marched in protests on important occasions such as March 10th, the commemoration of the Lhasa Uprising of 1959. Being in Delhi also gave Dupa and me a chance to loosen up. Our school was great, but it was more like a Buddhist monastery where drinking, smoking, partying, and even seeing movies were not allowed.

In Delhi, an open society, Dupa and I did as we pleased with no need to look over our shoulders to see if any of our teachers were watching us entering the movie theaters. And we weren't going to watch Hindi movies, which, in general, had too much singing while running around, and dancing while crying and arguing, and too much eating. The heroes never got hurt, even if buildings fell on them, and punches could be heard before they landed. My least favorite were the movies that were designed to make everyone cry. My first Hindi movie was called something like *Meri Dost aur Meri Piyaara*, which roughly means, "My Friend and My Love." It was a sad story about two friends, one blind and the other handicapped. While the blind man carried the handicapped man, two incomplete human beings became one complete human by using one's legs and the other's eyes. When the movie was over, I saw everybody crying and sobbing as if a grandmother had died. Due to my stubbornness, I couldn't even cry when my own parents were killed, so I certainly couldn't cry for a black and white movie in which nobody was actually dying or suffering.

Being Khampas, Dupa and I liked Western movies about cowboys, outlaw gunslingers, and characters like Billy the Kid. The other movies we enjoyed were action and adventure films, such as war movies, the James Bond series, and movies about the American Civil War and the Roman Empire.

And then our luck changed again.

ALTHOUGH AS ADULTS we knew that someday we might have to go separate ways, it happened too quickly. Two years before graduation, Dupa's mother fell ill and my brother, with whom I'd shared every crisis and joy since childhood, had to return to Nepal. With the help of Home Minister Kalon Wangdu, Dupa found work in a carpet factory in Kathmandu owned by an organization known as Chegdri-Tsokpa—the United Association of Tibet—affiliated with the Tibetan government-in-exile.

This left me by myself to finish school.

As determined individuals whose childhoods were transformed quickly into adulthood due to the Chinese occupation, facing challenges in life were not foreign to us. However, without my brother, there was a sense of something missing in my life. Although our separation didn't cause any problems in my studies, emotionally the reality was difficult. When Dupa was called home, I was not only separated for the second time from my brother, but I was left by myself to cope with the terrible memories of the slaughter of our family and the frustration over our inability to punish the killers. And I was also alone with the disappointment that we had been unable to fulfill my father's request that we seek guidance from the Dalai Lama. Since arriving in India, Dupa and I had made many unsuccessful efforts. We knew that to secure a private audience with Tibet's spiritual and temporal leader would be a rare privilege for two humble Tibetan refugees. However, I never gave up hope that one day we would be able to tell His Holiness our story and express our grievances about the tragic deaths of our families and the massacre of our friends, and to get the pain out of our chests and the negative thoughts out of our minds.

Ironically, the one time I did speak directly to His Holiness, it was in a room of a 100 people crowded together on the floor, elbow to elbow. After visiting our school—a grand event for which we Tibetans dressed in traditional costumes and in line to receive His Holiness with our traditional silk greeting scarves—His Holiness was conducting a special audience at the new International City near Pondicherry. Seated on a throne specially constructed for the occasion, His Holiness asked the audience specific questions. He was curious about the possibilities of establishing an independent international community with its own judicial and monetary system, one which would be like a sovereign state within the sovereign nation of India. However, when His Holiness asked what the Tibetans thought about the international city concept and its "eventual possibility of materialization," no one answered.

First he looked to the founder and head of the Tibetan school and then to a teacher from the Tibetan Education Ministry, both of whom sat in the front row. Following protocol, the founder was supposed to answer the questions, followed by the teacher and, then the other Tibetans in turn.

Instead of answering, both educators turned their heads toward me. Thinking they were looking for someone behind me, I turned my head, but—since I'd crowded into the back row at the last minute—no one was there. A little boy sitting in front of me, who thought they were looking at him, said, "Not me."

Okay. I raised my hand. Although the leaders may have looked to me because I was talkative by nature and knew something about the subject, the main reason I answered was that nobody else dared to respond.

His Holiness smiled at me. "Go ahead."

Choosing my words carefully, I answered his questions to the best of my knowledge. While I didn't know anything more than the other Tibetan students, they were afraid of speaking to His Holiness. Candidly, I expressed my own doubts about the project, adding, "But, at the same time, I admire such a noble ideal, a concept planned with the belief that anything is possible if all the conditions exist to make it happen."

Nodding, the Dalai Lama indicated he understood my point of view. He seemed satisfied with my answer.

Of course, while I was honored to have the privilege of talking to the Dalai Lama of Tibet, this was not the conversation I wanted to have with His Holiness. However, it was hardly the time—in front of 100 people, many of them strangers—to express my grievances over the massacre of our families.

It was clear. A private audience with Tibet's spiritual and temporal leader would require official help from high-standing Tibetan leaders in Dharamsala. When I didn't have the money to go to Nepal, I often spent school holidays in Dharamsala and continued to appeal for help—among others,from Home Minister Kalon Wangdu Dorjee, who became my key advocate. In addition to giving me a free room next to his residence, Kalon Wangdu found me a tutor in Tibetan writing and grammar, and, late in the evenings when I was up studying, we became very close friends as we shared personal histories for hours at a time.

I was inspired by the story of how he—a common Tibetan like myself, who had been the servant to an aristocratic family back in Lhasa—had risen to one of the highest positions in the government. When he was first appointed, Kalon Wangdu told His Holiness that he wasn't qualified because of his background as a servant, but His Holiness politely refused to excuse him. Although Wangdu had been very embarrassed at the time, he smiled when he told me that, while he was doing the usual customary three prostrations to His Holiness, his pack of Panama cigarettes fell from his pocket right in front of the Dalai Lama.

I was happy that this minister—who inspired everyone with his work ethic and his morality—showed a personal interest in me as a restless and curious young Khampa looking for the challenges of life. Kind and thoughtful, he took me seriously when I told him all about the massacre and everything I knew about Chushi Gangdruk operations in Mustang. However, from 1965 to 1972, even though the Home Minister and I trusted each other and became close friends, neither Kalon Wangdu nor any other official in the new government, was able to override Yeshi's power in Dharamsala and arrange an opportunity for us to share our story with the Dalai Lama.

Then, suddenly, in the summer of 1972, everything changed. Although no one ever directly made the connection for me, several things began to happen simultaneously. Not only were we granted a private meeting with the Dalai Lama to describe the massacre, but the officials in Dharamsala, who were finally making Yeshi's crimes against the state public, suddenly took an interest in our forgotten lawsuit. Although it wasn't public knowledge, Yeshi had finally been caught red-handed embezzling, and the Tibetan High Command was in the process of deposing him. As no one any longer was defending the corrupt former monk, Wangdu Dorje had seized the opportunity to resurrect our lawsuit and arrange for us to tell His Holiness about Yeshi's crimes. Although no action was ever taken on our legal petition, Tibetan officials used certain parts of it to build their case against Yeshi.

Of course, Yeshi the Cat outsmarted them. When Yeshi was summoned to Dharamsala and asked to step down, he agreed and then tricked the officials. Slipping away from his guards, he snuck back into Mustang, where he retrieved the trunks of money he had embezzled from the 1.5 million dollars sent by the CIA. Along with 150 Chushi Gangdruk loyalists, many of them from his hometown in Batang, Yeshi then fled to Pokhara, where they turned on their fellow Khampas and collaborated with Nepalese authorities to hunt down loyal Chushi Gangdruk members.

But none of that mattered to Dupa and me. Because Yeshi had finally fallen from grace, His Holiness was going to hear our story. When Kalon Wangdu Dorje gave me the news, I got word to Dupa, who caught the next bus for India.

Finally, we would pay tribute to my father's dying wish. Eight years after the brutal massacre of my parents, we would be able to tell the leader of Tibet about one of Yeshi's most sinister crimes—the slaughter of fellow Tibetans and the true heroes in the Tibetan struggle for freedom—our family. What would His Holiness say?

CHAPTER ELEVEN

THE DALAI LAMA AND THE WIDER WORLD

1972–77: INDIA, ENGLAND, AND THE UNITED STATES

A S DUPA AND I FOLLOWED Kalon Wangdu to the Dalai Lama's residence, a sacred silence spoke louder than speech, the spiritual atmosphere one experiences in special Buddhist temples. Instead of the bungalow where the Dalai Lama first lived in exile, His Holiness was now in a palace, mansion, and temple combined, an environment most fitting for a Dalai Lama of Tibet. And maintaining complete quiet around his residence was important to avoid disturbances during the Dalai Lama's meditations, prayers, meetings, and studies.

We were speechless anyway. After many long years of waiting, Dupa and I could feel each other's awe at such a golden opportunity—an audience with the Fourteenth Dalai Lama, known to the world then as one of the greatest men living in the 20th century, who inspired millions of people worldwide.

To prepare us for this meeting, the home minister had brought with him two very long white silk greeting scarves (*khatas*) folded into bundles, which we were to offer to His Holiness. After instructing us in how to present them according to traditional protocol, he also reminded us that, even though His Holiness was called by many names—such as *Chubgong Rinpoche*, the Precious Protector; *Yeshen Norbu*, the Wish-fulfilling Jewel; *Gyalwa Rinpoche*, the Victorious Precious One; and *Tenzin Gyatso*, the Ocean of Wisdom—in his actual presence, we were to address the Dalai Lama as *Kundun*.

Then, we were on our own. Dupa and I caught each other's eye. It would have been absolutely impossible in old Tibet for ordinary persons like ourselves to talk to the Dalai Lama.

After an attendant led us into a well-lighted room decorated with wall hangings and pictures of historic significance, important artifacts and altarpieces, we were left alone to contemplate our good fortune. It appeared this was to be a special audience, especially arranged for us to tell our sad and tragic story to the Dalai Lama with no one else present.

Minutes later, when His Holiness entered with a smile—young, handsome, energetic, and radiating compassion—I held my breath. He seemed encircled by a pale gold light. Stumbling to our feet, we performed the customary prostrations. With our palms touching, we placed our hands on the tops of our heads, then over our mouths and noses and chests, after which we lay on the floor—which was covered with beautiful Tibetan rugs—and stretched out our bodies fully with our hands reaching over our heads.

Once we had repeated the prostrations three times, Dupa and I then unfurled our long white silk greeting scarves to full length. Following protocol taught to us by Kalon Wangdu, we draped them over our outstretched hands, bowed, and offered them to the Dalai Lama. If you give a scarf to a friend, you just put it around his or her neck. But, of course, we wouldn't touch the Dalai Lama. Lifting the scarves from our hands one by one, His Holiness blessed them and then draped them around our necks instead. Although His Holiness conducts the greeting scarf ceremony a bit differently today, touching the scarves and giving them back to us was his blessing.

After the scarf ceremony, we sat on the floor facing his Holiness, excited to see what would happen next. What happened next was that His Holiness the Dalai Lama insisted we sit on chairs. This seemed wrong, but we reluctantly rose from the floor and sat. This definitely felt wrong. When His Holiness took his own seat, we slid off the chairs back to the floor.

When His Holiness asked us again to take the chairs, in something close to a whisper, I said, "Kundun, no Tibetan would dare to sit on chairs that were at the same level as your seat."

Laughing, he motioned for us to rise. "But you must sit. Protocols don't matter much if we're going to have a long conversation. We might as well be comfortable."

A long conversation? I was holding my breath again. Slowly we moved back into the chairs. Dupa and I had wanted to approach this audience without expectations—as expectations usually lead to surprises or disappointments.

This was beyond anything we had hoped for. A long conversation. And it was with me doing most of the talking.

For an hour and a half, I blurted out every detail. I opened the contents of my heart to His Holiness, and the fullness of my emotions about the massacre of my family and other innocent Tibetans in the killing field of Mogum, Nepal in April 1964. After waiting for this moment for years, I wasn't going to spoil it by letting my mind go astray. I told myself, *focus, focus, focus.* I told him everything—the corruption in Mustang under Yeshi's command, our father's leaving Mustang, Tsewang being dragged behind one of Rara's horses, the three CIA–issued bullets that had killed my mother, and my uncle's suffering and death. When I finished, my jaw relaxed. I had never felt so relieved.

After His Holiness listened to my story patiently and without interruption, he was no longer smiling. Now that he had heard the whole true story in person from us, the Dalai Lama's voice was low and serious. "For all these years, I was not aware that such incidents took place. It's very tragic that such a situation occurred within the Tibetan community."

I glanced at Dupa and continued. "Dupa and I are finding it very difficult to decide whether or not to forgive those responsible for the deaths of our parents." I explained that, as Khampas, Dupa and I, by tradition, were required to take revenge or lose respect. "But we didn't come to seek your support in punishing the perpetrators. Following my father's wish, we're seeking your help in ridding ourselves of our anger and hatred against those responsible. We want to get this terrible anger out of our hearts so that we can continue with our lives and help with the struggle for Tibet. To do that, we need your blessings and spiritual guidance."

After pausing for a few seconds, His Holiness said, *"Nyingjey, nyingjey"* (compassion, compassion), which roughly means, "You have my compassion." His voice was soft. "I appreciate your desire and effort to forgive our Tibetan foes. It's right to forgive one's enemies. We should think about the larger meaning of things. We should always work for positive results that benefit others."

Something about His Holiness couldn't be put into words, but Dupa and I felt a change in our attitudes towards others, especially toward Yeshi and his killer dogs. Because His Holiness was so kind, understanding, transparent, and human in the manner in which he received us—with tremendous compassion for our tragedy—he inspired us to forgive our enemies, both Tibetan and

Chinese alike. Anger had always been my worst enemy—as when I punched the Tibetan from Amdo who called himself a "Japanese tourist." Solemnly, Dupa and I promised the Dalai Lama that we would never seek vengeance.

Then His Holiness changed the subject. "I'm grateful for your vision to work together as nonviolent freedom fighters for a free Tibet. But I urge you to work on yourselves first so you may stand on your own feet. Then go about helping the Tibetan people as well as humanity at large."

This was the other important lesson I would never forget. If I couldn't take care of my own spiritual needs, then I couldn't think about helping others and doing great works in the world. I had to walk the walk before talking the talk. Over the years I have come to know many great talkers who talk a great deal and write many thick books but end up doing nothing of great substance. For me, the life of His Holiness was the example.

Although I still had nightmares about the massacre and fantasies about killing my parents' killers, our "long" conversation with the Dalai Lama had given me the means for spiritual healing. I vowed to overcome my anger and seek to live helping others. His Holiness helped me let go of my dualistic thinking—I and others, we and them, friends and enemies, and the list goes on without limit—and realize the oneness of everything. This was also one of the lessons my father taught me when I was a young boy in Kham—"Treat everyone as equals, including enemies." Now I knew what he meant. We were all part of one continuum.

As we were leaving, His Holiness told me that if I wanted to see him in the future for important reasons, either personal or Tibetan, to simply ask.

And within a year, I had a reason.

AFTER MY PROSTRATIONS, I gave His Holiness my news. "Kundun, I'll be leaving to study in England on a scholarship, but I want your blessing."

When the Divine Mother died, I explained to him, the opportunity to study in the West appeared in the form of a scholarship to a British school. A guest teacher at the Pondicherry School and close friend of the Divine Mother named George Bennett had offered me the chance to study comparative philosophy and religion studies at his school in Shelbourne, England. The International Academy for Continuous Education attracted students from all over the world. I would be the first Tibetan pupil.

Here, I told His Holiness, was my opportunity to fight for Tibet by becoming educated in the ways of the West. "But it's all for my country. After finishing my studies, I'm determined to work for the Tibetan cause."

Once His Holiness blessed my plan to study in England, he smiled warmly at my youthful dreams. "To work for the cause of your country is good. Very good indeed." He then gave me three pieces of advice by which I still try to live.

First, he told me, "The future of Tibet will be in the hands of younger generations." And it's true now more than ever that we Tibetans living in exile have heavy responsibilities to shoulder and wisely crafted decisions to make. We face a crisis over the institution of the Dalai Lamas of Tibet and must fight to maintain genuine Tibetan-chosen Dalai Lamas in the face of the impending danger of Chinese-chosen Dalai Lamas. Any Chinese-chosen Dalai Lama would work in the interest of continuing Chinese domination over Tibet. At the same time, living as a cultural group without a homeland, we must fight to maintain what is fundamentally indispensable to our survival—the separation of religion and the democratic government founded by the Fourteenth Dalai Lama. I understood that His Holiness was making me personally responsible for the future of my country and my people and telling me I had an obligation to set a good example for generations to come.

He delivered the second piece of advice in a serious tone. "As a young man, do not disgrace your people. This is the first step in the right direction to help your country." I understood this as both a personal and a general message. Because I was young and inexperienced in the political world at large and a risk-taker, I could possibly do more harm than good for my people. Especially as displaced refugees living in foreign countries, we young Tibetans might behave in ways that shed a poor light on the Tibetan cause. We could also be easily influenced by the new cultures in which we found ourselves.

He was sounding a warning. In Western industrialized society, where materialism is a strong and influential component of civilization, anyone born in Tibet or brought up in Tibetan families-in-exile and now living in Western-influenced societies must face two different worlds simultaneously. It would not be easy to carry on my cultural heritage and national identity while living in somebody else's backyard. This would be my challenge. In the West, I had to properly represent Tibet, not simply become another Westerner.

Finally, he told me, "Always recognize when opportunities come your way, and use them properly." As I would learn throughout my years in the West, opportunities are rare, and sometimes difficult to recognize. They don't keep knocking on your door every day like the postman. They come in the same magical way as they disappear. Often we have to create the opportunities ourselves, not wait for them.

As then and since, I've always been grateful for the messages I received from His Holiness, which have always been simple, down to earth, and very practical. After thanking him, I rose and walked backwards until I reached the door.

As I turned headed down the steps of the residence, completely lost in my excitement, somebody called my name. "Paljor, are these yours?"

His Holiness was standing at the door smiling.

I looked down at my feet. I had walked away without my shoes. Now we both smiled.

If I were to follow the Dalai Lama's advice, I couldn't go into the wider world dressed like the barefoot yak herder I used to be. But I would always be a Tibetan.

TTHE MINUTE I GOT OFF THE TRAIN in Kathmandu to get Dupa's blessing for my plans to study in England, everyone urged me to re-board and head back to India.

For Tibetans living in Nepal, 1973 was a dangerous year. Some 100 of Yeshi's pack of armed killer dogs were hunting down other Chushi Gangdruk who had opposed the former monk. In exchange for Yeshi's spying for the Nepalese government, the Nepalese army eventually arrested and imprisoned eight of Yeshi's former unit commanders who had deserted him, including Rara—my father's killer. Yeshi himself was in deep hiding from his former commanders—the same fighters he had previously led—who were actively hunting down Gyen Yeshi the Cat. But Yeshi's men, having become Nepalese citizens under the protection of the Nepali army, were free to make their enemies simply disappear.

And I could be next. Following the wisdom of the Dalai Lama, I no longer wanted to take revenge on Gyen Yeshi for murdering my family. But this was not the moment to seek him out and offer my forgiveness. My telling the story of the massacre to His Holiness and filing the lawsuit against Gyen Yeshi and his men had contributed to the whole Tibetan community turning on the former Chushi Gangdruk leader. The Tibetan officials in Dharamsala had also reopened my lawsuit as part of their case against Yeshi.

But it wasn't just Yeshi and his henchmen who made Nepal unsafe for former freedom fighters. With the CIA backing withdrawn and the Chushi Gangdruk operation officially shut down, the Nepalese government had begun disarming the former freedom fighters. This left many of the old guerrillas—who had devoted decades of their lives to the Mustang resistance movement—in despair, some committing suicide, and others stubbornly forming renegade guerrilla bands in the hills. Afraid of becoming victims of the impending war between the Chushi Gangdruk and the Nepalese army, Tibetans closed all the businesses in Kathmandu that had Khampa names on the signboards. Because many former players in the Chushi Gangdruk and other activists had gone into hiding, I couldn't find some of my old Khampa friends.

Over buttered tea, Dupa and I renewed our commitment to fight for our country. But this was not the time or place. Backing up my plan to seek an education and allies in the West, Dupa then insisted that, for my own safety, I leave Kathmandu on the next train. Back in Dharamsala, I would tell officials there what was happening to Tibetans in Nepal.

I will always wonder about the reception I received. When I immediately contacted officials in the Tibetan government-in-exile, including the home minister, telling them they needed to help their fellow refugees in Nepal and to stop Yeshi once and for all, even the highest officials were mysteriously uninterested in what I had to say. Having shut down the Mustang military operation, the government was no longer investigating Yeshi's embezzlement of millions from the Tibetan resistance, his role in the death of Gompo Tashi's nephew, or any of his other crimes, including the massacre of my family. In fact, as a new Nepalese citizen, Gyen Yeshi—the brutal murderer and traitor—was soon prospering by opening several businesses in Kathmandu.

While the Dharamsala government seemed to have no interest in explaining their reluctance to pursue Yeshi or any inclination to assist the terrorized Tibetans in Nepal, the Tibetan leaders were eager to help me leave town. Looking back, I wonder if I was asking too making questions. While many Tibetans waited for years for an ID card—a document in lieu of a passport for "stateless refugees"—with the influence of friends in high places, my identity card was issued in only three months.

Even today I question just how far Yeshi's reach extended. On the same note, I still wonder about the files around my lawsuit that have been kept under seal.

But I needed to leave behind the past and these unanswered questions.

I was a young man heading West.

MY NEW SCHOOL IN SHELBOURNE, ENGLAND, looked to me like a castle built by English lords. Housed in a gray stone mansion, the Bennet School was surrounded by groves of trees where countless pheasants perched at night. Standing in the entryway, I stared at the marble floors and the chandeliers hanging from the high ceilings. In accordance with the Dalai Lama's personal advice to me— "Don't disgrace our own people"—I would have to work hard to represent my people well in this world so far from home. I was much more comfortable on the dirty, raucous streets of India. Negotiating clashing cultures requires wisdom and skillful means, which I didn't have at the time.

But my new classmates were welcoming. I was exotic, the school's first and only Tibetan. From their studies, they knew about Buddhist culture, about the Dalai Lama and his government-in-exile, and about China's invasion and its brutal attempt to exterminate the Tibetan culture.

And the Bennet School was no ordinary school. Almost all of the hundred students were college graduates. And our teacher, Mr. B, was no ordinary professor. A great mathematician, a spiritual master, a well-known scholar of philosophy and religions, and a famous author who wrote many books including *The Dramatic Universe*, Mr. B was the purest Christian at heart with a Buddhist outlook who had a profound knowledge and appreciation of all the major religions of the world. At Mr. Bennett's school, we all became more aware of the coexistence of all schools of thought and human psychology. And, ironically, I developed my enthusiasm for Tibetan Buddhism from him, a Western teacher.

Even though I was born into a Buddhist family and had met and listened to many great teachers from Tibet, I had never considered myself as a Buddhist practitioner. When I was fighting to kill or to be killed, my belief in Buddhism had been growing in scope. Killing enemies and losing friends, I came to realize the fragility of human life and the nature of impermanence, which dominates everything. I had also come to believe in karma, the law of cause and effect. But these were beliefs, not actions.

Listening to Mr. B, who sounded like a Tibetan Buddhist Master, something clicked in my head, and I became the practicing Buddhist for which my family and His Holiness had hoped. Under Mr. B's teaching, the Buddhist view broadened my mind, enriched my vision, and increased my ability to look at things from different perspectives and to comprehend things with a much deeper sense of meaning. The karmic law of cause and effect was now guiding my actions in terms of choosing between virtuous and non-virtuous deeds. With Mr. B's explanations, my understanding of dualistic perception was reducing my self-importance in the light of my ego, and lessening my "self-cherishing." I was accepting the laws of karma, life after death, rebirth and reincarnation, and the concept of two truths—the relative truth and the ultimate truth. Understanding the nature of impermanence and emptiness has helped me personally to accept things in life as they are, in essence both good and evil, to understand and rise above the dualistic view of myself and others, and to embrace the path of the Middle Way that transcends what Buddhists call the two extreme views of externalism and nihilism. Perhaps Mr. B's words touched me because there had been some karmic connections in our past lives, or perhaps I was looking from a Western perspective as an outsider looking at Buddhist thoughts from a different angle. It was like viewing myself in the mirror.

At the same time—maybe because I was his first Tibetan student or the student of the Divine Mother—Mr. Bennet had a soft place in his heart for me. Often, his family took me to their house in London, a city which represented yet another complete cultural departure from India. In the big cities in India, things were always in chaos—children running half-naked in the streets along with cows, pigs, chickens, and dogs. Everything was noisy, dirty, and smoky. And everybody in India seemed to be in the business of cheating somebody else, especially in trains, taxis, and rickshaws. London, on the other hand, was comparatively clean, and there was no pushing and shoving at bus stations, taxi stands, and airports. On our visits to London, Mr. Bennet showed me many places of great interest, including the British Museum. And sometimes, when Mrs. B was not available, Mr. B drove the car himself. He was color-blind and sometimes ran through red traffic lights. He would joke, "I did it again."

Even though some students were jealous of the special attention Mr. B gave me, in my one year there, I made many friends. When I wasn't in London with Mr. B's family, I was with other students drinking and dancing at a party. Almost every other day was some student's birthday, so there were lots of celebrations. With one group of friends, I formed a rock 'n' roll band called Rosy and the Rockets. With other friends, I hitchhiked to different parts of England performing English folk dances at country fairs in exchange for beer. For extra pocket money, I sold my ceramic whistle birds, which sounded like flutes, and my bears—which I renamed "Yetis."

Then, an auspicious event marked my final connection with the school and Mr. B.

Without any idea what I was going to do with it, one evening before dinnertime, I found the exact rock I was looking for near the school's vegetable garden. Some friends helped me move it into the school library. It took four people to carry it. When everyone wanted to know what I intended to do with the rock, I had no answer. I wasn't sure myself.

Then, in my dream that night, Mr. B said, "Hail the jewel in the lotus," which was a brief translation of the six syllables of the Tibetan mantra, *Om Mani Padme Hum.* The next day, I started to carve that mantra onto the rock. While many students were amused, others were irritated by the noise of my chipping at a rock in the library. On the third day, when Mr. and Mrs. B came by, I told them I was making a carving of a Tibetan mantra for Mr. B. Without asking which one, he said, "Hail the jewel in the lotus," exactly in the same manner I had heard him say it in my dream. Smiling at me, he looked happy as he left the room.

On the morning I finished engraving the mantra in the rock, all was normal. As always, Mr. B had looked happy and healthy as he was serving porridge to the students for breakfast. Pausing beside me, he asked if I was present when the Divine Mother passed away. When I said, "Yes," he nodded. "I was hoping you were there."

After completing a final touch-up on the correct color for each of the six syllables in the mantra, I went to work at my morning assignment in the gardens. All was well.

No one was prepared when, at a 10:30 a.m. emergency meeting in the great hall of the school, Mrs. B announced that, suddenly and peacefully, Mr. B had passed away an hour earlier. While everyone in the great hall cried, some sobbing uncontrollably, I sat stunned. Mr. B knew that that day, the day I finished carving the mantra, was his last. Later, Mrs. B told me that Mr. B wanted the stone mantra to be permanently placed in their house in London. The spirit of Mr. B's teachings and his compassion remained strong for all his students, and he had changed my life forever.

But now it was time to move on. Maybe at one time the sun never set on the British Empire, but by 1975 the sun hardly shined there.

With Mr. B's death, it was time for me to realize the final step in my plan to gain allies for Tibet. I was going to the United States, a superpower, and the richest country in the world.

1
7
8

THE WOMAN INTRODUCED HERSELF as "La Scala," and the other person meeting me at the airport in Albuquerque introduced himself as "Professor Mark Nelson, also known as Horse Shit."

Sure I misheard him, I smiled. "I beg your pardon. What's your name?"

Picking up my bag, he smiled back. "Horse Shit is my nickname."

"Okay. I see." I didn't see, but what else could I say to a man who looked like a professor and called himself Horse Shit?

I had arrived from Heathrow Airport in London, via Chicago, at Albuquerque, New Mexico with $37 in my pocket—which probably made me the poorest Tibetan in the richest country in the world. I was eager to see whatever came next.

La Scala and Horse Shit took me to Synergia Ranch fourteen miles outside of Santa Fe, where I would be joining the Synergetic Civilization of the Theater of All Possibilities—whatever that was. What I heard was one word—"possibilities." With some luck, and more likely through past karmic connections, my opportunity to head across the Atlantic to the land of possibilities had appeared in the person of John Allen. One of the many great thinkers who lectured at the Bennet school, Allen was a worldwide traveler and explorer. When, in our few brief conversations, I had expressed an interest in the U.S., Allen was enthusiastic about my joining his new age group in New Mexico and working with him for the Tibetan cause. After Mr. B died, John wasted no time. Within three weeks, I had an air ticket and a visa.

In the United States, I hoped to have a better chance of making a difference for my fellow countrymen. I would try to carry on the fight for a free Tibet begun by the great Khampa resistance leader Gompo Tashi. When the Chinese invaded our homeland, Tashi and other Khampa businessmen left behind the world of trade for submachine-guns and fierce warfare. In 1975, as former guerrillas, we survivors had to fight for the survival of Tibetan culture with different weapons—global diplomacy and public pressure.

I was also the first and only Tibetan in New Mexico. Again, I would be representing my country to Americans and couldn't "disgrace" my country. I needn't have worried. This was no ordinary group of Americans. Happy and excited to meet their Tibetan guest of honor, each person introduced themselves to me by a given name and an "also known as" nickname. It sounded a little as if I had landed among the Sicilian mafia. In addition, because it happened to be one of the monthly cultural days, this one being "Russia" day, everyone was dressed up in Russian costumes and drinking vodka. Laughing and raising their drinks, they poured me—soon to become "Paljor, also known as Thondup the Terrible"—a glass.

When I woke the next morning with a hangover, I wondered whether I had landed in some Third World country by mistake. Someone was going door to door ringing a bell, like they do in Tibetan monasteries for morning prayers, and, in the daylight, I saw that all the buildings were constructed of mud bricks, locally known as adobe, just like the Tibetan houses back in Kham. Neither the ranch nor the city of Santa Fe looked anything like the America I expected. While my images of the U.S. had been based on the high modern buildings in New York, Chicago, and Las Vegas, the local architecture in Santa Fe was very much like that of Tibet—with mud bricks, round wooden pillars, and carved corbels. In fact, the people at Synergia Ranch even had characteristics similar to Khampas. Straightforward in their talk and independent in their character, their emotions burst out like firecrackers.

Under the supervision of my great friend John Allen, who never ceased to surprise me, the people at Synergia Ranch were conducting several projects simultaneously, including the Theater of All Possibilities—which performed worldwide—and the Institute of Ecotechnics, which organized scientific conferences globally, working on ecology and environmental conservation projects, including the Biosphere II near Tucson, Arizona. Sometimes I thought of Allen as a crazy bodhisattva with wrathful compassion and untested crazy wisdom, someone who had figured out how everything in the universe worked, yet never learned how to drive a car. At the time I joined them, the group was rapidly expanding their work into Australia, France, England, and Nepal.

After breakfast on the first day, I learned John Allen's future vision for me. Overlooking a small valley near Synergia Ranch, he pointed to fifteen acres. "This is your place for Project Tibet." He nodded at the empty land. "Doesn't this valley look to you like the place where Milarepa may have meditated?"

Although I responded, "Sure, sure," John had underestimated my commitment. At the time, most of my new friends, including John, might have supposed my dreams of continuing the fight for Tibet in America were wishful thinking, or at least modest. My American supporters had no idea how far I would go. Although Milarepa may have been happy here so far away from the commotion of civilization, my idea of going to the West, especially America, to start a nonviolent cultural revolution to preserve, to promote, and to pro-tect Tibetan identity as an independent nation and free people wasn't going to happen in a remote valley fourteen miles from the center of business and activity. I had my eye on bustling Santa Fe. This small city would be the home of Project Tibet.

Without developing the land near the ranch or revealing my plan to open a center in Santa Fe, I spent my time making "Tibet" a familiar name in New Mexico. The U.S. was not an easy place to gain support for the Tibetan cause. I was still the first and only Tibetan resident of New Mexico, and most people had never heard of this country located somewhere in central Asia. Like the rest of the world, they knew about the Dalai Lama, Mount Everest, and the Yetis. What they didn't know was that this marvelous ancient civilization was near death at the hands of the brutal and relentless Chinese. It would be my job to educate them while I waited for an opportunity to build Project Tibet. The Dalai Lama had told me, "Recognize when opportunities come your way, and use them properly." I was waiting.

In 1976, the right opportunity appeared in the person of Edward P. Bass, a multibillionaire from Texas and friend of Tibet who was working with John Allen and his new age group on a unique construction project called Synopco. When Bass and I bonded over our love of Tibet, he hired me at Synopco—first as a quality controller and later as the financial vice president. I was fasci-nated by this project.

Financed entirely by Bass, the project to build 30 residential houses with adobe bricks was based on revolutionary thinking and very un-American—not a capitalistic approach and not profit-minded. Synopco supported local art-ists by giving them day jobs as electricians, surveyors, plumbers, carpenters, bricklayers. Unlike in any other construction company in the world, Synopco employees worked for four hours a day and only four days a week to give the artist/workers enough money to live on while allowing them time to create works of art. Although there was not much money to be made with this sched-ule, the workers were more efficient and less exhausted. And eventually, be-cause of their work on this project, many people became professionals, some later starting their own companies and working as contractors for larger com-panies. Because Bass's motivation was to help others, it could rightfully be called the Bodhisattva Construction Company.

Very wealthy and very generous, Bass was also very careful with how he spent his money. One day, Ed gave me $1.50 that he said he owed me from a year earlier. I was shocked. It was amazing that a man who was worth billions of dollars could care about small change like that. As it turned out, however, my friend Ed Bass would not hesitate to spend millions for good causes. Including mine.

When the Santa Fe historical association blocked Bass's application to build a five-star hotel on a property located on upscale Canyon Road, Bass sold much of the empty land but gave me a parcel on which sat two existing buildings. This was my miracle. By 1977, two years after I had arrived in America, with my initiative, John Allen's vision, and the financial backing of Ed Bass, we gave birth to Project Tibet, Inc. While its completion was a few years away, the Project Tibet compound with its lecture halls, galleries, and shops, on a multimillion-dollar property in the heart of the Santa Fe art district known as Canyon Road, was underway.

Although one person's war against China didn't seem and doesn't look practical, I was a man with a purpose. In order to increase awareness of Tibet, I organized functions celebrating and commemorating all Tibetan major historical events such as the Dalai Lama's birthday on July 6th, the Tibetan New Year in February, and the Tibetan national uprising against the Chinese occupation on March 10th. I invited Tibetan lamas to give Buddhist teachings, scholars to give talks on Tibet, and supporters to provide slide shows and movies on the Tibetan culture, people, and landscape—anything I could think of that was Tibet-related.

But gaining allies in the West was only a stepping stone. I wanted to do something meaningful for my fellow refugees living in exile in Nepal. Even though Yeshi and his bandits were no longer a threat in Kathmandu—the Nepalese government had confiscated all his weapons except the handguns carried by his bodyguards—and the Chushi Gangdruk had come out of hiding, the former freedom fighters couldn't make a living in Nepal. Yet this was where they lived. And they needed jobs.

CHAPTER TWELVE

PUTTING DOWN
PA JATA'S SWORD

1978-90: KATHMANDU, NEPAL

IT WAS THE ONLY HOTEL IN NEPAL built to be earthquake-proof. Constructed in the traditional Tibetan architectural style and based on Western technology, Hotel Vajra was also the first joint venture on a large scale ever attempted between Tibetans and Americans. As a guerrilla-turned-businessman, this initiative was my way to provide jobs for out-of-work guerrillas and help hundreds of my fellow refugees to endure in a foreign land. It worked.

With a multi-million-dollar investment from Ed Bass, John Allen behind the scenes making things happen, Dupa as executive chairman and general manager of the operation, and me as the coordinator between the Tibetans and Americans, our concept was to integrate the wisdom of the East with the scientific knowledge of the West—a meeting of minds combining the best of two major civilizations. Based on the interdependence and interconnectedness of the world economy in the 21st century, we saw our joint venture as potentially a global model for a new generation of management. We were making history.

Of course, there were three nations involved.

In 1978, Dupa and I consumed an ocean of Johnny Walker Black Label and other whiskey (from foreign countries only), mountains of chicken chili to go with the whiskey, as is the Nepalese custom, and countless packs of 555 ciga-rettes. Although Dupa and I normally didn't party to this extreme, Nepalese officials, who were heavy drinkers and chain-smokers, needed to be either en-tertained lavishly or bribed to encourage them to do their official jobs for us. And, in their country, their way was the highway.

What we couldn't know was that the lengthy process of incorporating the hotel business into a legal entity was so complicated and politically sensitive that we were looking at a year of paperwork before we could ever break ground. Things move very slowly in Nepal. Every other day was a holiday. When the King left the country, it was a holiday, and when he returned home, it was another hol-iday. There is an old Tibetan proverb: "Every other day is a new year in Nepal."

Because it would be years before the hotel could start paying dividends to the American shareholders and provide jobs for my Tibetan partners and the rest of the Tibetan community, I needed to make another "opportunity" happen. While Hotel Vajra was a work-in-progress, I proposed we expand our American/Tibetan joint venture to include a second and separate legal entity completely independent from the hotel project—a handicraft center and rug factory—that could open its doors immediately. With everyone signing on, we partitioned a three-story building originally used for chicken farming to accommodate a car-pet factory, residential housing for the Tibetans, a small school, and a gift shop.

For this project, however, we included a third group in the partnership, the original freedom fighters who deserted Yeshi and called themselves Tobtsang—the name in the Tibetan resistance for one unit of ten guerrillas sharing the same tent and operations together. For Dupa and me, Tobtsang, which included our friends Thusam and Lochap, became family and we were *pha-ma mechig dorjee pun*—"Vajra brothers of different parents."

For our carpet factory and handicraft center, which we called Tobtsang Zoda, each one of us had different talents and expertise. I was their foreign minister and chief adviser. Dupa, who knew everybody in Nepal, and was highly respected in the Tibetan community, was the expert in the carpet busi-ness, and in charge of public relations. Thusam was a natural-born diplomat who spoke Nepali well and had a connection with the royal family of Nepal. Lochap knew the antique market, had strong connections with the monaster-ies and the older generation in the larger Tibetan community in Nepal, and was a founding member of Nangchen Nyer-ngak, the Tibetan Association of United Districts of Nangchen. As a group, the Tobtsang became the most pop-ular Tibetan family in the Kathmandu valley.

Within a few months, the noise of wool swishing in the dye buckets, water splashing in the rinsing process, and the thrum and clack of looms, mingled with the chatter of happy-go-lucky workers gossiping, singing, and teasing each other in the newly opened carpet factory. As foremen wandered through the factory chatting with the men and women who were spinning Tibetan wool into threads, dying the wool, creating balls of yarn, weaving the rugs, and trimming the borders, humans weren't the only ones creating commotion and clamor. Kathmandu is the land of monkeys. Dozens of them scampered about unnoticed, exchanging meaningless chatter. The Tobtsang Zoda always felt more like a party than a factory.

In addition to employing hundreds of men and women, the handicraft center also supported hundreds more—the workers' relatives, friends, and many people from our own districts in Tibet who relied on us for their well-being. Providing residential accommodations for unskilled Tibetan workers who then were trained as professional weavers, Dupa and his Tobtsang partners made the workers feel part of their family.

By 1979, after a year of drinking and smoking with Nepalese officials and the royal family, new sounds—the buzz of drills, clang of hammers, and singing and shouting by workers—mingled with the sounds on the crowded, noisy streets of Kathmandu where everyone and everything—bikes, cars, motorbikes, three-wheelers, cows, pigs, chickens, babies, and beggars—shared the same pothole-littered roads. The construction of Hotel Vajra was also underway.

While I was spending half the year in New Mexico—1980 saw the official opening of Project Tibet—among the Tibetan refugee community in Nepal, Dupa and I saw a renaissance of our Gonatsang and Khurutsang families. Everyone in Nepal knew of us and our success helping our fellow Tibetans. From what was left of our original home and extended family in Kham—two orphans, Dupa, and myself—we were creating families with children and grandchildren to carry on the Khampa legacy. Neither the Chinese nor Yeshi's killer dogs had exterminated us. In my fantasy, our two families would continue growing large enough to found an entire town in Tibet one day—in a free Tibet, that is.

As tourist buses pulled into the Project Tibet Compound in Santa Fe, the looms hummed in the Tobtsang rug factory, and guests registered at the Hotel Vajra, it was the realization of a dream by a humble yak-boy to keep his promise to himself and to the Dalai Lama.

There was just one problem. According to Nepal's laws at the time, for joint ventures with foreigners, the chairman of the company had to be a Nepalese citizen, and Dupa, who was running both the hotel and the factory, was still in the process of applying.

And there was only one person in Kathmandu who could help.

BECAUSE YESHI'S SECURITY TEAM was suspicious of people waiting in cars, I had followed the advice of our intermediary, Zatsap Nganglo—a chieftain of one of the twenty-five districts in Nangchen and a friend of Yeshi's as well as mine—who suggested we not take the family car but arrive by taxi. However, when Nganglo suggested that I bring a traditional Tibetan greeting scarf—which would have represented an act of respect and submission on my part—I refused. I wasn't going to offer a greeting scarf to the man who ordered the slaughter of my parents. Instead, beside me on the seat in the taxi, I brought a large basket of fruit.

When Zatsep Naganlo had told me months earlier that Bawa Yeshi wanted to meet so he could tell me "his side of the story about the Mogum massacre," I recognized an opportunity to honor the Dalai Lama and forgive my enemy.

I also recognized the chance to do something I hadn't done as young nomad boy—kill two birds with one stone.

We needed to make Dupa's position legal and official. The only person who had the connections to help Tibetans like Dupa get Nepalese citizenship was Bawa Gyen Yeshi. Not only was he a Tibetan who had taken on Nepalese citizenship and opened several businesses in Kathmandu, he had gained importance with the government because he had spied for the Nepalese against other Tibetans.

On the ride there, Nganglo jokingly asked me if I would have "any second thoughts about forgiving Yeshi" when I finally met him face-to-face. Although occasionally my fellow Tibetans had spotted Yeshi circumambulating some Buddhist temples with his bodyguards, I had never even seen a photograph of the former head of the CIA-sponsored resistance movement, much less met him. Smiling, I said, "I'll decide when I see his face." Humor, as my uncle and my father had taught me, relieved tension before confronting the enemy.

When the taxi dropped us by the iron gate at the entrance to Yeshi's lavish, walled, and well-fortified compound, Yeshi's right-hand man and a few armed bodyguards were waiting. I assumed more guards were watching from the windows, ready for action. I was ready too.

Although Yeshi and his men no longer posed a physical danger to former Chushi Gangdruk enemies, Yeshi and his pack of renegades were still estranged and isolated from other Tibetans. In a person-to-person meeting, I would urge Yeshi to reconcile with the other Tibetans in Nepal, and, ultimately, help Dupa and our other Tibetan partners get the Nepalese citizenship they needed to control their share of Hotel Vajra. At this point in 1982, Yeshi's people were still considered outlaws in direct conflict with the exiled Tibetan government and the Tibetan community at large. In person, I would encourage him to stop turning his men against the wishes of the Dalai Lama and unite with the Tibetan government under His Holiness.

I planned to take advantage of what I suspected was Yeshi's real motive for seeking peace with me. Yeshi's usefulness as a spy for the Nepalese government was on the decline, and, although Yeshi owned a few businesses in Kathmandu, by 1982, my star was rising over his. As a successful entrepreneur who was politically well-connected—and the only Tibetan able to initiate a multi-million-dollar joint project with American investors—my popularity in the Kathmandu business community and with the Royal Family of Nepal was increasing. No doubt, Yeshi would see my growing influence as a threat to his increasingly tenuous position—although, looking back, perhaps his willingness for a détente with me may have been based on a more complicated motive. He may have feared I had the clout to turn Nepalese political leaders against him as my way to avenge the massacre.

Why else would he want to see me, a person whose efforts had contributed to his fall from grace?

As I waited for Yeshi in his large, formal, and well-furnished meeting room—which had several doors behind which guards could be listening and waiting—I was suddenly uneasy.

I needn't have worried. When Yeshi arrived in the large room in traditional Buddhist monk's robes instead of a guerrilla's uniform, my preconceived notion of him as a tough and vicious-looking Khampa killer vanished. Instead, I saw a simple old Buddhist monk wanting to talk.

Taking my hand warmly in both of his, he said pleasantly. "I'm very pleased to finally see you."

In fact, he was very pleased to exonerate himself. And, for the next hour, as we drank buttered tea, he tried. Insisting that he was "not involved directly or indirectly" in the massacre of my family, he told me, "It was a terrible mistake committed by my men." It was easy for Yeshi to place all the blame on Rara, the man who had actually pulled the trigger and murdered my father and Tsewang. Yeshi certainly had no loyalty to Rara, one of his eight former commanders whom he had helped the Nepalese government send to prison in 1974. By the best definition, Rara was a useful idiot as well as a born killer. He had been the very character Yeshi wanted on his side to do his dirty work—a ruthless killing machine who wasn't that politically smart. Rara may not have even known he had been manipulated by Yeshi to carry out the massacre.

Even though I knew that Yeshi was the true killer, I listened politely. I hadn't come to hear his side of the story. There was no other side. Everyone knew the truth. No Chushi Gangdruk soldier would have acted without Yeshi's orders.

When it was my turn to speak, I followed another piece of advice my father had given me when I was young, "Always be honest, candid, and straightforward." Meeting his eyes, I told Yeshi, "Let's not speak of this anymore. I've promised His Holiness I wouldn't seek vengeance either against you or your people." I paused and took a sip of tea.

While I hadn't accepted his version of events or used the word "forgive," I felt him relax when he understood that I was offering peace, not revenge.

"What most interests me," I told the man who ordered the murder of my parents, "is persuading you to give up any disobedience to the Dalai Lama's leadership and to give up your fight against our government."

He nodded for me to continue.

As I looked Yeshi in the eye, I remembered my father's other advice, "Never flatter or beguile people to do you favors." Yeshi and I both had something to gain. I had to remember that.

Choosing my words carefully, I made my case. "As a man of your status, the leader of the Tibetan resistance organization and a high-ranking member of the Chushi Gangdruk, I hope you'll consider turning your people over to the Tibetan authorities and living under the leadership of the Dalai Lama— so that you and your people will not lose your cultural heritage and national identity as Tibetans."

To my surprise, Yeshi didn't seem to disagree with me and nodded again.

Taking a final breath, I concluded, "We need you to engage in the Tibetan freedom struggles against our common enemy by unifying your group with other Tibetans, not isolating them from mainstream Tibetan-exile society."

Motioning for one of his attendants to bring me the gift of a large Tibetan rug, Yeshi took my hands again. "Thank you for meeting with me. And thank you for your thoughtful discussion on this matter."

As I walked to the taxi, I was convinced that I did the right thing to leave the past behind. For myself, letting go of my anger toward Yeshi was a relief. A sad-looking man in monk's robes, he had seemed honest and straightforward with me during our meeting. Simply seeing him as another human being in the form of old monk, not an enemy, I even felt compassion for him.

Apparently Yeshi was equally pleased with our meeting. He told Nganglo that he was "impressed" with my "candid talk and self-confidence" as a young man and my willingness to not dwell on past events.

But, I wondered, did he hear my request for reconciliation with his fellow Tibetans? Without asking Yeshi directly, I also hoped that my urging him to be responsible to his fellow Tibetans would prompt him to help Dupa and the other hotel partners secure the required Nepalese citizenship for them to have their names on the hotel. Did my meeting with Yeshi really touch the heart of the corrupt traitor?

To test Yeshi's willingness to associate with me and the Tibetan community in Nepal, I sent him a formal invitation to my wedding, which was taking place that same year in Kathmandu.

Of course, this presented a dilemma. Even though no one spoke of Yeshi anymore and tensions had cooled down, several guests at the wedding would be Yeshi's sworn enemies—the Tobtsang—as well as friends of the recently released Khampa commanders whom Yeshi had helped jail. Rather than party with Yeshi or his men, many of my guests would be more inclined to kill them.

On the first and most important day of the wedding ceremony, when religious rituals were performed and gifts were presented, we escorted Yeshi's men separately to the wedding reception where they presented their greeting scarves and gifts away from the rest of the party. Although Yeshi himself didn't attend, he offered a symbolic gesture of goodwill by sending several of his top men armed with many gifts—and handguns. As it was a three-day ceremony with 800 people in attendance, keeping the two sets of killers apart required extra precautions and a security detail.

During the second two days, which were just for fun and entertainment, only friendly people—those who were of no danger to others—were invited to the largest hall for the all-night party, where my wife's sister Dolkar was the hostess for a drinking game which left most of the guests happily drunk. Although Yeshi's men were very friendly, I kept my security personnel on extra alert, making certain that the most overtly dangerous people were kept far away from each other.

The wedding was also a test of loyalty for my own people, to see who showed up and who didn't. With over 800 guests, including several from America, the three-day ceremony was the largest wedding ever held within the Tibetan community in Kathmandu. It was also the only wedding to bring together so many diverse groups of people. My American guests, John Allen and Ed Bass, were impressed by how well everything was organized.

Certainly things were organized sufficiently to avoid any incidents, which made it all worth the risk of having Yeshi's men at the wedding. Although I'll never be sure whether it was my détente with Yeshi that made the difference, that year Bawa Yeshi surrendered all his people to the Tibetan authorities, agreeing to live under the leadership of His Holiness. And when Dupa and our other partners sought Yeshi's support obtaining Nepalese citizenship, he helped them willingly.

I had fulfilled my promise to the Dalai Lama by forgiving Yeshi, the man who ordered the slaughter of my parents. But the real test was to come. Could I forgive the men who actually shot them?

WHEN THE OWNER of my favorite Mahjong house in Kathmandu showed me to a table, I immediately recognized the man who had pumped dozens of sub-machine-gun rounds into my unarmed father. Even though I had only met Rara once—when Dupa and I were forced to engage with the killers right after the massacre—I had never forgotten any of their names or faces. I took a few shallow breaths. For decades I had been fantasizing about which gun to use when I met Rara in one of the thirty-four hells. Now here he was across the Mahjong table from me.

All around us in the noisy, small, crowded room, players chattered loudly, shouting "Zemok" when they won, and focusing all their attention on the game—which was costing them money.

Even though he didn't recognize me, he knew my name at once. Oddly enough, although I'm not sure if it was on purpose or by chance, the owner called me by my full name "Paljor Thondup-la," instead of "Paljor-la," when introducing me to the table. Rara, who had been talking when I entered the room, grew quiet. Clearly uncomfortable, he fumbled for something to say. "You live in America, don't you?"

I nodded. "Yes, I do. But now I'm here."

But what the hell was Rara doing in Nepal? Wasn't he in India? Everyone knew that when the Chushi Gangdruk commanders had been released from prison in 1980, they had been exiled to India. I had even heard that Rara had a job there. It didn't make sense. Had he returned to Kathmandu? But why? Just to play Mahjong? I didn't think so. Was it possible that Rara was here to kill Yeshi? He didn't say.

On the other hand, did Rara imagine that I was in Kathmandu to kill *him*?

I had certainly thought about it every day. Now that I was face-to-face with my father's killer, my immediate reaction was—what the hell was I supposed to do? The mixed emotions crackled like a contained bonfire. I tried to remember what the Dalai Lama wanted. Could I feel the forgiveness His Holiness had counseled? Not really. When so unexpectedly meeting the devil who had shot my father, I found that compassion didn't come easily at all.

Although Rara didn't look physically weaker, the fact that he was elderly, poorly dressed, and not the glamorous killer he used to be, helped to calm me down. I took a breath. Why would I kill this man? I pitied him. Rara was old and pathetic. In truth, although Rara was a killer by nature, he had been Yeshi's henchman who just followed orders. Instead of killing Rara, I drank tea with him.

As it would turn out, Rara would soon be punished without my intervention. Rara's failure to stay in India with his comrades was a fatal error. Within a year—again with Yeshi behind the plot—the killer of my father was arrested a second time by Nepali authorities and sent to a Nepalese jail.

I couldn't think about Rara. Although I still revisited the massacre in my nightmares, during the waking hours I was living my dream—Project Tibet fully active in New Mexico, and the joint ventures with our American partners thriving in Kathmandu—that is, until the laws of impermanence intervened, and we Tibetans had to go it alone in Nepal.

I LOVED THE SOUNDS—wool swishing in the dye buckets, water splashing in the rinsing process, and the thrum and clack of looms—especially when they mingled with the workers' laughter. But this time I was standing in a different carpet factory, a new one.

What worked well in John Allen's American group had not worked that well with the Khampas. In the late 1980's, our Tobtsang family had split, with Thusam and the Tobtsang joining forces with the American partners, and Dupa, Lochap, and I going a separate direction. In order to compromise, and to reconcile things so that we could get on with our lives, I offered the Tobtsang the original carpet factory, along with the property it stood on, and Dupa and I kept shares in the Vajra Hotel.

The ultimate failure of our joint venture still feels unnecessary and simply due to a lack of understanding of our cultural and temperamental differences. By nature, Khampas are stubborn and hotheaded, as John Allen himself turned out to be—an intellectual "American Khampa," as viewed by some of my Tibetan associates. Perhaps it was by way of a cosmic accident, yet for some universal purpose, that I happened to bring these two very different groups together. I like to think of our experiment as a great educational experience, a good introduction to Western psychology, and hands-on experience dealing with people from different parts of the world.

While we were unhappy about the breakup of our Tobtsang family—as we had lived together for so many years as *phama mechig dorjee pun*, "Vajra brothers of different parents"—we were happy to have been part of the project that provided employment for Tibetan refugees and Nepalese citizens as trained employees in management skills. A former taxi driver has become one of the top managers today. Thus we put our ideals into practice. I'm very proud of our hotel, which still operates as one of the most beautiful and modern in Nepal.

But now Dupa and Lochap needed jobs. My question was, "Why not produce the highest-quality Tibetan handmade rugs in all of Nepal by yourselves?" Suggesting they open their own business independent of American investors, I secured enough capital by mortgaging the hotel property to open the doors of this busy place where I now stood with Dupa. When he took me into the new showroom filled with beautiful handwoven traditional rugs, we paused at the back of the room. On a stand protected by a glass case was a large, gold-framed portrait of His Holiness. I was excited that I would be able to tell the Dalai Lama about this business, run and owned by Tibetans, which in a short time had become one of the major producers of Tibetan carpets in all of Kathmandu. As the demand for their carpets skyrocketed, instead of having trouble finding buyers, they now had trouble producing enough to supply the demand.

Then, while I was back in the West looking for support to retake our homeland, Dupa actually did it. He reclaimed some of Chinese-occupied Tibet. In the early 1990's, when the Chinese were encouraging foreign investors, Dupa—who once fought the Red Menace as a guerrilla—engaged in a cultural revolution through the backdoor. While the Chinese were always suspicious of Tibetans, now that Dupa was a Nepalese citizen, it had been possible for him to open a business in our country. In the Holy City of Lhasa, which had been ravaged during the invasion, Dupa and his partners built a hotel with a typical Tibetan building design like that of the destroyed Potala. They also opened a successful rug factory that was the talk of the town. Providing residential accommodations for Tibetan workers from all over Tibet, many coming far from their homes, Dupa and his partners, as they had in Kathmandu, treated the workers as family, not employees, servants, or slaves.

Dupa had proved that Tibetans didn't need Western gurus to succeed in business.

However, we still needed Western support for the Tibetan political cause.

During the months I spent each year in New Mexico, I continued raising awareness to the West of China's illegal occupation of Tibet. I registered Project Tibet as a Tibetan Charitable NGO; "Free Tibet" bumper stickers appeared on the backs of every 30th or 40th car on the roads in New Mexico; residents of Santa Fe were wearing "Save Tibet" T-shirts; and, eventually, with my initiative, the Tibetan population in New Mexico increased from one person (myself) to about 170 through the Tibetan Resettlement Program.

By 1989, I was participating in conferences about Tibet in Dhamasala and the United States. As our NGO became more known, I was also asked to join other Tibetan organizations working for our common cause and became a board and sometimes founding member of those, including the International Campaign for Tibet, the United Districts of Nangchen Association, and Friends of Tibet New Mexico. With Project Tibet and my affiliation with other Tibetan NGO's and international NGO's, such as Amnesty International and other human rights groups, my efforts were beginning to make an impact in the media and in reaching the general population to gain more support for Tibet.

I also turned to politics. In response to both the Tiananmen Square massacre of students, where several thousand deaths were claimed but not confirmed, and the brutal crushing of Tibetan Buddhist monks' peaceful protests in Lhasa, resulting in an unconfirmed great number of deaths reported by witnesses, I formed a new Political Action Committee, Friends of Tibet, New Mexico. Our mandate was to pressure political leaders both at the state and national level to take up the Tibetan cause by challenging U.S. relations with China. With the publicity from the Dalai Lama receiving the Nobel Peace Prize that same year, I was able, with the help of my friends in the political world, to push through several legislative bills at the state and national levels in support of Tibet.

However, Project Tibet hosting this Nobel Prize winner in New Mexico in 1991 was the highlight of my career as a political activist for the cause of Tibet.

AS WE ACCOMPANIED HIS HOLINESS to a reception for him hosted by our Native American sisters and brothers, the 19 Honorable Governors of the 19 Indian Pueblo Tribes of New Mexico, a squirrel running across our path paused and looked at us with curiosity. "What's up, Dalai Lama?" Nearby, two ravens perched on a telephone pole were facing east, which portended a lucky day in Tibet.

It was certainly an auspicious day in Santa Fe, the capital of New Mexico, "the Land of Enchantment," and my second home away from my home in the Land of Snows, the Roof of the World, and the home of the Dalai Lamas. The bright blue sky empty of clouds seemed to symbolize the nature of emptiness, a day of peace and harmony. As usual, His Holiness was smiling and shaking hands with the crowd that followed him everywhere. Over a thousand members actively worked organizing seven major events for his five-day visit.

While His Holiness spent most of the week with his American supporters, this memorable meeting between Native American leaders in the home of the Red Indians, the true owners of America, and His Holiness, the true leader of Tibet, was one of the most moving and historic events of his visit. There was a feeling of true brotherhood in the tribal community center as 700 Native American men, women, and children, many of them in bright rainbow-colored clothing, crowded toward the stage to watch His Holiness place a scarf about the neck of each governor. Then His Holiness was decorated with Indian jewelry such as warrior's bracelets and silver and turquoise pendants. When the Dalai Lama admired the warrior bracelet worn by a Pueblo governor's son, the young man immediately removed it from his own arm and offered it to His Holiness. Before the Dalai Lama could say "no," I jumped in to tell him that to refuse a gift is an insult according to Native American tradition. With a warm "thank you," His Holiness accepted the bracelet and slid it onto his own wrist.

The ceremony was all done according to Native American tradition—except for the dress code. Although the current governors did wear traditional dress for ceremonial occasions, having seen how other VIPs received the Dalai Lama, many of the governors chose to blend into this international gathering by observing a special protocol for His Holiness. Many wore business suits with ties. Only the performers were in bright traditional dress of rainbow colors for a show of dancing and singing in the Dalai Lama's honor.

In individual speeches, each of the nineteen governors then praised the Dalai Lama's commitment to nonviolence, world peace, and universal responsibility. All nineteen jointly issued a proclamation stating that Tibet was an independent nation. His Holiness remarked on the good-natured and open-hearted friendliness of his Native American brothers. He told them that it was very important to preserve, protect, and promote their cultural heritage by using native language within their tribes and, if possible, developing their own writing system.

It was truly a rare meeting of minds and hearts as two peace-loving brothers from opposite sides of the world came together to share cultures and exchange ideas in the spirit of brotherhood and their common humanity.

The next stop was a meeting with the white man's political leaders. But first I had to find His Holiness. On our way to a private meeting among His Holiness, the Governor of New Mexico, the Mayor of Santa Fe, and Congressional delegates consisting of two U.S. Senators and three U.S. Congressmen, I turned to discover the Dalai Lama had disappeared. This wasn't the first time. In the early 1980's, on my first day on the job working as the Dalai Lama's bodyguard during his first visit to the United States, I had lost His Holiness at least once a day. In fact, during my years working the Dalai Lama's security detail on U.S. visits, his disappearing from the scheduled route became routine.

While it was a great honor and privilege to serve my country's leader—who also happened to be one of the world's most famous leaders—it was not an easy job. Although my former training in martial arts, special training in the tactical use of various types of weapons, defensive driving, and crowd control made me well-suited for the position, His Holiness was not fond of protocols and formalities and had little concern for his own security when interacting with the public. Eventually, I found His Holiness on the other side of the Santa Fe street, holding the hand of a man in a wheelchair, and we headed into our meeting.

Having just bonded with our Native American leaders, His Holiness now was equally at ease with U.S. political leaders. In an atmosphere of friendship and open-minded dialogue, the Americans seriously discussed what we as Americans could and would do for the Dalai Lama and the people of Tibet. As a result of this meeting, the first-ever meeting between a U.S. President and the Dalai Lama of Tibet took place later that same year.

As we now had a few hours before the Dalai Lama's final speech, I signaled his driver to take His Holiness back to the hotel to rest. As usual, the Dalai Lama had his own ideas about how to spend his free time on his visit to Santa Fe. Instead, His Holiness moved to the front seat of his limo and instructed the driver to go to the Santa Fe Ski Basin. My friends and I followed, along with the whole entourage of seven cars, including the State Police escort car. With His Holiness, we took the ski lift to the top of the mountain for a great view of the surrounding areas. While everyone was enjoying the view, I kept my eyes on His Holiness. Because the ski lift didn't have seat belts or anything to hold onto, it swung back and forth whenever it stopped to drop off or pick up people. As I knew from having been his bodyguard for years, the Dalai Lama rarely worried about his own safety.

In large crowds, His Holiness was also completely fearless, as dozens of strangers always trailed beside and behind His Holiness, touching his robes and reaching to shake hands. When His Holiness gave a sermon on the Karma Kagyud Lineage of Tibetan Buddhism to an audience of about 870, more would have attended if the crowd hadn't reached the maximum capacity allowed by the Santa Fe Fire Department. Capacity crowds—all pushing forward to get closer to the bright light surrounding Tibet's spiritual leader—also attended his lectures on "Peace through Compassion and Nonviolence" and "Universal Responsibility." Then, for his final talk, there was no crowd limit! Broadcast on live television, "World Peace through Compassion and Nonviolence" touched millions of people all across North America and Canada.

After the Dalai Lama's historic visit, I was soon holding events for as many as 400 people at the Project Tibet compound, dedicated to the preservation and promotion of Tibetan cultural heritage and national identity. Everyone enjoyed Tibetan dancers and cultural performers, as well as hosting many high lamas and scholars—such as Tai Situ Rinpoche, Drikung Chetsang

Rinpoche, Ganden Tripa Rinpoche, Chagduk Tulku, Namkhai Norbu Rinpoche, Khenpo Katak, and Bhorka Tulku—lecturing about Tibet.

Of course I couldn't have done this alone. Without key American members of Project Tibet and Friends of Tibet New Mexico, there would be no Project Tibet—today, one of the oldest and most popular Tibetan organizations in the United States—or any historic visit from Tibet's spiritual leader. His Holiness and I wanted to thank them.

My plan was a spiritual journey in which I would introduce my American friends to Tibetan culture in its incarnation-in-exile in Dharamsala, and to two high holy men of Tibet, both in exile—His Holiness in India and a famous high lama in Nepal. However, Tibetans aren't just the good. My delegation would, accidentally, also meet the bad and the ugly. Our first stop was the good.

AS EVERYONE REMOVED THEIR SHOES and entered the hall, the silence was sacred. No one spoke. A few months after the Dalai Lama's 1991 stay in New Mexico, I took nine of our U.S. sponsors to Dharamsala where, rather than just meeting with His Holiness while he was in Santa Fe, my U.S. friends had an audience in Dharamsala, a much greater honor for us all. The Dalai Lama had visited our home. Now we visited his.

In India, my friends could also experience true Tibetan culture in Dharamsala, India, the temporary home of the Dalai Lama and his government. When Dupa and I were first there in the 1960's, Dharamsala had been a sparsely populated area of northern India with some small villages known as "hill stations" in the Himalayan foothills. With few buildings, houses, shops, or any sizable hotels, everything in Dharamsala was small and old-fashioned. Very few houses had indoor plumbing, and public restrooms were nonexistent. Visible on the roads back then were only a scattering of public buses and a few jeeps owned by the exiled Tibetan government, the local Indian government, or private individuals. Because of the rapidly growing fame and popularity of His Holiness on the world stage, Tibetans kept pouring into Dharamsala from all over India, Nepal, Bhutan and even still from Tibet, risking their lives to see and hear His Holiness. Dharamsala became known as "Little Tibet." Observing in person the Renaissance of Tibetan Civilization outside of Tibet, the American friends of Tibet were able to witness the willpower, perseverance, and indomitable spirit of the Tibetan people in exile.

By the time of our visit in 1991, the city had also been magically transformed. Due to the efforts of the Tibetan government-in-exile in India, with
the support of the international community, and especially the Indian government, the city attracted international tourism, foreign journalists, writers,
scientists, scholars, dignitaries, and government officials from around the
world. In addition to new government buildings, tourist hotels, banks, restaurants, and chains of shops, there were services such as tourist buses, taxis,
rental cars, beauty salons, and movie theaters. The Tibetan Children's Village
looked more like an actual village, in itself large and impressive, improving
the local economy and raising the living standards of the Indians in the State
of Himachal Pradesh.

After receiving a blessing from His Holiness, the One Victorious Jewel of
Tibet, we moved on to Nepal, where we had an encounter with my family's
root lama and personal spiritual leader.

FOR NONBELIEVERS and most Westerners, it's a fairy tale. When my American
delegation and I arrived that day to see the Tibetan settlements in Nepal and
other "things Tibetan," I didn't tell them in advance they might witness this
phenomenon. I didn't want to surprise or shock them. And I asked that no one
make a sound.

In the marble courtyard of Dupa's guest house, Serze Tulku, our root lama
and the spiritual teacher of our families, was dead in the lotus position, the
meditative posture of sitting with crossed legs, both hands on knees, head
straight, gazing slightly downward, like the Buddha's statues. Clinically he
was dead, but his body appeared fresh and radiant.

Before I brought the group to Dupa's house, I took time to explain they
were about to witness *thugdam*, the Tibetan name for it, an extraordinary
event which no Westerners ever heard of, not to mention had never seen. I had
witnessed this rare phenomenon two other times in my life, including when
the *thugdam* of the high lama's tutor had to be "shortened" because we were
on the run. Only highly realized Tibetan lamas or great yogic practitioners die
in this meditative pose and remain in that position for several days. In some
cases, I told the Americans, the body completely disappears, leaving only the
hair and nails. That is called the attainment of Rainbow Body.

Glancing at each other, my friends stood for a long time before the body.
Just a week earlier when we had arrived for a sight-seeing trip to Nepal, Dupa

and I had introduced them to Serze Rinpoche a week earlier. We had brought him a wheelchair from the U.S., which he enjoyed playing with like a child enjoying a toy. They knew he was a famous high lama who meditated day and night with hardly any sleep, one of few such practitioners in the world today. However, I didn't tell them he had predicted his own death to occur while they were in Kathmandu. Although Dupa and I had expected his death to occur as it did, we might have been wrong.

Everyone left Dupa's house speechless. No words were needed.

What we witnessed was a once in lifetime experience. And my guests were about to have another one.

WHEN I WHISPERED to my American friends that the man serving us tea in a Kathmandu handicraft center was the man who murdered my mother, they stared at me, shocked. One man spilled his tea.

I was in shock also. Although Khalap Jampa didn't know who I was, I immediately recognized the murderous traitor who came from behind a rock and shot my brave mother three times in the head at point blank range with a CIA-issued Colt 45 as she tried to defend her dying husband. My mother's body had been just feet from my father's when I found them after the shooting stopped.

To honor His Holiness and remain focused on Tibet's future, I had let go of my anger toward Yeshi and Rara. But could I do the same for a coward who had killed an unarmed woman in cold blood. This was an unexpected and true test of my capacity to forgive.

It took me a few minutes. I had no idea he was alive, much less in Kathmandu.

As my guests stared at me, I stared at him. What I saw was no longer the proud and arrogant man who had commanded a unit of the Chushi Gangdruk and spied for Yeshi at the trial against our men in Mustang. Now he was just an old man whose job as a freedom fighter was to wait on visitors at the Tobtsang Zoda operated by retired Tibetan guerrillas. I felt pity for him. Without the glory he had enjoyed in the Tibetan resistance movement in Mustang during the prime of his life, he was now nothing. But he was alive. Sometime in the 1980's, my father's killer Rara had died in jail.

Those were my thoughts as I looked at this sad old man. He had no idea he was serving tea to the son of a woman he had murdered. And I didn't tell him.

To serve Tibet, I needed to focus on the real enemy—Mao and his murderous Communist regime that was trying to obliterate my culture. Bad karma would send the miserable individuals who killed my parents to somewhere far worse than jail.

Although the images of the massacre would always continue to flash through my dreams on dark nights, during my waking hours I had work to do.

As tourist buses pulled into the Project Tibet Compound in Santa Fe, the looms hummed in the Tobtsang rug factory, and guests registered at the Hotel Vajra, I was realizing a humble Khampa boy's promise to himself and the Dalai Lama. And for the next few years, I was at peace.

But the promise of a free Tibet was still a distant dream for all Tibetans. Would I ever see my country again?

CHAPTER THIRTEEN

YAK-BOYS COME HOME

1995-98: DRONGPA MEDMA, TIBET

T WAS A HORRIBLE SIGHT. All Dupa and I could see for miles and miles were mountains of skeletons of dead yaks, sheep, goats and horses. Extremely cold snowstorms during the winter of 1995 had killed several million animals throughout the whole of Nangchen kingdom, including our district, leaving nomad families with nothing to live on. Dupa and I stood on the icy hillsides trying to figure out what we could do.

Having high expectations of Tibetans who lived in foreign countries, especially America, dozens and dozens of area families had traveled many days' journey by horse to greet us like returning warriors. One man shook his head, his palms out. "You were such a young small boy when you left, yet you've come after so many years to help us? Why? Why have you done this?" That was the reaction of many of the locals from my district. They couldn't believe it. Metaphorically, we had walked in from the back door, landed in the center of attention, and instantly become local heroes who brought in foreign money to invest in the homeland.

In our first return home in almost forty years, many elders were still alive and tearful to see us. Several had known our families—and some even knew that my parents were killed by Tibetans. Most emotional was my reunion with the one survivor among the eighteen of our men whom the Chinese had taken prisoner when I was a boy. "I am the unlucky one to survive," he said, his voice sad and soft. I understood him to mean that he wished he had died with his cousins and friends. When I asked about the labor camp, he became too emotional to answer. We hugged each other and shed many tears. Although he never told me what happened to him or the others, he told me a story about my great-grandfather that I had never heard.

As the story went, when my great-grandfather Gona Tensong and his reckless and restless friends came across a *drimong*, a grizzly bear, to everyone's surprise, my great-grandfather stepped back as if to run away. Instead, he took the moment to throw away his sword and rushed forward to wrestle the beast with his bare hands. After he brought down the *drimong* by its ears, his friends rushed in to finish off the animal. Fighting the bear without a weapon was one more way Gona Tensong proved his bravery. But he wasn't the only brave Tibetan.

When Dupa and I went from village after village and from home to home talking to nomad families who had lost their animals, each family greeted us hopefully and warmly, but had little to say. Without their animals, which they loved like their own children, nomads had no way to make a living. Even though they had nothing, they were incredibly generous to us. We received so many invitations that it would have taken at least a month to accept them all, so, to not disappoint anyone, we ended up visiting one family every hour every day for the whole week. Although we couldn't possibly eat a dozen breakfasts, a dozen lunches, and a dozen dinners in one day, we appreciated the hospitality and good-heartedness of our former hometown. And the numbers of nomad homesteads in the district had grown to five times more than when we lived in Kham. Because the Chinese couldn't survive the harsh winters in highlands where the nomads lived and chose the comforts of cities and towns, the grazing land and rivers were still pristine, and the nomads had been able to thrive. Until now.

While Dupa and I couldn't possibly replace the millions of animals lost in that snowstorm, we left determined to help our fellow nomads who had already been living as second-class citizens under the Chinese.

However, we had a few more stops in Tibet before we returned west to raise funds for Drongpa Medma.

IN THE MIDDLE OF AN ICY RIVER, our path was blocked on both riverbanks by foot-and-a-half-high ice walls. On the way to visiting what was left of the local monasteries, we had been battling freezing weather and rocky terrain. Now we were stuck. After many attempts to pull the jeep from the water, all our chains broke. At a loss, Dupa looked at me, as the brains of the operation.

Of course, I had an idea. Without a way to light a fire on our teenage camping trip, I had solved the problem with a gun. Maybe I could use one here. A local friend had given us an AK-47 with 700 bullets and a pistol to take with us for sport shooting, a favorite pastime in Kham. By emptying one magazine of thirty rounds into one ice wall, chunks of ice breaking off and flying, I cleared a path. When our host asked the customary question—had we run into any problems on the way—I said, "We ran into a river of enemies, but we shot our way out." He took this literally and thought we had actually run into bandits. But any humor was lost in sadness.

When we saw the mud walls and piles of stones the Chinese marauders had left behind, Dupa and I both became emotional. On this grass-strewn rubble had been Barmed Gon Monastery, which was richest in our district and the one most important to my family, the home of the four reincarnated lamas who had followed us to central Tibet during the exile. Here had lived my monk uncle, Serze Tulku, our root lama who had predicted his own death and passed away in the lotus position, and Bhayu Tulku, our childhood friend who knew through intuitive vision that Dupa and I had killed a rat. There were only foot-high walls where this ancient monastery had stood. With little to say, we each drifted into silent contemplation.

It was time to scheme. We had to help the nomads in a way that wouldn't make the regional Chinese government officials raise objections to any foreign aid. Dupa decided he would send money and supplies to the devastated homesteads in our district and raise funds to rebuild the destroyed monasteries.

During the freezing night, as nine of us slept in the one large room of a nearby stone structure, with the fire going the whole night, I had a mysterious dream. In the dream, I was walking toward a monastery on streets paved with river rocks, smooth with rounded edges. Unlike the temple halls of other monasteries, which were filled with statues, *thankas*, long rows of seats and long tables, this hall appeared to be almost empty except for one huge statue of Guru Rinpoche (Padmasambhava). Instead of walking to Guru Rinpoche's statue to pray, as I usually would have done, I walked to a large door. Next to it was a huge boulder with water pouring from its middle, making a small pond. As I stepped on the slippery river rocks that were the stepping-stones across the pond, I gripped one edge of the boulder for support. My right hand and its fingers made a dent into the rock as it if were soft butter, and my feet sank into the stepping-stones as if they were wet mud, leaving deep footprints. Then I walked through the door. Only some high lamas can walk through walls. I had personally seen three of them do it. But I was far from being a high lama. The killer instinct in me was still kicking like an untamed mule. Did the dream have a message for me about how to help my nomad brothers?

The next night, I had another mysterious experience while contemplating these questions. At about 4 a.m., after going outside to relieve myself, I had the urge to sit quietly for a moment next to the ruins of a small shrine that had been ruined by the Chinese. As I meditated quietly, I felt as if I were in a different time and space. It was the dawning of a moment of lucid awareness of the naked truth of the primordial, intrinsic nature of things. When a nearby dog barking woke me, I realized I was out in the cold in only my underwear.

When I went back to the room, our driver, who was sitting by the fire smoking a cigarette asked me where I had been "all this time." I had been sitting nearly naked for at least two hours in freezing temperatures. I looked at my bare legs and arms. I wasn't even shivering. I had clarity.

ON OUR LAST STOP in that winter of 1996, for the first time since we were nine, as Dupa and I stood on the banks of the Chedchu River, the River of Happiness, that flowed through the backyard of our childhood home, we relived the day when the swollen currents had swept us up in a flash flood and almost drowned us. We remembered two little boys tossed up on the bank by a flash flood, our fingers locked. We had never forgotten. Now, because it was winter, the river was frozen and looked smaller than it did in the summer—and less dangerous. When we arrived at the big village which now sat on the site of our old tents, we were welcomed by special performances of dances and songs.

As Dupa and I walked the land underneath two circling ravens, we relived our pastoral childhood as young princes on the Roof of the World, roaming through flower fields and hillsides shooting birds and making weapons from animal bones to pretend we were King Gesar's famous warriors. Now this centuries-old way of life had disappeared in a blizzard. That world was gone.

But our fellow Tibetans were still alive. And we wouldn't desert them.

I showed Dupa a site about a hundred yards from the riverbank. My mission for Drongpa Medma would be about the future. The nomads' herds were gone. The families had nothing to pass on. Their children needed an education and new skills, something the Chinese wouldn't provide for nomads. The Chinese leaders, who were still in the business of eradicating our ancient culture, feared educated Tibetans (as well as educated Chinese, for that matter) and found it easier to keep the ignorant and uneducated masses in the dark than to fool well-informed and educated people.

The Beijing leadership has too many things that they don't want others to know, such as what really happened in the Tiananmen Square massacre, the whereabouts of the young Panchen Lama, the monks who went missing during Chinese raids on Tibetan monasteries, and many more such incidents in both Tibet and China. The freedom to choose one's destiny is the mark of evolved human beings, and a good education could offer Tibetans that opportunity. I would build schools in the nomadic communities most devastated by the snowstorm. In addition to following my father's model to "think broadly, deeply, and, in the long term," I was also going to honor his specific advice to me that I could move beyond the limitations of the nomadic life.

Dupa and I were nomads who had become businessmen. And other nomad children could do that too.

CHILDREN WERE SLIDING DOWN the shiny *pang* grass of the Drongpa Medma hillsides and dashing about with pretend swords along the Chedchu River. Surrounded by miles of wildflowers, our first school, a boarding school in my home district, was ready to open its door to nomad children. Because it was the end of June, the roads were no longer icy, and everyone was home after the season of harvesting caterpillar fungus (*yertsa gunbu*), which is the biggest cash crop for nomads—and, for most, the only cash income they have— everyone was already in a celebratory mood. In addition to singing and dancing, the locals held special events like horse and yak races—just like the fairs and festivals of my childhood. The air was pristine, the birds plentiful, the river rippling. And the school, with its solid brick walls was ready for its teachers and pupils. And this was just one of the three schools that would be built over the next three years. I had raised enough money from several anonymous donors and from NGO's including the Tara Foundation in Germany to build two more schools, both near Gar Monastery.

It started with countless drinks, chain-smoking, laughing, joking, singing and telling funny stories at my expense. Just as with the Nepalese officials, securing the building permits from the Chinese required bribery disguised as parties. While Tibetans still held minor administrative posts in the region, the Chinese, on behalf of Beijing, were the decision-makers behind the scenes. In other words, Tibetans did the hard work to serve the local people while the Chinese authorities sat around and gave orders. At these parties, the Chinese never talked business, of course. It was all part of the Chinese game. Having been drinking with a government director for hours the night before made it possible to conduct business in their official offices the next day. I'm not sure what the Chinese saw when they looked at me, but they were friendly.

To the citizens of Drongpa Medma, when I returned in the summer of 1996, I could have been King Gesar. When I also rebuilt a very important Buddhist Stupa, originally erected in the 19th century, that had been completely destroyed during the Cultural Revolution, I was a kid who had left our homeland and come back to help our people.

Before arriving to celebrate the new school, I stopped to check on Dupa's project. As usual, with Dupa, the promises he made were the promises he kept. He's the kind of man who does what he says. The year after we returned from Tibet, Dupa had already begun to rebuild Barmed Gon Monastery. By the time I was back in Nepal to work on the school, Dupa had completed the portion of the monastery which included the residential house for the newly reincarnated Serze Tulku Rinpoche, now an eight-year-old child. After watching the *thugdam*, the amazing passing away of our family's spiritual teacher, it was very moving to see him as a child in a different life form in a different time, a person who needed us for his material needs. By caring for this child, we could repay the kindness and compassion that we had received from our teacher's previous incarnation. What goes around comes around in the wheel of life. After all, we didn't lose our teacher—we had just lost sight of the old body of our teacher, who had come back in a smaller new one.

While visiting the monastery, I also relived my strange spiritual experience at this site the previous winter—meditating for hours in my underwear without contracting frostbite.

During the three years I returned to my hometown, from 1996 to 1998, to build the schools, I also gained notoriety among the locals for my magical connection with the local spirit world. While local spirits aren't considered enlightened deities, like Tara and Mahakala—spiritual protectors who remove obstacles to the pursuit of enlightenment—one can befriend the local spirits with offerings and invocations of their names in praise of their good qualities. In return, they protect against danger from enemies, and they bring good luck, fame, power, and prosperity.

My Gonatsang family had always made such invocations and offerings to our local spirits, who therefore were supposed to be my family's friends. Growing up, I had been only a half-believer, a skeptic with an attitude of "Who cares?" That is, until I visited Drongpa Medma for the third summer in July and, for the third year in a row, my arrival was greeted by a brief rain followed by a double rainbow. Although it would be sunny when I arrived, as soon as I entered the home of my host family and the first cup of tea was served, the rain started, followed by the double rainbow. It soon became major town gossip.

I made an even more dramatic impression while camping with friends near our new school. On our third day of camping, picnicking, and playing mahjong, a big hailstorm headed toward us from the valley, which could have easily blown away all our tents, blankets, and sleeping bags. Without thinking, I tossed a cup of tea in the air as an offering to the local spirits, as done traditionally, and put my hand out towards the coming clouds like a traffic officer. When the storm halted in mid-air and changed direction, everybody looked at me with their eyes and months wide open, as if they were seeing Milarepa, or a ghost appearing from nowhere. More surprised than they were, I asked, "How the hell did I do that?" Given the time to think about it, I never would have tried to stop a hailstorm.

When the same thing happened in another town just weeks later, my friends and the local people decided I must be a highly accomplished Buddhist practitioner possessing spiritual powers like the great yogis. At a town fair, the tents belonging to the Police Department had already been blown over by a windstorm, and our tent was being held down by at least seven people. Again, in the same the way as before, I tossed the tea first and then held my hand up to stop the storm. It stopped. Although, I didn't think I had any super-spiritual power of my own, I was becoming a believer. Local spirits were there if we took the trouble to befriend them.

My spiritual calling, however, was not to stop the weather. Providing an education turned out to be more practical for the nomads than trying to replace the yaks lost in the snowstorm. In the three schools I built, several hundred students finished seventh grade and went on to join secondary schools.

I funded thirty-seven college scholarships, and all the students graduated and found jobs in local government offices. Building a small furniture factory to produce Tibetan-style furnishings and training the local people in carpentry skills, I also helped to insure that Tibetans could manufacture their own products without outsiders taking their jobs away from them.

Not only was I seeing tangible results from each new project I brought to Kham, each year I spent several days camping on the land where Dupa and I were happy nomad boys. At different times, at different sites—Lake Nyimo near Lhasa, the military encampment with the legendary warriors on the western border, and even our camp at Dolpo—I had fantasized that we were about to reestablish our nomad lives. But these were silly dreams. It was a time of war. We were on the run. Nothing was stable. No return to a bucolic life was possible. Yet now here I was each year in Kham, at my family's homestead, the site where I had lived my entire childhood as a nomad.

These were my thoughts in the summer of 1998 as I was lying on my back watching the circling ravens and crows. Above my campsite near my family's former home hovered brown eagles strong enough to carry away lambs, cats, puppies, rabbits, and other small creatures. Closing my eyes, I was a ten-year-old nomad boy again, amidst the beauty and the danger. Here Dupa and I soothed baby lambs, slept under the stars tending the horses with Uncle Chopak, and pretended we were warriors like King Gesar's thirty superheroes, with sticks imagined to be horses, shouting Tibetan war cries like, *"Kee hee hee hee, lha gyalo"*—"Victory to the gods!" Other times, we pretended that we were lamas and monks performing fake rituals, mumbling varieties of meaningless words that sounded real from a distance. Khampas, the legendary people of Eastern Tibet, range from the most fierce and accomplished fighters and warriors to the most spiritual monks, scholars, and lamas, all of whom were present in our families.

Unfortunately, I have to hold that visit in my heart forever, because it was my last.

THE CHINESE NEVER EXPLAINED THE DECISION. In 1998, when I attempted to return to Tibet to build more schools and support the existing ones, the Communist officials wouldn't approve my visa.

On my trips to Tibet, I had been careful to stay under the radar by obtaining my China visas through a travel agency in San Francisco. They took hundreds of passports at a time to be stamped at the Chinese Consulate. Because the Chinese didn't bother to check each and every passport from travel agents, I was able to travel as just another tourist coming from the U.S. If I had applied independently as a Tibetan expatriate and a Chinese official saw my face and Tibetan name on my passport, they would never have let me in.

So how did they flag my passport? Perhaps they discovered I was a board member of International Campaign for Tibet, an organization which the Chinese hated and feared. I suspect I'll never know.

Unless the karmic wind blows me back to our fatherland to defend the Land of Snows and the home of the Dalai Lamas, I must continue the struggle for a free Tibet from Kathmandu and the West.

For me, however, the fight to preserve our culture and our memory on our home soil will never be over. For those I love—my mother, my father, my brother Dupa, Dupa's father, Uncle Chopak, and all my relatives who were there when I lived the blessed life of a nomad boy—I will never stop fighting for my true homeland.

I was and will always be a son of Tibet.

OM MANI PADME HUM

अ་རེ་བོད་ཁང་
TIBET HOUSE US
PUBLICATIONS

TIBETAN CULTURE

Dreams and Truths from the Ocean of Mind   2019
    Pema Lodoe (the Sixth Sogan Tulku of Tibet)
    (Ed. and Trans. by Robert Warren Clark)

Man of Peace—The Illustrated Life Story of the Dalai Lama of Tibet   2016
    Robert Thurman, William Meyers, and Michael Burbank

My Appeal to the World   2015
    H.H. the Dalai Lama XIV (Compiled by Sofia Stril-Rever)

The Dalai Lama and the King Demon: Tracking a Triple Murder Mystery   2013
    Raimundo Bultrini

A Drop from the Marvelous Ocean of History   2013
    Lelung Tulku Rinpoche XI

TIBETAN ART

A Shrine for Tibet: The Alice S. Kandell Collection   2010
    Marylin Rhie and Robert A.F. Thurman

Vanishing Tibet   2008
    Catherine Steinmann and Danny Conant

Visions of Tibet: Outer, Inner, Secret   2006
    Photographs by Brian Kistler; Introduction by Robert A.F. Thurman

The Tibetan Wheel of Existence   2000
    Jacqueline Dunnington, M.A.

Wisdom and Compassion: The Sacred Art of Tibet   2000
    Marylin Rhie and Robert A.F. Thurman

Mandala: The Architecture of Enlightenment   1997
    Denise P. Leidy and Robert A.F. Thurman

Worlds of Transformation: Tibetan Art of Wisdom and Compassion 1991
    Marylin Rhie and Robert A.F. Thurman